GENDER AND AMERICAN JEWS

HBI SERIES ON JEWISH WOMEN

SHULAMIT REINHARZ, GENERAL EDITOR

SYLVIA BARACK FISHMAN, ASSOCIATE EDITOR

The HBI Series on Jewish Women, created by the Hadassah-Brandeis Institute, publishes a wide range of books by and about Jewish women in diverse contexts and time periods. Of interest to scholars and the educated public, the HBI Series on Jewish Women fills major gaps in Jewish Studies and in Women and Gender Studies as well as their intersection.

The HBI Series on Jewish Women is supported by a generous gift from Dr. Laura S. Schor.

For the complete list of books that are available in this series, please see www.upne.com

Gaby Brimmer and Elena Poniatowska, *Gaby Brimmer*

Harriet Hartman and Moshe Hartman, *Gender and American Jews: Patterns in Work, Education, and Family in Contemporary Life*

Dvora E. Weisberg, *Levirate Marriage and the Family in Ancient Judaism*

Ellen M. Umansky and Dianne Ashton, editors, *Four Centuries of Jewish Women's Spirituality: A Sourcebook*

Carole S. Kessner, *Marie Syrkin: Values Beyond the Self*

Ruth Kark, Margalit Shilo, and Galit Hasan-Rokem, editors, *Jewish Women in Pre-State Israel: Life History, Politics, and Culture*

Tova Hartman, *Feminism Encounters Traditional Judaism: Resistance and Accommodation*

Anne Lapidus Lerner, *Eternally Eve: Images of Eve in the Hebrew Bible, Midrash, and Modern Jewish Poetry*

Margalit Shilo, *Princess or Prisoner? Jewish Women in Jerusalem, 1840–1914*

Marcia Falk, translator, *The Song of Songs: Love Lyrics from the Bible*

Sylvia Barack Fishman, *Double or Nothing? Jewish Families and Mixed Marriage*

Avraham Grossman, *Pious and Rebellious: Jewish Women in Medieval Europe*

Iris Parush, *Reading Jewish Women: Marginality and Modernization in Nineteenth-Century Eastern European Jewish Society*

Shulamit Reinharz and Mark A. Raider, editors, *American Jewish Women and the Zionist Enterprise*

Tamar Ross, *Expanding the Palace of Torah: Orthodoxy and Feminism*

Farideh Goldin, *Wedding Song: Memoirs of an Iranian Jewish Woman*

HARRIET HARTMAN

AND MOSHE HARTMAN

GENDER AND AMERICAN JEWS

Patterns in Work,

Education, and Family

in Contemporary Life

BRANDEIS UNIVERSITY PRESS
Waltham, Massachusetts

Published by University Press of New England
Hanover and London

Brandeis University Press
Published by University Press of New England,
One Court Street, Lebanon, NH 03766
www.upne.com
© 2009 by Brandeis University Press
Printed in the United States of America
5 4 3 2 1

Library of Congress Cataloging-in-Publication Data
Hartman, Harriet.
  Gender and American Jews: patterns in work, education, and family in contemporary
life / Harriet Hartman and Moshe Hartman.
      p.   cm. —   (HBI series on Jewish women)
  Includes bibliographical references and index.
  ISBN 978–1–58465–756–9 (pbk. : alk. paper)
  1. Jewish women—United States. 2 Jewish family—United States. 3. Sexual division of
labor—United States. I. Hartman, Moshe, 1936– II. Title.
  HQ1172.H36 2009
  305.892'4073—dc22   2009015973

University Press of New England is a member of the
Green Press Initiative. The paper used in this book meets
their minimum requirement for recycled paper.

We dedicate this book to the loving memory of our parents,

Lola and Laçi Hartman, Bernard and Florence Stillman,

who first made us aware of both Jewishness and gender;

and to our grandchildren,

the girls (Elisheva, Shira, Yikrat, Netanya, and Chana Esther)

and the boys (Ephraim, Binyamin, Oriyah, Yoseph Meir, and Maor),

who in their own way are already contributing to Jewish gender equality.

CONTENTS

Preface by Sylvia Barack Fishman, ix

Acknowledgments, xi

Chapter 1   An Introduction to Gender and American Jews
and the Significance of the Inquiry, 1

**PART I   THE DISTINCTIVENESS OF GENDERED
PATTERNS OF SECULAR ACHIEVEMENT
AMONG AMERICAN JEWS**

Chapter 2   Education Patterns: The Foundation of Family
and Economic Roles, 13

Chapter 3   Family Patterns of American Jews, 25

Chapter 4   Labor Force Participation and Occupational
Achievement, 44

Chapter 5   Dual-Earning Patterns of American Jews, 88

**PART II WAYS OF BEING JEWISH AND THE
DISTINCTIVE SECULAR ROLES OF
AMERICAN JEWISH WOMEN AND MEN**

Chapter 6   Gendered Patterns of Jewishness, 121

Chapter 7   How Jewishness is Related to Family Patterns of
American Jews, 152

Chapter 8   How Jewishness is Related to Gendered Patterns
of Secular Achievement, 172

Chapter 9   How Jewishness is Related to American Jews'
Dual-Earning Patterns, 203

Chapter 10 Intermarriage and Gendered Patterns of Secular
Achievement, 230

PART III CONCLUSIONS

Chapter 11   Conclusions and a Look to the Future, 253

Appendix: Statistical Tables, 269
Notes, 277
References, 283
Index, 295

Many observers have assumed that gender is no longer a major factor in American Jewish life, but—according to this carefully argued, brilliantly documented analysis of male and female life cycles, roles, behaviors, and values—gender is more important than ever. Working from the two most comprehensive recent national surveys of American Jews, Harriet and Moshe Hartman examine the similarities and differences in men's and women's lives, compared both to each other and to men and women in the past. Their findings are critical to an understanding of how American Jews function as individuals, in families, and in societies. The Hartmans prove that scholars and policy planners alike ignore gender at their own peril.

American Jewish men and women continue to be much more highly educated than the American population in general. In the single decade from 1990 to 2000, Jewish women in particular showed significant progress in terms of their educational and occupational achievements. Today, more than one in five Jewish women who earn graduate degrees go beyond the master's degree. Although Jewish men continue to exhibit higher educational levels than women, the gap is decreasing. Those gender differences that persist are greatest for Jews over age 45. Indeed, among men and women ages 35 to 44 who earn graduate degrees, a larger proportion of Jewish women than men earn them in the professions—a statistical snapshot, perhaps, of the return of Jewish men to the business world and their declining attraction to professional life.

The Hartmans show us that highly educated American Jews continue to have strong biases toward both married life and work outside the home. Jewish women who earn higher degrees get married later and have fewer children than their less educated sisters, but they are "more likely to be married, less likely to be divorced, [and] less likely to be married more than once" than other women. In contrast, less educated Jewish men are more likely than their highly educated brothers to be divorced, and to remain unmarried after divorce. Strikingly, married American Jewish men and women are typically educated at similar levels. This educational homogamy is especially common among younger American Jews and Orthodox Jews.

Despite the much-publicized putative trend of young women to cease working outside the home and reclaim homemaker roles, the Hartmans show that more than 80 percent of Jewish women with bachelor's or master's degrees—and more than 90 percent of Jewish women with doctoral or professional degrees—are in fact employed. The Hartmans compare these and related data, including male and female earning power, to other non-Hispanic white Americans and to Jews in the past, creating a well-rounded and fascinating portrait.

Defining "Jewishness" is a complicated enterprise. When the Hartmans analyze gender differences in Jewishness, they allow various categories of behaviors, beliefs, and values to speak for themselves, subjecting the data to statistical tests in order to include several possible prisms of interpretation. They show that branches of Judaism still matter—despite post-denominational claims to the contrary—in the way American Jews act and think. Orthodox men and women have few significant gender differences in levels of Jewish involvement. However, women who identify with the Conservative or the Reform/Reconstructionist branches of Judaism are more engaged and active than similarly identified men.

Age matters as well—in sometimes surprising patterns that challenge expectations. For example, while older American Jews are more likely to see Judaism as a moral guide, younger American Jews are more likely to observe religious rituals. The Hartmans show that, overall, women are significantly more strongly identified in almost all Jewish expressions, "even when age, education, and denomination are controlled." However, these gender differences are reduced when Jews receive extended years of formal Jewish education, and when they marry Jews.

From simple bar graphs to complicated regression analyses, the Hartmans present their data in ways that are suitable for the interested public as well as for students and scholars. Like other volumes in the Hadassah-Brandeis Institute Series on Jewish Women, this important study takes a fresh approach to the interface between gender and Jewishness. By providing the definitive analysis of the impact of gender on American Jewish societies today, the Hartmans will change the way American Jewish life is understood.

Sylvia Barack Fishman
Professor of Contemporary Jewish Life
Co-Director, The Hadassah-Brandeis Institute
Chair, Near Eastern and Judaic Studies Department
Brandeis University

ACKNOWLEDGMENTS

This book would not have been possible without the generous support of the Hadassah-Brandeis Institute, Brandeis University, and in particular, the encouragement of Professor Sylvia Barack Fishman. The authors are most grateful for this support, but of course remain solely responsible for the content of the book.

GENDER AND AMERICAN JEWS

CHAPTER 1

An Introduction to Gender and American Jews and the Significance of the Inquiry

I think gender is no longer the essential issue of American Jewry. . . .
Egalitarianism has become so pervasive and normative in American Jewish
life that it rarely makes headlines.
—Rela Geffen, 2007

A recent book questions the "declining significance of gender" in the U.S. population (Blau, Brinton, and Grusky, 2006). Geffen (2007) considers egalitarianism to be so pervasive and normative in American Jewish life that it is no longer a topic of interest. Yet here we are, writing a book about gender roles and Jewishness among American Jews. Are we beating a dead horse? Has egalitarianism been achieved and is gender no longer an issue for American Jews? Are we setting up a "straw person," only to knock it down with negative findings? Perhaps. And yet we cannot help but feel the questions still need to be asked, particularly of this subgroup in U.S. culture. Few other subgroups can claim such high educational and occupational achievement, coupled with strong leadership in the feminist movement for gender equality. Few other subgroups are positioned between religion, ethnicity, and secularism the way American Jews are. Few other subgroups can claim unique status as family oriented yet as having one of the lowest fertility rates in the country. So we raise the question: Has gender equality in secular achievement been attained by American Jews? And whatever the answer, is it because of or in spite of Jewish religious and ethnic identity?

We did not approach the question with a blank slate. We built on a previous study we had done, *Gender Equality and American Jews* (Hartman and Hartman, 1996a), using data from 1990. Then, too, we compared the educational achievement and economic roles of American Jewish men and women and related them to "Jewishness," in an attempt to explore whether there was a "Jewish" pattern of gender differences in secular achievement. We had reasons to suspect gender equality: strong human capital of both men and women; small family size, which diminished the negative effect of childcare on mothers' secular achievement; a historical tradition of wives participating in the labor force and often supporting the family economically while the husband engaged in religious studies; Jewish women's involvement in the movement for gender equality in the third wave of U.S. feminism; and support for gender equality by highly educated Americans like most American Jews. On the other hand, the centrality of the family in Judaism implied a strong investment in family roles, which often conflict with women's investments in higher education or a career; and a tradition of gender inequality in religious roles was suspected of spilling over to secular roles. We noted that some interpret gender inequality in religious roles as gender difference rather than status ranking; and in some denominations (the most numerous), religious roles have become increasingly accessible to women and men, which weakens the impact of this factor.

We confirmed tendencies toward equality in secular roles that we were expecting, but we also found some unexpected inequalities, and the sources of both equality and inequality were somewhat surprising. Although both American Jewish men and women are better educated than their counterparts in the broader U.S. society, American Jewish men retained an educational advantage over women, just that they did so at a higher level than in much of the rest of U.S. society. As in the broader society, Jewish women had achieved parity with men in terms of high school and undergraduate degrees, but there were still fewer graduate degrees awarded to women. Cohort analysis showed us that there was movement toward educational parity, but it had not yet been achieved according to the 1990 data we were analyzing. Although American Jewish men and women had high labor force participation rates compared with their counterparts in the broader population, a sizable minority of women, many more than men, were not participating in the labor force or were working part time rather than full time. This pattern was more common when women had children, especially young children at home, as might be expected.

In this book we focus on whether there remains a distinctive secular behavior among American Jews, and whether those who identify themselves as more "Jewish" in a variety of ways are more likely to engage in this distinctive secular behavior. American Jews' distinctively high secular achievement has long been recognized (Smith, 2005). Several explanations for this have been offered: human capital (e.g., education, long work hours); cultural capital (e.g., placing a high value on education and achievement); social capital (e.g., networking among Jews); and marginality (a motivator of creativity) (Burstein, 2007). However, as Jews have become more integrated into American life ("white," per Brodkin, 1999), their marginality has become increasingly part of the cultural legacy rather than an everyday experience; and their cultural particularity has become less self-conscious and salient, so much so that a sizable minority (about 20%) that others would term "Jewish" do not identify themselves as such (United Jewish Communities, 2003c). The question then arises as to whether the cultural basis for secular distinctiveness is eroding or can be traced primarily to human capital factors.

Even more interesting, perhaps, than the distinctiveness of American Jews from the broader population is the variation among Jews. In trying to capture the "cultural" capital imparted through Jewishness, we find ourselves with the daunting task of trying to define "Jewishness." Fishman has captured the myriad "varieties of Jewishness" (2006), clearly showing that there is no unique way of being Jewish. Jews differ not just by their origins or their denominations. They may emphasize Jewishness as a religion or an ethnicity, they may be communally involved or privately spiritual, they may be involved with other American Jews and/or Jews in Israel or the rest of the world, they may see being Jewish as being a member of a race or tribe, or they may consider themselves purveyors of a universal morality—the variations are truly astounding. One would expect that those who define their Jewishness as more pervasive might find their secular roles and achievements influenced more by their Jewish identity, such as it may be, and that those who compartmentalize their Jewishness might be detached from "Jewish" ways of behaving.

In our 1990 work, we attempted to relate some varieties of Jewishness to secular (in)equality between Jewish men and women. When analyzing the contribution of Jewishness to this pattern of inequality, we found it was less the direct influence of Jewishness than the indirect influence of Jewishness on family roles that accounted for the different labor force patterns between men and women. More traditional and more strongly identified Jews tended to have more children, which curtailed labor force participation to some extent. However, among traditionally and more strongly identified Jews, there was more likely to be gender equality in education, occupation, and occupational prestige, including within their marriages. We concluded that American Jewish women were particularly responsive to family roles but that Jewishness per se did not bring about unequal secular achievements.

The collection of the 2000–01 National Jewish Population Survey (NJPS) data affords an opportunity to reexamine these issues, with an expanded data set that includes much more information about ways of "being

Jewish," a larger sample that allows better comparisons between subgroups of respondents, and an updated social context that brings us into the twenty-first century.

Since 1990, the broader U.S. context has changed, and so has the context for American Jews. Marriage is increasingly delayed, divorce and single parenting have become more common, women are more likely than men to complete undergraduate and master's degrees, and the labor force participation rate of women and especially mothers is at an all-time high (though still not as high as men's). We cannot ignore the differences in family status as we analyze gender differences in American Jews' secular achievements. Twenty-one percent of American Jewish mothers with children under the age of 18 at home were not married at the time of the survey (though the vast majority had been married before giving birth); nearly 10% of the women were in their second marriage (or beyond). We examine whether these differences in family status influence the secular achievement of American Jewish women and whether they affect gender equality.

In the United States, women's representation in many previously considered "male" occupations has doubled or tripled, and in some cases women have achieved parity with men (Chao and Utgoff, 2005), and the gap between men and women's earnings has narrowed (though not disappeared) (Sweet and Meiksins, 2008). Within the increasingly "post-industrial" economy, there has been an expansion of occupations in which representation by American Jews has traditionally been disproportionately high (information processing; professional, retail, and wholesale trade) (Sweet and Meiksins, 2008; Wyatt and Hecker, 2006), challenging perhaps the distinctiveness of the American Jewish occupational structure.

Yet another difference is the change in the context of the feminist movement. Whereas in the 1970s and 1980s, stay-at-home moms and labor force dropouts were devalued in much discourse, the 1990s and 2000s have seen a renewed sense of the value of family contributions; there is less disparaging of family-oriented women and more bemoaning of how much career may take away from family involvement for both women and men (Edlund, 2007; Muñoz, 2007; Newcombe, 2007; Steiner, 2007). Dual-earner couples have become the norm (Bond, 2002), but research and public discourse recognize that extensive hours in the labor force affect the family adversely by taking parents away from their children and sapping their time, energy, and other resources (Accenture, 2007; Becker and Moen, 1999; Crompton, 2006; Shellenbarger, 2008). With such awareness, one can legitimately ask whether couples, if they can afford to, cap the number of hours they collectively spend in the labor force, and whether it is still the mother or wife who bears the brunt of family demands or whether economic and family roles are shared. A highly qualified subpopulation like American Jews, in which women and men both have strong human capital, presents a case study for exploring how gender roles are managed in contemporary society. Insight into gender differences among American Jews, especially when children are present, may help us understand the limits of gender equality among those who are family oriented.

Gender roles are not only a product of intimate arrangements. Riv-Ellen Prell (1999) has shown us how much gender relations among Jews reflect the relations between Jews and the broader society. American Jews are becoming increasingly accepted as part of the mainstream majority of whites, so much so that many of the boundaries between Jews and non-Jews are increasingly blurred. One clear implication is easier intermarriage; intramarriage may occur just as much by chance as by intention, or it may be socioeconomically rather than culturally or religiously based. In 1990, the sections of our book dealing with couples focused solely on Jewish adults married to Jewish adults. If in 2000 we had considered only intermarried couples, we would have been leaving out one-third of the couples in our sample of American Jews. Secular achievement is actually important to examine as it interacts with intermarriage, as we will show. Jewish men married to Jewish women tend to have higher educational and occupational achievement than Jewish men married to non-Jewish women. The dynamics of this are beyond the scope of the data we use (i.e., does intramarriage promote educational and occupational achievement, or does lower educational or occupational achievement promote intermarriage?), but they are interesting to speculate about.

At the same time, because Jews are more widely accepted as part of the mainstream, they are freer to express their "Jewishness" in a variety of ways, which may strengthen (or weaken) their "Jewish" identity in multiple respects (Kaufman, 1999). So the question again arises, how are various expressions of "Jewishness" related to the distinctiveness (or lack thereof) of secular roles of Jewish men and women? The rich variety of questions in the 2000–01 NJPS enabled us to explore such expressions more fully because of the larger number of data related to Jewish identity collected in the survey. There are questions related to religious identity, ethnic identity, public participation in Jewish culture, private observance of home-based ritual and prayer, and more (as we present in Chapter 6). Among contemporary Jews, there appear to be two tendencies with regard to "Jewishness": one toward less involvement and engagement and one toward more involvement and engagement (Cohen, 2005). We can examine whether one leads to less or to more distinctiveness from the broader U.S. population. The answer, which we address in our analysis, may be surprising.

Another change related to gender equality among Jews is the development of women's roles in the contemporary Jewish community. Women have always been active in the American Jewish community, but there have been several ways in which their activity has developed in the past few decades (Geffen, 2007; Prell, 2007b). Across the denominational spectrum, women have become more involved in both lay and professional leadership, prayer and study circles, philanthropic giving circles, life-cycle rituals relevant particularly to women's issues, and more (Geffen, 2007). They still face obstacles to reaching the pinnacles of public leadership in secular, voluntary organizations like the Jewish Federations, but as our opening quote shows, gender no longer drives strong ressentiment (Geffen, 2007, p. 9). This book examines whether there is "pervasive and normative egalitarianism" in Jewish secular roles as well.

THE DATA

Our primary data come from the National Jewish Population Survey undertaken in 2000 and 2001. Sponsored by the United Jewish Communities (UJC), it constitutes the largest survey of a national sample of American Jews ever conducted. It also encompasses the widest range of questions on Jewish topics (including education, religious behaviors and attitudes, ethnic attitudes, engagement with Jewish culture, organizations, Israel, and intermarriage) of any other large survey of contemporary American Jews. (More information on the survey can be found in Kadushin, Phillips, and Saxe, 2005; Kotler-Berkowitz, 2006; United Jewish Communities, 2003b and 2003d; see also the Web site www.jewishdatabank.org, where registered users can freely download the data.)

The survey was conducted by telephone using random digit dialing (RDD) techniques and a stratified sampling frame, oversampling areas of high Jewish population density. More than 170,000 households were screened, resulting in 5,148 respondents, who received various versions of the questionnaire, depending on how closely they fit a number of criteria of Jewishness. The sample that we used for this study includes 4,144 respondents, who fulfilled two of the following criteria: they said that their religion was Jewish/Judaism,[1] their parentage was Jewish, they were raised Jewish, and/or they considered themselves Jewish. Because we broke down the sample by age, marital status, and sometimes gender, education, labor force participation, and occupation, some of our sub-samples are very small, as we note throughout the text.

For simple calculations, "person-weights" were used to estimate actual numbers in the wider Jewish population with the same attributes. These person-weights were provided with the data set and are explained in more detail in the study documentation provided by the United Jewish Communities (2003b and 2003d). For analyses based on correlations, including factor analyses and multiple or logistic regressions, or to conduct significance tests, the unweighted data were used. Most of the tables report unweighted sample sizes, even if the calculations were performed on the weighted sample. Notes clarify this for each table. Unless otherwise noted, the data source for each table and figure is the NJPS 2000–01.

Considerable attention has been devoted to the limitations of the survey (see Kadushin, Phillips, and Saxe, 2005; Saxe, Tighe, Phillips, and Kadushin, 2007), including a low rate of response in general and to certain questions in particular, an underrepresentation of young non-Orthodox and baby boomer Jews (owing either to sampling errors or to lack of response) (Saxe et al., 2007), as well as missing data because certain questions were not asked of certain subpopulations. Regarding the low response rate overall, estimates have been made as to whether parts of the American Jewish population are so underrepresented as to present a bias in the results. This is a problem for us, particularly with regard to the underrepresentation of baby boomer Jews, whether for non-response or sampling reasons, as they are likely to be in their prime career years and their labor force behavior and achievement may not mirror those of other cohorts. The underrepresentation of younger Jews poses a less serious problem, because they are often not married and are more likely to be excluded from much of the analysis anyway. With regard to particular questions, the biggest problem is the low response rate regarding income, which is always a sensitive question. Chiswick and Huang's (2008) analysis suggests that the non-response on this topic is biased toward higher-income respondents, as might be expected.

These limitations are real and must be kept in mind so that we exercise appropriate caution when interpreting the results. However, since there is little reason to expect that these problems affect men and women differently, when we are analyzing comparisons between men and women in various subpopulations of the sample, we may have more confidence in the results. Furthermore, these are the most comprehensive data available for a reasonably sized national sample of Jews. Therefore, we believe that this is the best data source for our analysis, but we try to be mindful of the data's limitations.

The survey was constructed to yield information on the American Jewish population for both planning and policy-making purposes as well as for academic research. At times this meant that theoretical considerations were compromised in the interest of keeping the survey brief enough that respondents would be motivated to answer all of the questions. We find this particularly troubling when we attempt to understand what "Jewishness" means, as we shall note in Chapter 6. We apologize for the limitations the available questions placed on our analysis, but we trust the reader will find there is certainly much in this rich data set that is worth considering.

For comparison purposes, we use the 1990 NJPS, wherein the population of Jews is defined as meeting two of the following criteria: (1) born Jewish; (2) raised Jewish; (3) consider themselves Jewish. For comparison with the broader U.S. population, we use published and unpublished data from the 1990 and 2000 Censuses, the 2004 Current Population Survey, and the 2001 Survey of Income and Program Participation (SIPP) conducted by the U.S. Census Bureau. Where possible we concentrate on non-Hispanic whites aged 18 and older in our comparisons, as nearly all of the Jewish population is white, and we focus on the education and labor force participation of Jewish adults 18 and over (unless otherwise noted).

STRUCTURE OF THE BOOK

The first part of the book focuses on the distinctiveness of American Jews as compared with the broader U.S. population in terms of men's and women's educational attainment, familistic behavior, labor force patterns, and occupational attainment. Following something of a life-cycle approach, we begin with an examination of the educational attainment of American Jews, according to the 2000–01 NJPS findings; we discuss the distinctiveness of American Jews compared with the broader U.S. population in 2000 and examine whether this distinctiveness has changed since 1990 (Chapter 2). A major focus is the difference in educational attainment of Jewish men and women. We briefly look at lifelong learning as well. Chapter 3 examines the family behavior of American Jews with a similar purpose, to show its distinctiveness in comparison with the broader U.S. population. We consider a number of measures of "familistic behavior," including marriage, age at first marriage, age at birth of first child, number of children, divorce, and number of times married. We also examine educational homogamy among American Jews. Chapter 4 continues with labor force participation and occupational achievement, relating them to educational attainment and family roles, and examining whether the patterns we find among American Jews differ from those seen in the broader population. In Chapter 5, we consider the dominance of dual earning among American Jewish couples, examining the extent to which that phenomenon is related to equal economic contributions of the spouses and equal occupational attainment, and whether the patterns we find are similar to or different from those within the broader U.S. population.

The second part of the book deals with the second way in which we examine the relationship between gender, "Jewishness," and secular behavior. We examine the various meanings of "Jewishness" in Chapter 6 and compare their manifestations among men and women. In Chapter 7 we relate the various expressions of "Jewishness" to familistic behavior, examining whether "more" Jewishness in any sense is related to a particular pattern of familistic behavior among men and/or women. In Chapter 8 we relate expressions of Jewishness to secular attainment—education, labor force, and occupational status and rewards—and to the patterns of gender equality we find in each. Chapter 9 relates Jewishness to dual-earning patterns among Jewish couples. Chapter 10 focuses on the differences between intermarried Jews and intramarried Jews in terms of their family behavior and secular attainment, addressing the question of whether intermarriage results in "less Jewish" patterns of behavior.

We conclude in Chapter 11 with a summary of our findings, indications of trends, implications for Jewish communal policy, and suggestions for further research on the topic.

PART I

The Distinctiveness of Gendered Patterns of

Secular Achievement among American Jews

CHAPTER 2

Education Patterns

The Foundation of Family and Economic Roles

We start by looking at gender differences in educational attainment among contemporary American Jews. Education is a good starting point, for (at least) two reasons: (1) It is basic to considering achievement in secular activities. By providing access to the training and credentials attesting to occupational "fitness," education acts as a gatekeeper to occupational status and rewards. (2) It is related to many considerations regarding family roles, which further interact with secular achievement. Entrance into a permanent intimate arrangement may be postponed until education is completed, or childbearing may be delayed until education is completed and a career established. Thus, the years a person spends pursuing education may condition decisions about family roles. Education may also provide information that affects decisions about family roles (e.g., about the economics of family life or contraception). And educational settings serve as marriage markets, where potential partners congregate, thus influencing the homogamy later found among intimate partners.

Contrary to what might be expected, American Jewish men and women do not have equal educational attainment. This fact is sometimes camouflaged in comparisons with the broader U.S. population, because the gender differences are concentrated at the top end of the educational spectrum, which is sometimes conflated with all those receiving college degrees. But if we look at the proportion of those who earn graduate degrees or professional degrees, men and women are not equal (as we shall show later in the chapter). The inequality common to the rest of the U.S. population is simply transferred up the educational ladder, as we found in 1990 (Hartman and Hartman, 1996a).

But the inequality between men and women is not great and certainly does not resemble any gender gaps seen in developing countries, for example. Nor does it resemble the gender gap in formal Jewish education (see

Chapter 6), which has been influenced by a tradition that emphasizes men's formal training for the widespread public ceremony of Bar Mitzvah (which for many entails a knowledge of Hebrew and reciting or chanting at least some portion of the weekly Torah reading) and for public religious leadership roles. Although women have made inroads into both of these public arenas, particularly among the non-Orthodox, it would be inaccurate to conclude that gender parity has been achieved in the celebration of Bar or Bat Mitzvah or in rabbinical or cantorial roles (Geffen, 2007). But it is not at all clear that the inequality in formal Jewish education spills over to secular education. On the contrary, because traditionally more men were involved in formal Jewish education and the culture valued men's immersion in such study, there is a parallel historical tradition of Jewish women's immersion in secular training, especially for economic roles that would help support the family (Katz, 1973; Webber, 1983).

If we were to consider "college education" a single category, we might indeed conclude that there is gender equality in the educational attainment of American Jews, especially among those under 65. But patterns of gender equality in educational training raise new questions about family dynamics. We cannot assume that all parties concerned view educational homogamy as desirable, especially if it challenges traditional statuses within the family. Furthermore, it may or may not imply class and status homogamy within the family. Even when their educational attainment is similar to that of men, women do not usually earn the same wages as men (Padavic and Reskin, 2002), although the gender gap is narrower than it used to be. We need to examine whether the differences in educational attainment that we find among American Jews are sufficient to maintain traditional roles within the family, or whether there is a greater likelihood of spousal equality in this respect among American Jews than in the broader population. We also need to examine how the level of educational attainment among Jewish men and women is reconciled with the importance of the family, which is central to Jewish tradition. These are some of the threads our analysis will follow.

But first, let us turn to the educational patterns themselves—the subject of this chapter. Gender differences in Jewish education are considered in Chapter 6.

EDUCATIONAL ATTAINMENT OF AMERICAN JEWISH MEN AND WOMEN

By any standard, and especially compared with non-Jews in the United States, American Jews are well educated (Table 2.1). Less than 4% have not completed high school, 80% have completed more than a high school education, and 58% have completed at least an undergraduate degree. A quarter

Table 2.1 Education of American Jews and U.S. White Population by Gender

Education	American Jews, 2000–01			U.S. white population, 2000		
	Men	Women	Total	Men	Women	Total
Less than high school	3.8	3.1	3.4	22.1	22.0	22.1
High school graduate	13.2	18.3	15.9	28.7	32.9	30.9
Some college	19.7	25.7	22.9	27.2	28.2	27.7
Bachelor's degree	33.1	30.5	31.7	13.7	11.7	12.7
Master's degree	18.8	17.9	18.3	4.7	3.9	4.3
Doctoral, professional degree	11.3	4.6	7.8	3.5	1.3	2.3
Total	100.0	100.0	100.0	100.0	100.0	100.0
(*n*, thousands)[a]	(1,569)	(1,752)	(3,321)	(380,521)	(414,702)	(795,223)
Bachelor's degree or higher (%)	65.2	52.0	57.8	21.9	16.9	19.3

Data source for American Jews: NJPS (2000–01); for U.S. Whites: 2000 U.S. Census.
[a]NJPS data weighted by person-weights provided with dataset.

of Jews have earned graduate degrees, and nearly 8% have earned professional or doctoral degrees, including 1% who have earned medical degrees and about 2%, law degrees.

Both Jewish men and women are highly educated, and overall the gender differences are small.[1] However, as education increases, the gender gap widens: while more than 96% of both men and women have completed at least a high school education, nearly two-thirds of men have earned at least a bachelor's degree, compared with slightly more than half of women; 30% of men have earned some graduate degree, compared with 22.5% of women; and 11% of men have earned a doctoral or professional degree, more than double the 5% of women. Among Jews who earned a graduate degree, more than a third of the men went beyond master's degrees, compared with only 22% of the women; 23% of the men earned doctoral degrees, and 13% earned first-professional degrees (D.D.S., M.D./D.O, or law); whereas only 14% of the women earning graduate degrees earned doctoral degrees, and only 7.6% earned first-professional degrees.

Gender differences in education are greater for American Jews aged 45 and older than for younger cohorts. As in the broader U.S. population, American Jewish men had greater access to higher education than women until about the 1960s, partly because of the association of higher education with preparation for professional careers that were not open to women

(Hunter College, 2005) and partly because of assistance with higher education offered by the GI bill to (male) veterans after World War II (McLaughlin et al., 1988). Only after 1960 did the proportion of women with a higher education begin to catch up with that of men. The results can be seen among American Jews: more than 72% of American Jewish women between the ages of 25 and 44 have earned undergraduate degrees, compared with 65% of women 45–54, less than half of women 55–64, and only about a third of the women 65 and over (Figure 2.1). Unlike women, men between the ages of 45 and 64 are as likely to have earned undergraduate degrees as are men 25–44. Among men, a lower level of education characterizes only the age group of 65 and older.[2]

Therefore, among American Jews under 45, there are few gender differences in the proportion earning undergraduate degrees, and they are not statistically significant. However, from age 35 and older, the gender gap is wider, and it increases with age.[3]

Among those who received graduate degrees, women are more likely than men to have discontinued their education after earning a master's degree, in all cohorts (Figure 2.2). However, there are some interesting differences between the cohorts. Among men, the proportion receiving doctorates is greater in the 35–44 cohort than in older cohorts, while the proportion earning

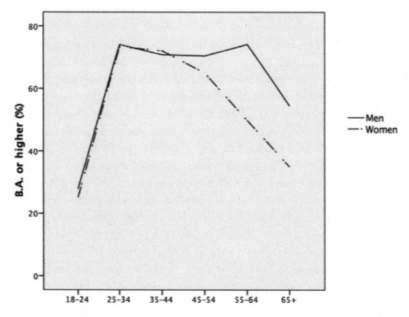

Figure 2.1. Percentage of American Jews achieving a B.A. or higher, by age and gender. *Data source:* NJPS, 2000–01.

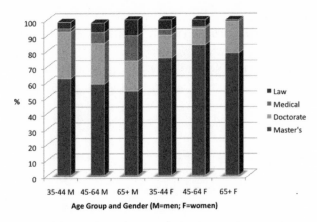

Figure 2.2. Distribution of graduate degrees, by gender and age (35 and over).

professional degrees is greater in the older cohorts than in the 35–44 cohort. Among men 65 and older, more than 16% of those earning graduate degrees went into medicine or dentistry and more than 10% went into law; among men 35–44, only 2% of those earning graduate degrees went into medicine or dentistry, and less than 5% went into law. Among women, on the other hand, the proportion earning professional degrees is greater in the 35–44 cohort, reflecting a proportion increasing from less than 1% among women 65 and older earning graduate degrees to nearly 10% of women 35–44. As a result, in the age cohort 35–44, the proportion of women's professional graduate degrees is actually greater than that of men's.

EDUCATIONAL DIFFERENCES BETWEEN AMERICAN JEWS AND THE BROADER WHITE U.S. POPULATION

Compared with the broader U.S. white population, American Jews are much more highly educated. The modal educational attainment of American Jews is a bachelor's degree, whereas that of the rest of the white population is a high school degree (Table 2.1). Seventy-eight percent of those in the U.S. white population have completed high school, compared with more than 96% of the Jewish subpopulation. Less than 20% of U.S. whites had completed an undergraduate degree in 2000, compared with 57.8% of Jews, and less than 7% had completed graduate or professional degrees, compared with more than a quarter of Jews. Nearly four times as many Jews have completed graduate or professional degrees than the broader white population, while nearly seven times as many whites have not completed high school as American Jews.

These general comparisons are reflected in the comparisons of each gender. Jewish men are much more highly educated than men in the broader white population: 21.9% of white men have received an undergraduate degree or higher, compared with nearly two-thirds of Jewish men; and the proportion of Jewish men who have received graduate degrees is almost four times that of white men. On the other hand, the proportion of white men in the broader population who have not completed a high school education is nearly seven times that of Jewish men.

Similar differences are found when white women in the broader population are compared with Jewish women. Twenty-two percent of white women have not completed a high school education, more than seven times the percentage of Jewish women who have not completed high school. Only 16.9% of white women have earned an undergraduate degree, compared with more than half of Jewish women. The proportion of Jewish women who have completed a graduate degree is more than four times that of white women.

These differences can be expressed by dissimilarity coefficients, which measure the differences in educational distribution from one (sub)population to another (Table 2.2). The coefficient of dissimilarity is defined as $D = {}^1/_2 > S \, |P_{ai} - P_{bi}|$ where P_{ai} and P_{bi} are the percentages in each educational level (or other percentage distribution) from the first in a pair of distributions (*a*) and the second in a pair of distributions (*b*), respectively. (This formula applies wherever a coefficient of dissimilarity is used in this book.) In this case, the coefficient of dissimilarity tells us what percentage of the subgroup would have to change its educational distribution to have the same distribution as the subgroup with which we are comparing it. For example,

Table 2.2 Dissimilarity Coefficients of Educational Distributions for American Jews and U.S. Non-Hispanic Whites, by Gender

Population	American Jews, 2000–01			U.S. white population, 2000		
	Men	Women	Total	Men	Women	Total
American Jews, 2000–01						
Men						
Women	11.0					
Total	5.9	6.5				
U.S. white population, 2000						
Men	20.0	23.0	21.3			
Women	27.4	23.3	25.2	10.7		
Total	21.7	21.6	20.5	7.1	7.4	

Data source for American Jews: NJPS (2000–01); for U.S. whites: 2000 U.S. Census.

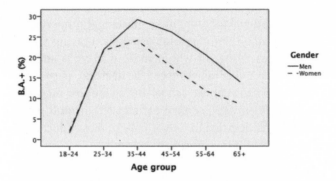

Figure 2.3. Percentage of U.S. non-Hispanic whites achieving a B.A. or higher, by age and gender, 2000. *Data source:* U.S. Census, 2000.

the coefficient of dissimilarity of 20.5 between the total white population of the United States and the Jewish population in the NJPS sample tells us that over 20% of the white population would have to change its education to have similar educational achievements as American Jews (or vice versa). The differences between Jewish and white women are slightly greater than those between Jewish and white men, with their dissimilarity coefficients 23.3 and 20.0, respectively. In each of these cases, it is the broader population that would have to increase its education to have achievements similar to those of American Jews.[1]

The gender gap in education among American Jews is very similar to the gender gap in education among the broader white population (about 11% of women in each population would have to change their education to have achievements similar to those of men). In both populations, these differences reflect a higher proportion of women than of men who do not continue their education after high school graduation or drop out of college before completing a degree, while a higher proportion of men than women complete doctoral or professional degrees. A higher proportion of Jewish women go on to some college than do women in the broader white female population, but the pattern of gender differences is the same in both populations.

There is virtually no gender gap in the proportion completing high school or obtaining a higher degree in any age group in the broader white population. However, as among Jews, from age 35 on, there is a gender gap in the proportion receiving undergraduate degrees (Figure 2.3). The lack of gender difference among those under 35 may reflect the trend toward equality in educational achievements (or may simply be camouflaging gender differences in higher educational degrees, as we find among American Jews).

Even with their high educational attainment, a substantial proportion of American Jews are continuing their education as adults. Leaving out the youngest respondents (ages 18–24, of whom more than 70% attended school, many of whom were still completing college degrees), 15.5% of respondents aged 25 and over had attended school during the year preceding the survey (1999–2000). Twenty-five percent participated in adult Jewish education. A total of 32% participated in one or both of these educational pursuits. This was equally true of men and women over 25.

The proportions decrease with age, but even among those 65 and over, 11.9% had attended school that year, and 21.6% had received some adult Jewish education; 27.5% had participated in one or both (Table 2.3). Note also that, among women, there is an increase in school enrollment in the 40–59 age groups, indicating a pattern of "re-entry" as mothers return to continue their education after their children are older. In these age groups, women are more likely to be enrolled in school than are men.

The proportions enrolled in school as adults are higher than in the broader population: more than a third of American Jews aged 25 to 29 are enrolled in higher education, compared with only 11.4% of the broader population (Swail, 2002), but because many may be completing graduate degrees, a fairer comparison might be of older age groups. Among those, only 6.7% of those in the broader population between the ages of 30 and 39 were enrolled in school during the year 2000, compared with 16.8% of American Jews.

American Jewish adults enrolled in school are also more likely to be attending full time than are adults in the broader population. Among those between the ages of 25 and 29 in the broader population, 51% of those enrolled attend full time, compared with 55.6% of Jews; among those 30–34, the respective percentages are 39% (broader population) and 44.4% (Jews). Of those attending school, women are more likely to attend part time than men (62% compared with men's 56%). But during the most intense work years (ages 35–54), men are more likely to be attending part time than women. In those age groups, men enrolled in school are also more likely to be employed than women (less than 10% of the men are not employed, compared with about a quarter of the women). This may reflect both work-related schooling and the increasing proportion of "nontraditional students" who are re-entry women returning for college degrees, often after their main childbearing and childrearing years—both trends increasing in the broader population as well.

Most of those enrolled in higher-education classes are married, among Jews as well as the broader population; this is especially true after age 35 for

Table 2.3 Percentage Enrolled in School and Percentage Who Receive Some Adult Jewish Education, by Age and Gender[a]

Age	Enrolled in school, 1999–2000			Received adult Jewish education[b]		
	Men	Women	Total	Men	Women	Total
25–29	40.6	31.5	36.0	22.3	19.0	20.6
	(126)	(144)	(270)	(126)	(145)	(271)
30–34	20.9	17.2	19.0	24.0	16.6	20.2
	(140)	(155)	(295)	(140)	(155)	(295)
35–39	13.0	12.8	12.9	16.8	25.1	21.1
	(139)	(155)	(294)	(139)	(154)	(293)
40–44	8.1	17.9	13.3	31.6	32.4	32.0
	(169)	(204)	(373)	(169)	(201)	(370)
45–49	12.6	20.5	16.6	30.4	35.6	33.0
	(188)	(232)	(420)	(188)	(232)	(420)
50–54	12.7	17.3	14.9	25.9	26.5	26.2
	(212)	(242)	(454)	(212)	(241)	(453)
55–59	8.8	16.1	12.9	18.9	32.9	26.6
	(127)	(181)	(308)	(127)	(181)	(308)
60–64	11.5	10.6	11.0	17.5	24.2	21.0
	(106)	(140)	(246)	(104)	(139)	(243)
65+	12.6	11.3	11.9	22.8	20.7	21.6
	(415)	(606)	(1021)	(412)	(601)	(1013)
Total	14.7	16.2	15.5	23.9	25.4	24.7
	(1661)	(2128)	(3789)	(1656)	(2016)	(3772)

[a]Unweighted sample size in parentheses; calculations performed using person-weights provided with dataset.
[b]Respondents were asked, "During the past year, did you attend any adult Jewish education classes or any other kind of adult Jewish learning, such as synagogue programs, a book group, a study group at home or work, or a Bible study group, but excluding any college courses you may have taken?"

Jews. A higher proportion of women than men who return to school as adults over the age of 35 are divorced or separated (or, among those 65 and over, widowed). Among men, a higher proportion of those returning to school between 35 and 65 who are not currently married have never married (rather than being divorced or separated).

In summary, the patterns of learning that established higher educational attainment among American Jews than in the broader population appear to be evident in their patterns of lifelong learning as well. But the gender inequality characterizing more traditional education is different in these patterns, and even reversed. Thus, women make up more of the adults attending school between the ages of 40 and 59, and more of the adults receiving Jewish education between the ages of 55 and 64. Such gender differences are not unique to American Jews, but they may increase the extent of gender parity in education over the life course. Non-married men engaging in later education are less likely to have ever married than are non-married women continuing their education; the women are more likely to be divorced or separated, presumably using their education to train for a better occupational position with which to support themselves and/or their families.

CHANGES SINCE 1990

Among both Jewish men and women, the proportion who did not go beyond high school in 1990 was more than twice the proportion of those who did not in 2000–01 (Table 2.4). About four and a half times as many men completed some college in 2000–01 as compared with 1990; and nearly five times as many women completed some college in 2000–01 as compared with 1990. There is only a small increase in the proportion earning bachelor's and master's degrees among both men and women in 2000–01 as compared with 1990, but the proportion of women completing doctoral and professional degrees increased, while the proportion of men completing such degrees actually decreased. In 1990, 85% of the graduate degrees

Table 2.4 Education of American Jews, 18 and Over, by Gender

Education	American Jews, 1990 (%)			American Jews, 2000–01 (%)		
	Men	Women	Total	Men	Women	Total
Less than high school	4.5	3.0	3.1	3.4	3.8	3.7
High school graduate	29.6	40.3	18.3	15.9	13.2	34.9
Some college	4.3	5.2	25.7	22.9	19.7	4.7
Bachelor's degree	31.1	28.9	30.5	31.7	33.1	30.1
Master's degree	16.2	19.1	17.9	18.3	18.8	17.6
Doctoral, professional degree	14.2	3.5	4.6	7.8	11.3	8.9
Total	100.0	100.0	100.0	100.0	100.0	100.0
(n, thousands)[a]	(1,874)	(1,821)	(1,752)	(3,321)	(1,569)	(3,696)
Bachelor's degree or higher	61.7	51.5	52.0	57.8	65.2	56.6

Data sources: NJPS (1990, 2000–01).

[a]Weighted by person-weights provided with datasets.

Table 2.5 Education of U.S. Non-Hispanic White Population, by Gender

Education	U.S. white population, 1990 (%)			U.S. white population, 2000 (%)		
	Men	Women	Total	Men	Women	Total
Less than high school	22.7	22.6	22.6	22.1	22.0	22.1
High school graduate	29.8	33.9	32.0	28.7	32.9	30.9
Some college	26.1	26.9	32.0	27.2	28.2	27.7
Bachelor's degree	13.5	11.5	12.4	13.7	11.7	12.7
Master's degree	4.6	3.8	4.2	4.7	3.9	4.3
Doctoral, professional degree	3.3	1.2	2.2	3.5	1.3	2.3
Total %	100.0	100.0	100.0	100.0	100.0	100.0
(Weighted *n*, thousands)	(3,692)	(4,052)	(7,744)	(3,805)	(4,147)	(7,952)

Data sources: U.S. Population Census (1990, 2000).

earned by women were master's degrees; in 2000–01, this proportion dropped to 78% (the rest being doctoral or professional degrees).

Changes in the education of the broader white population of the United States have been much less dramatic (Table 2.5). There is a slight increase in the proportion of those finishing high school and also in the proportion of those going on to some college, but the proportion earning bachelor's, master's, and doctoral degrees is remarkably stable. Women's enrollment in undergraduate, graduate, and professional degree programs has increased at a rate greater than men's enrollment (NCES, 2003), but these changes are not reflected in major changes in educational distribution between 1990 and 2000.

In summary, increases in the education of Jews since 1990 are more dramatic than in the broader white population. The increase of Jewish women going on to doctoral and professional degrees is also more dramatic than in the broader population, although enrollment trends suggest that such changes will become apparent in the broader population in the near future.

SUMMARY AND CONCLUSIONS

We see that Jews' educational attainment continues to be higher than that of the greater U.S. population of non-Hispanic whites, extending into patterns of lifelong learning. In fact, the education of American Jews appears to have increased at a more dramatic rate than that of the broader population, maintaining and even increasing the gap in achievement.

We also see that the patterns of gender inequality in education among American Jews remain very similar to such patterns in the broader population—small but persistent, even at the higher levels of education of American Jews. Some indications that this is changing can be seen in the greater educational similarity of younger cohorts, especially in the higher proportion of Jewish women aged 35–44 who have completed master's and first-professional degrees than men of similar age. However, this may only reflect women finishing their degrees faster than men (Buchman and Diprete, 2006).

In the coming chapters we will see whether the small but persistent differences in education influence educational patterns in marriage, labor force participation, or occupational attainment.

CHAPTER 3

Family Patterns of American Jews

This chapter explores the distinctiveness of American Jewish family patterns and analyzes the gender differences within them. As mentioned earlier, historically Jews have demonstrated two contradictory tendencies, which make this an interesting case. On the one hand, the family is central to Jewish life and values, and much of Jewish life takes place within the family. Children are highly valued and not only are central to the transmission of Jewish identity, but also are related to heightened Jewish practice and communal involvement. The family's importance was strengthened by the diaspora experience, as in many settings the family was the only intact Jewish institution. In the United States today, however, the family institution may be seen as weakened, with a declining rate of marriage, a higher rate of divorce, and a decreasing size of families (Coltrane and Collins, 2001, ch. 5). At issue is the extent to which American Jews have been affected by declining familism in the broader society. Furthermore, Jewish integration into U.S. society may also have diminished the need for family centrality, as institutions of formal and informal Jewish socialization, such as supplementary and day schools, summer camps, and youth trips to Israel, flourish (Cohen, 2004). As immigrants to the United States, Jews relied heavily on the family to perpetuate Judaism (Heschel, 2004; Prell, 2007b), but with a majority of American Jews now being at least third generation, the immigrant experience may have less influence, and with this, the family's centrality may diminish.

Their traditional familistic orientation contradicts a second tendency among American Jews: their relatively high educational and occupational achievement, factors that are usually associated with smaller families and low fertility. High educational and occupational achievement also undermines traditional gender roles based on the centrality of women's domestic role. Although Jewish women have a long history of providing or helping to provide for the family's economic needs, their primary focus has been the good of the family rather than self-actualization (Fishman, 2005). In contemporary U.S. society, individualistic motivations predominate (Bellah, Madsen, Sullivan, Swindler, and Tipton, 1985/1996; Fishman, 2005), which may further undermine familistic motivations for secular achievement. The norm of small families might easily be reconciled with strong individualistic secular ambitions. Therefore, traditional Jewish familism may be further undermined by contemporary patterns of secular achievement and their ramifications in family life. This chapter examines contemporary American Jewish family behavior to determine how distinctive it is from the broader U.S. society, focusing particularly on comparing American Jewish men and women with those in the broader society who share similar educational characteristics. The chapter also lays the foundation for examining how family behavior is related to the secular achievement of men, women, and couples, which we address in subsequent chapters.

The distinctiveness of American Jewish families has not gone unnoticed in previous research. Based on the General Social Survey compiled from 1972 to 2000, Smith's (2005) "statistical portrait" of the distinctiveness of American Jews provides evidence of the traditional familistic tendencies of American Jews, as well as the smaller family size. In comparison with the national sample of the broader U.S. population, American Jews have a higher rate of marriage, a lower rate of divorce, and a higher proportion of individuals growing up in intact families. At the same time, American Jews have smaller families than the broader population. Although American Jews remain distinctive in these respects, because the number of children among the broader population has been decreasing at an even faster rate than among American Jews, the differences are narrowing. The initial report on the 2000–01 National Jewish Population Survey (United Jewish Communities, 2003c) suggested that the overall percentage of American Jewish men and women ever married was comparable to the percentage of those who had ever been married in the broader U.S. population (based on data from the 2000 U.S. Population Census), although American Jews delay marriage and therefore have much lower rates of marriage until around age 45 for men and age 35 for women (see also Xu, Hudspeth, and Bartkowski, 2005). In this respect, distinctive American Jewish familism appears to have waned. American Jewish women continue to have fewer children than do women in the broader U.S. population, partially owing to delayed childbearing (the gap narrows with age). However, in every age group, a significantly higher proportion of American Jewish women appear to remain childless than among women in the broader U.S. population (United Jewish Communities, 2003c). Hurst and Mott (2003) suggest that many of the differences in fertility between American Jews and the broader population can be explained by education. Fishman (2005), however, notes that education interacts with intended fertility in a different way among Jews than in the broader population. Our analysis addresses the extent to which education explains differences in family behavior between American Jews and the broader U.S. population.

Of particular interest among American Jews, as a highly educated subgroup, is how education is related to family behavior. A number of researchers have noted a recent trend whereby the highly educated are more likely to marry, albeit after some delay, and to have more children once they begin childbearing than are less educated women who delay childbearing. Thus, Goldstein and Kenney (2001) found higher marriage rates among college-educated women; Martin (2000) found that college-educated women who had postponed childbearing until after age 30 had increased their fertility from the 1970s to the 1990s, in contrast to the fertility of less educated women who had postponed childbearing and childrearing. The proportion of highly educated women with two or more children had also increased. Similarly, Weeden, Abrams, Green, and Sabini (2006) did not find a negative relationship between education and fertility, despite expectations to this effect. Thus, there is ample evidence that marriage and childbearing are becoming increasingly compatible with women's higher educational training and presumably labor force participation. This chapter addresses where American Jews fit into these trends.

DATA

Family behavior indicators that we consider include the proportion of respondents currently or ever married, the proportion currently or ever divorced, age at first marriage, duration of first marriage for those whose first marriage ended in divorce, childlessness (of women), age at birth of first child (for women), and number of (live) children born (to women).

For comparison with the broader U.S. population, we use primarily the U.S. Census Bureau Survey of Income and Program Participation (SIPP) of 2001 (original analysis and published analysis in Kreider, 2005). The SIPP data have the advantage of including detailed marital history for men and women of all ages, as well as extensive information about the characteristics of adults, their households, and those with whom they live, including data about husbands and wives currently married. We focus on non-Hispanic whites, as nearly all American Jews are white. The proportion of Jews among this broader population is estimated to be less than 2%; to the extent that Jews are included in the survey, the effect would be to reduce the differences between the two populations, but only minimally.

At the time of the 2000–01 NJPS, 21.3% of the adult American Jewish population had never been married, 61.5% of the population was currently married, and another 1% was separated, 1.2% cohabiting,[1] 8.7% divorced, and 8.2% widowed.[2] More than three-quarters had been married at least once, and more than a third had been divorced at least once.

This distribution does not tell us much unless we introduce some comparisons. In discussing family behavior, it is important to consider these patterns separated into different age groups, for both cohort and life-cycle considerations. That is, some patterns indicate change in social norms relating to marriage and divorce, such as delayed patterns of marriage or greater acceptance of divorce (cohort effects), while some of the differences may simply have to do with the fact that the younger cohort is not old enough to marry (or divorce) or to have experienced much death or widowhood (life-cycle effects). Through the main first-marriage and childbearing ages, until about age 45, both life-cycle and cohort effects contribute to variations; after age 45, most of the differences between age groups can be attributed to birth cohort variation. We also separate men and women, because women typically marry earlier than men (see the mean age at first marriage in Table 3.1, which shows a difference of from 1 to 5 years, depending on the age group).

Looking first at the proportion currently married (Table 3.1), we see that the proportion ever married increases through the 35–44 age group, suggesting that some first marriages are still occurring in this age group, especially among men. The proportion currently married peaks in the 65 and older age group for men, but earlier for women, as women typically live longer than men, and therefore in the older age groups there is an increasing proportion of widows. In the 65 and older age group, more than 95% of both American Jewish men and women have been married at least once.

About a fifth of the population has been married more than once, and this proportion peaks for men in the 55–64 age group, among whom nearly 30% of the men have been married more than once; for women the peak is in the 45–54 age group, among whom 22.5% have been married more than once. The lower proportion of women who have been married more than once may reflect a higher proportion of both widows and divorcees who do not remarry. Among those women who have ever divorced, for example, 42% have never remarried, compared with less than a third of the men.

About 18% of the men and women have been divorced at least once. The proportion divorced peaks in the 55–64 age group for both men and women, indicating a cohort difference between those 65 and over and those 64 and younger. Close to a third of the men and women aged 55–64 have divorced at least once, compared with 17% of the men and 15% of the

Table 3.1 Family Behavior of American Jews, by Age and Gender

Family indicator	18–24	25–34	35–44	45–54	55–64	65+	Total
				Age			
Men							
Currently married (%)	8.9	46.1	66.6	72.7	70.0	75.7	61.5
Ever married (%)	9.2	50.4	74.2	91.2	89.6	96.2	75.2
Mean age at first marriage	21.0	26.3	29.0	29.2	29.8	30.0	29.1
Married more than once (%)	0	1.5	15.6	26.6	29.1	21.5	21.8
Divorced (%)	0.3	3.4	6.2	13.2	14.2	5.6	7.7
Ever divorced (%)	0.3	4.2	16.4	33.3	32.2	17.2	19.0
Mean duration of first marriage before divorce (years)	na	1.0	6.3	7.9	13.8	14.4	10.4
(*n*, thousands)[a]	(163.1)	(230.0)	(247.5)	(352.8)	(204.0)	(381.0)	(1,578.3)
Women							
Currently married (%)	17.6	55.9	69.8	71.6	65.0	54.1	57.9
Ever married (%)	17.7	60.2	83.5	88.5	95.3	97.4	79.7
Mean age at first marriage	20.4	25.6	27.1	27.2	24.4	25.2	25.8
Married more than once (%)	0	4.7	15.3	22.5	17.6	20.3	15.9
Divorced (%)	0.2	3.5	10.1	14.0	21.2	7.1	9.6
Ever divorced (%)	0.2	6.1	20.5	28.8	31.8	14.5	18.1
Mean duration of first marriage before divorce (years)	na	4.0	6.5	9.4	13.4	13.4	10.2
Childless (%)	89.7	63.8	28.9	27.0	14.3	9.2	32.6
Mean age at birth of first child	20.0	25.0	28.0	27.0	23.0	25.0	24.5
Mean number of children	0.1	0.8	1.7	1.6	2.0	2.1	1.4
Four or more children (%)	0	5.2	9.5	6.2	9.9	10.0	7.5
(*n*, thousands)[a]	(179.7)	(237.4)	(271.3)	(363.5)	(238.7)	(461.9)	(1,752.4)

[a] Weighted by person-weights distributed with dataset.

women 65 and over (the lower percentage of women 65 and over may in part be a reflection of their older age, on the average, in that women live longer than men). Among those whose first marriage ended in divorce, the first marriage lasted on average 10 years; in the older cohorts (55+), this first marriage lasted on average even longer—more than 13 years.

More than two-thirds of all the women have children, and 83.5% of those who have been married at least once have children. Up to the 35–44 age group, it is difficult to determine how much of this is temporary, that is, whether the women will still give birth. But after age 45 it is unlikely that a woman will give birth. In the 45–54 age group, 17.5% of those ever married remain childless, compared with 11.0% of the 55–64 age group and 7.0% of the women 65 and over. This suggests a trend of increasing childlessness, even among those married.

Single mothers (mothers who are currently not married) make up 18.3% of all the American Jewish women who have given birth; less than 4% have never married. Perhaps of more relevance is the percentage of mothers who have children under 18 at home: 12.3% are currently not married, including only 2.8% who have never married. This is quite comparable to the broader U.S. population. Among single mothers who have finished college, all but 3% have also been married (Ellwood and Jencks, 2004, p. 11).

Overall, Jewish women have on average fewer than 2 children. This too varies by cohort. Among women 55 and over, the mean number of children is 2 or more, whereas in the 35–44 and 45–54 cohorts, the mean number of children is 1.7 and 1.6, respectively. (It is likely that women in younger age groups will bear children later; hence, the mean number of children may not be a final statistic.) The mean age at birth of first child peaks in the 35–44 age group at age 28, and is lower in other age groups, especially among women 65 and older. Few women in the sample had their first child after age 35 (2.5% ages 35–39 and less than 1% over age 40), so it is hard to know to what extent American Jews are part of a growing trend of late motherhood (Gregory, 2008).

Education and Family Patterns among American Jews

Their higher educational level explains some of the distinctiveness of American Jews' family behavior, as we shall explore later in comparison with the broader population. Among Jews, level of education is also related to variation in family behavior. In Table 3.2 we focus on men and women between the ages of 35 and 64 (after most have completed their education and most childbearing has been completed, but before widowhood becomes a major factor). American Jews with higher education are more likely to be married, less likely to be divorced, and less likely to be married more than once; among women, higher education is also associated with later marriage, later birth of first child, fewer children, and especially much lower percentages of four or more children (less than 3% of those with graduate degrees compared with 22.1% of those with high school education or less). Some of this gap may narrow slightly after age 35, as women with graduate degrees also give birth to their last child later than women with less education, but as Table 3.8 shows, even when the sample is restricted to

Table 3.2 Family Behavior of American Jews, Ages 35–64, by Education and Gender

| Gender | Family indicator | Education | | | | |
		High school or less	Some college	B.A.	Graduate degree	Total
Men	Married (%)	61.4	64.5	66.8	77.6	70.6
	Ever married (%)	85.4	86.5	82.6	89.3	86.2
	Mean age at first marriage	25.1	27.3	27.3	27.1	26.9
	Married more than once (%)	35.5	23.3	27.5	19.3	24.5
	Divorced (%)	15.2	16.8	10.8	8.6	11.5
	Ever divorced (%)	39.2	33.0	27.7	22.0	27.8
	Mean duration of first marriage before divorce (years)	11.9	9.1	10.3	11.1	10.6
	(n, thousands)[a]	(98.1)	(127.5)	(253.3)	(304.0)	(782.9)
Women	Married (%)	64.3	64.4	70.7	70.2	68.2
	Ever married (%)	88.9	88.0	89.3	88.0	88.5
	Mean age at first marriage (%)	22.4	22.7	25.2	26.2	24.5
	Married more than once (%)	16.7	25.2	18.4	16.3	19.2
	Divorced (%)	16.9	17.6	14.1	13.0	15.0
	Ever divorced (%)	28.7	31.7	26.4	23.8	27.2
	Mean duration of first marriage before divorce (years)	9.6	10.4	10.9	12.4	11.0
	Childless (%)	20.9	24.7	24.5	26.2	24.6
	Mean age at birth of first child	23.2	24.8	27.7	30.0	27.1
	Mean age at last birth	29.0	30.1	32.1	33.6	31.6
	Mean number of children	2.3	1.9	1.6	1.5	1.7
	Four or more children (%)	22.1	11.1	5.0	2.9	8.1
	(n, thousands)[a]	(103.4)	(207.1)	(270.9)	(248.4)	(830.9)

[a]Weighted by person-weights distributed with dataset.

women 45 and older, women with higher education have fewer children than women with less education. Our analysis reveals that, on average, the shorter the span of years of childbearing (age of last birth—age of first birth), the higher the level of the woman's education.

On the other hand, education appears to have very little effect on the chances of ever marrying, the duration of first marriage before divorce (especially for men), or women's likelihood of being married more than once. The last result is somewhat surprising, because there is an expectation that highly educated women will remarry at lower rates than men (Coleman, Ganong, and Fine, 2000); it does not appear to be supported by the data on American Jews, however. Women with graduate degrees are less likely to divorce and are as likely to be remarried as women with a high school education or less. Among those who do divorce, women with graduate degrees have longer first marriages on average than those with less education.

We can also consider the educational characteristics of Jews by their marital status. Married Jews have higher educational attainment than non-married Jews (Table 3.3). More than 60% of currently married Jews earned at least an undergraduate degree, compared with only about half of those who have never married and 55% of the divorced or separated. The lower education of the never married is partially related to their younger age, so that a relatively high proportion of them have not yet completed their education. The lower education level of the divorced or separated may be related to the greater likelihood that divorced men and women with a higher education will remarry, whereas the less educated may remain divorced (a similar pattern was found among Jews in 1990; see Hartman and Hartman, 1996a). Only 40.9% of widowed Jews have at least a bachelor's degree, which results from most of them being older than 55 and, as we noted earlier, the educational attainment of that age group is lower.

These differences based on marital status are apparent for both men and women. However, divorced women do not differ from currently married women as much as divorced men differ from currently married men. On the other hand, widowed women have much less education than women with other marital statuses, mainly because most of the widowed are older women who have a lower level of education. As a result, the largest gender gap is among the widowed, less because of their marital status

Table 3.3 Percentage of American Jews Achieving a B.A. or Higher, by Marital Status and Gender[a]

Marital status	Total	Men	Women	M/F ratio
Never married	51.1	53.7	48.2	1.11
	(933)	(476)	(457)	
Currently married	62.9	68.0	58.1	1.17
	(2,213)	(1,015)	(1,198)	
Divorced, separated	55.4	57.2	54.1	1.06
	(524)	(215)	(309)	
Widowed	40.1	59.5	32.3	1.84
	(460)	(114)	(346)	
Total	57.8	63.2	53.0	1.19
	(4,130)	(1,820)	(2,310)	

[a]Unweighted *n* in parentheses; calculations performed using person-weights provided with dataset.

than because of their age. Among the other marital statuses, the proportion of men and women earning at least a bachelor's degree is much more similar. Gender differences are smallest among the divorced and separated, mainly because divorced and separated women have almost as much education as the currently married, unlike divorced or separated men.

Because the majority of those never married are in the youngest age group (18–24), some of whom have not yet completed their education, and the majority of those widowed are in the older age groups, especially 55 and older, we looked at these relationships between marital status and education for each gender within age groups (Table 3.4).

In the youngest age group, the currently married are less likely to have completed a bachelor's degree than those who have never married; this difference results primarily because married women are less likely to earn a bachelor's degree. Consequently, the gender gap in education is much greater among the young who are married (with an M/F ratio of 1.48) than among the young who are single (with an M/F ratio of 1.16). For men, in all age groups under 65, the currently married have the highest education; for women, this is true for ages 35 and older (in the 25–34 age group, apparently, some women's education is still interrupted by marriage).

Among men, those who are divorced have the lowest level of education in each of the age groups. This is probably because of the tendency of more highly educated divorced men to remarry (as shown in Table 3.2). Divorced women, however, do not generally have less education than married or single women; in fact, among the older women (55 and over), divorced women are the most highly educated. This probably reflects the tendency of highly educated divorced women not to remarry—a pattern also found in the broader population (Bramlett and Mosher, 2002; Coleman et al., 2000); interestingly, however, it is found only among the older groups in this population.

The 45–54 age group is the first in which the number of widowed in the sample is large enough to compare with the other groups. The widowed show the largest gender gap in education in each of the older age groups (45–54, 55–64, 65+), mainly because widowed women (even in the 45–54 age group) are much less likely to have earned a bachelor's degree than women with other marital statuses.

In summary, we find that married Jewish men and women tend to have higher educational attainment than the non-married, in every age group except the youngest (presumably, young married women interrupt their education when they get married). Divorced and separated men are characterized by less education in almost every age group; divorced and separated women do not have less education than other women (with the exception of the 35–44 age group). Therefore, the gender gap in education is lowest

Table 3.4 Percentage of American Jews Achieving a B.A. or Higher, by Marital Status, Gender, and Age[a]

Age group	Marital status	Total	Men	Women	M/F ratio
18–24	Never married	34.2 (282)	36.7 (140)	31.7 (142)	1.16
	Currently married	29.6 (56)	35.0 (21)	26.5 (35)	1.48
	Divorced, separated	na	na	na	na
	Widowed	na	na	na	na
	Total	33.7 (338)	36.9 (161)	30.9 (177)	1.19
25–34	Never married	75.2 (266)	73.8 (141)	76.8 (125)	0.96
	Currently married	74.0 (278)	75.0 (116)	73.3 (162)	1.02
	Divorced, separated	70.6 (34)	66.7 (15)	73.7 (19)	0.91
	Widowed	na	na	na	na
	Total	74.4 (579)	74.0 (273)	74.8 (306)	.99
35–44	Never married	71.7 (165)	71.9 (91)	70.3 (74)	1.02
	Currently married	73.4 (421)	75.3 (183)	71.5 (238)	1.05
	Divorced, separated	58.5 (83)	68.8 (32)	52.0 (51)	1.32
	Widowed	na	na	na	na
	Total	70.8 (675)	72.3 (309)	66.8 (366)	1.08
45–54	Never married	67.0 (113)	70.5 (44)	64.7 (69)	1.09
	Currently married	70.4 (381)	74.0 (268)	67.4 (313)	1.10
	Divorced, separated	62.5 (170)	61.7 (82)	63.2 (88)	0.98
	Widowed	59.1 (22)	na na	46.2 (13)	1.68
	Total	68.2 (886)	71.2 (403)	65.7 (483)	1.08
55–64	Never married	54.4 (54)	66.7 (31)	47.8 (23)	1.40
	Currently married	54.8 (339)	77.2 (151)	53.2 (188)	1.45

Age group	Marital status	Total	Men	Women	M/F ratio
55–64 (cont'd)	Divorced, separated	58.3 (129)	76.7 (43)	63.5 (86)	1.21
	Widowed	39.1 (43)	75.0 (12)	48.4 (31)	1.55
	Total	51.1 (565)	75.6 (237)	55.1 (328)	1.37
65+	Never married	50.0 (50)	63.0 (27)	34.8 (23)	1.81
	Currently married	48.9 (528)	55.8 (271)	41.1 (247)	1.36
	Divorced, separated	46.0 (101)	50.0 (40)	43.3 (61)	1.15
	Widowed	37.2 (381)	53.5 (89)	32.3 (292)	1.66
	Total	44.4 (1,050)	55.2 (427)	37.0 (623)	1.49

Note: "na" indicates fewer than 10 cases in the sub-sample.

[a]Unweighted *n* in parentheses; calculations performed using person-weights provided with dataset.

among the divorced and separated. On the other hand, the difference between widowed men and women in terms of education is the highest of any marital status.

Educational Homogamy among American Jews

Education is also related to whom one marries, which may reinforce certain family patterns. Educational homogamy refers to marriages in which spouses have achieved the same level of education. Educational homogamy may be intentional, that is, potential marriage partners seek out spouses of a certain level of education; it may also happen by chance, because of patterns of association. Because both American Jewish men and women continue on to college in such large proportions, the likelihood of meeting a marriage partner with at least some college education is heightened.

Using six educational groups (less than high school, high school, some college, undergraduate degree, master's degree, doctoral degree, or professional degree), we find that 38.2% of American Jews have the same educational attainment as their spouse; another 46.8% are within one educational group of their spouse. When spouses' educational levels are not equal, it is

Table 3.5 Comparisons of Husband's and Wife's Education, by Age Group

Age group	Husband's > wife's education (%)	Husband's = wife's education (%)	Wife's > husband's education (%)	Total (%)	(n, thousands)[a]
25–34	25.1	44.2	30.7	100.0	(39.1)
35–44	39.5	34.9	25.6	100.0	(219.6)
45–54	40.3	35.3	24.4	100.0	(329.8)
55–64	44.0	35.9	20.1	100.0	(476.2)
65+	40.0	41.3	18.7	100.0	(277.8)
Total	38.6	38.3	23.1	100.0	(1,822.1)

[a]Weighted by person-weights provided in dataset.

more common for husbands to have received a higher education than their wives: in 38.6% of the cases, husbands have a higher education level than their wives; in 23.2%, wives have a higher education level than their husbands.

Educational homogamy is more common among young American Jews (under 35) and older Jews (65 and over). Homogamy among the young reflects increasing equality between men and women in their high educational attainment; among the old, it reflects the higher proportion of those with lower educational attainment. The traditional pattern of husbands having a higher education than their wives is not as common among those under 35—only 25.1% those aged 25–34 demonstrate this pattern, compared with more than 40% of those 45 and older. Similarly, it is more common to find wives with a higher level of education than their husbands among the young than the old (Table 3.5).

Compared with 1990, there is somewhat more educational homogamy and fewer "traditional" differences in which husbands have received more education than their wives. In 1990, in 31.6 of couples, husbands and wives had a similar educational attainment, compared with 38.3% in 2000–01; in 41% of couples, wives had more education than their husbands in 1990 (Hartman and Hartman, 1996a, pp. 176–77), compared with 38.3% in 2000–01. These trends toward homogamy and less traditional marriages mirror trends in the broader society, as we shall see later.

COMPARISON WITH THE BROADER U.S. POPULATION

Some of these patterns are similar to those seen in the broader population. Comparing the proportion of American Jews who have ever been married with the proportion among the broader, non-Hispanic, white U.S. population, we can see the effect of delayed marriage among American Jews, with

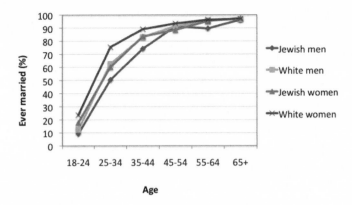

Figure 3.1. Percentage ever married, by age, of American Jews and non-Hispanic whites, 2000–01. *Data sources:* NJPS, 2000–01; SIPP, 2001 (Wave 2).

the gap between the Jewish and broader population of non-Hispanic whites larger through age 44 but virtually absent by age 65+ (Figure 3.1). (The data on which Figures 3.1 to 3.4 are based can be found in Table 3.6.)

The marriage delay results in a higher average age of marriage for Jews than for those in the broader white population, in the total and in every age group for both men and women, especially noticeable up to age 45, after which the gap narrows (Figure 3.2). Up to age 55, in fact, Jewish women marry even later than do men in the broader population, on the average. And even in the older age groups, Jewish men and women marry later than their white counterparts in the broader population.

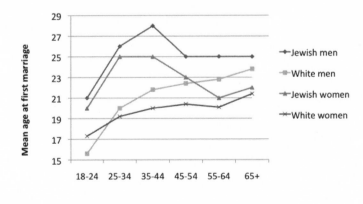

Figure 3.2. Mean age at first marriage, by age and gender, of American Jews and non-Hispanic whites, 2000–01. *Data sources:* NJPS, 2000–01; SIPP, 2001 (Wave 2).

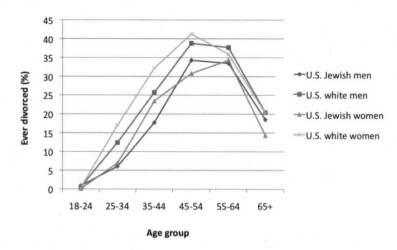

Figure 3.3. Percentage ever divorced for American Jews and non-Hispanic whites, by age and gender, 2000–01. *Data sources:* NJPS, 2000–01; SIPP, 2001 (Wave 2).

The proportion of Jewish men and women who are divorced is lower than that of men and women in the broader population in nearly every age group, although the differences are small for those 55 and over (Figure 3.3). When first marriages end in divorce, they are likely to have lasted longer among Jews, with a mean duration of more than 10 years, compared with around 8 years for the broader white population. A higher proportion of Jewish women remain childless, with differences especially notable through age 54 (Figure 3.4). Jewish women also wait longer to have their first child and have fewer children than women in the broader white population, in the

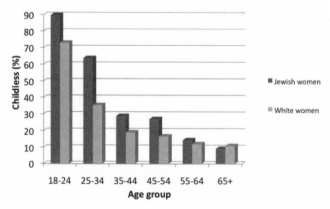

Figure 3.4. Percentage of women childless, for American Jews and non-Hispanic whites, by age, 2000–01. *Data sources:* NJPS, 2000–01; SIPP, 2001 (Wave 2).

Table 3.6 Family Behavior of U.S. Non-Hispanic Whites, by Age and Gender

Gender	Family indicator	Age						Total
		18–24	25–34	35–44	45–54	55–64	65+	
Men	Married (%)	11.2	54.0	68.6	72.0	79.5	77.0	61.9
	Ever married (%)	12.4	62.7	83.1	91.3	95.6	96.7	75.5
	Mean age at first marriage	15.6	20.0	21.8	22.4	22.8	23.6	22.4
	Married more than once (%)	0.8	11.3	18.9	31.3	33.8	23.1	23.4
	Divorced (%)	0.6	6.2	12.0	16.0	12.7	5.9	9.4
	Ever divorced (%)	0.6	12.4	25.7	38.8	37.7	20.4	23.3
	Mean number of years of first marriage ending in divorce	1.6	4.5	6.5	8.5	11.1	14.1	9.2
	(n, thousands)	(10,727.3)	(15,676.0)	(18,084.9)	(16,541.3)	(10,541.3)	(12,686.3)	(84,101.6)
Women	Married (%)	20.2	62.4	69.8	69.2	65.9	44.6	57.3
	Ever married (%)	23.6	75.5	89.1	93.4	96.2	96.7	82.4
	Mean age at first marriage	17.3	19.2	20.0	20.4	20.1	21.4	20.3
	Married more than once (%)	4.1	12.5	24.0	32.8	28.8	19.9	23.2
	Divorced (%)	1.4	9.3	15.0	18.0	15.6	7.2	11.6
	Ever divorced (%)	2.1	17.0	32.2	41.3	35.9	20.2	26.0
	Mean number of years of first marriage ending in divorce	2.9	4.2	6.4	8.2	10.7	12.8	8.5
	Childless (%)	73.0	35.4	19.0	16.6	12.0	10.9	25.1
	Mean age at birth of first child	19.2	23.2	25.0	24.5	23.6	Na	23.9
	Mean number of children	0.4	1.3	1.9	2.0	2.4	2.6	1.8
	Four or more children (%)	0.6	4.9	10.1	10.9	22.5	29.3	13.5
	(n, thousands)	(10,349.3)	(15,432.6)	(18,379.1)	(16,964.8)	(11,248.6)	(17,401.1)	(89,775.5)

Data source: SIPP, 2001 (Wave 2).

Table 3.7 Number of Biological Children for American Jewish and Non-Hispanic White Women Married at Least Once, Ages 45 and Over, by Current Marital Status

	Marital status					
	In first marriage		Now divorced		Now remarried	
Number of Children	Jews	Whites	Jews	Whites	Jews	Whites
Childless (%)	9.5	13.8	22.1	17.2	12.8	11.2
1 (%)	12.9	16.3	22.4	19.2	23.1	18.7
2 (%)	47.0	34.9	30.0	31.7	39.8	34.4
3 (%)	20.1	20.4	14.8	18.5	22.3	20.5
4 or more (%)	10.6	14.6	10.9	13.4	2.0	15.2
Total (%)	100.0	100.0	100.0	100.0	100.0	100.0
(n, thousands)[a]	(513.1)	(51,504.7)	(132.5)	(10,404.3)	(124.5)	(10,436.6)

[a]Weighted by person-weights distributed with each dataset.
Data sources: NJPS, 2000–01; SIPP, 2001 (Wave 2).

total and in each age group (Table 3.6). As can be seen in Table 3.7, the greatest differences in the percentage of those who are childless between Jews and the broader white population stem from those women who are divorced or remarried (i.e, not in first marriages). The other very striking difference is in the percentage of those who have four or more children, especially among those currently married (there being many fewer Jews having four or more children).

The Role of Education in Explaining Differences between American Jews and the U.S. Population

Not all of these differences between American Jews and non-Hispanic whites in the broader population are attributable to level of education. Controlling for level of education, and comparing only the population 45 and over (to reduce the confounding effects of life cycle), we find that the proportion of those ever married among men and women is quite similar, as is the proportion of those currently married at the time of each survey, respectively (Table 3.8). At every level of education, however, Jews marry later than whites in the broader white population, and this is true for both men and women.

At every level of education, Jewish men and women are less likely to have been married more than once and are less likely to have ever divorced—although differences between Jews and the broader population are

Table 3.8 Family Behavior of American Jews and Non-Hispanic Whites, Ages 45 and Over, by Education and Gender

Gender	Family indicator	High school or less		Some college		B.A.		M.A.+		Total	
		Jews	Whites	Jews	Whites	Jews	Whites	Jews	Whites	Jews	Whites
Men	Married (%)	71.8	73.5	71.8	74.7	72.9	77.9	77.0	82.2	73.9	75.6
	Ever married (%)	94.8	94.7	92.9	94.2	91.2	93.5	93.1	94.6	92.8	94.4
	Mean age at first marriage	24.6	22.3	26.5	22.7	26.9	23.6	26.7	24.1	26.4	22.8
	Married more than once (%)	23.9	29.6	19.5	33.3	22.9	24.8	19.2	25.4	21.1	29.3
	Divorced (%)	11.8	12.0	12.5	14.0	9.0	11.0	9.8	8.4	10.4	11.9
	Ever divorced (%)	26.3	32.1	27.6	37.5	22.7	28.7	27.6	28.8	25.9	32.6
	(n, thousands)[a]	(159.4)	(17,850.4)	(162.2)	(10,351.4)	(286.7)	(6,586.1)	(304.3)	(4,825.4)	(912.6)	(39,613.3)
Women	Married (%)	53.3	55.8	61.4	60.5	68.6	68.3	64.5	61.0	62.0	59.0
	Ever married (%)	94.5	96.5	92.1	96.5	95.6	94.0	90.3	87.4	93.2	95.5
	Mean age at first marriage	22.3	20.1	22.6	20.8	24.6	21.6	24.8	22.3	23.5	20.6
	Married more than once (%)	13.6	25.5	24.6	33.3	16.6	21.2	15.7	21.6	17.7	26.8
	Divorced (%)	11.0	11.3	12.8	17.1	12.6	11.8	15.5	16.7	12.9	13.3
	Ever divorced (%)	18.2	29.1	26.7	39.2	23.0	25.7	25.8	31.7	23.4	31.5
	Childless (%)	12.3	10.0	18.2	12.7	15.5	17.1	22.1	30.0	16.9	13.1
	Mean age at birth of first child	24.3	22.7	25.1	23.9	26.6	26.8	28.3	27.7	25.9	24.0
	Mean number of children	2.1	2.6	2.0	2.2	1.8	2.0	1.7	1.6	1.9	2.3
	Four or more children (%)	13.5	26.4	8.8	16.9	5.0	12.9	3.2	8.5	7.4	20.8
	(n, thousands)[a]	(245.7)	(24,254.4)	(283.0)	(12,153.2)	(273.0)	(5,774.0)	(218.8)	(3,432.8)	(1,020.6)	(45,014.5)

[a]Weighted by person-weights distributed with each dataset.

Data sources: NJPS, 2000–01; SIPP, 2001, (Wave 2).

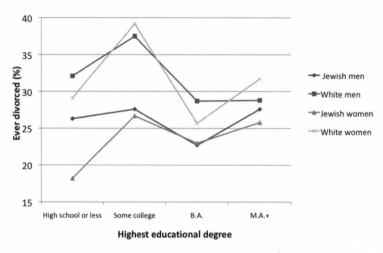

Figure 3.5. Percentage ever divorced for American Jews and non-Hispanic whites, by education and gender, 2000–01. *Data sources:* NJPS, 2000–01; SIPP, 2001 (Wave 2).

greater among the less educated than the more highly educated (Figure 3.5), especially for men.

Among the less educated (those who completed some college or less), a higher proportion of Jewish women remain childless than do women in the broader population; however, among women with college degrees, fewer Jewish women remain childless. Jewish women begin having children later in every education group, and they tend to have fewer children than women in the broader white population, except among those with graduate degrees, where there is little difference between Jewish women and white women in the broader population. Very large differences can be found at every level of education, however, among those with four or more children: the proportion of Jewish women at every level of education who have four or more children is less than half that of women in the broader white population.

Thus, we see that not all of the differences between American Jews and the broader white population can be attributed to the level of education of American Jews. Jews marry later, are less likely to divorce, are less likely to marry more than once, and have fewer children at nearly every level of education. In many cases, however, higher education reduces the differences between Jews and the broader white population.

Comparisons of Educational Homogamy

Collapsing the college degrees into a single category to make the educational classification more similar to that used by Schwartz and Mare (2005), and restricting the sample to wives aged 18–40 as Schwartz and Mare do, we can compare the educational homogamy among American Jews with that of the broader population. In 2000–01, there was educational homogamy in 69.6% of the American Jewish couples (wives aged 18–40) compared with 55% in the broader U.S. population (Schwartz and Mare, 2005, Figure 2, p. 633). American Jews may be seen as illustrating the trend of increased educational homogamy among the highly educated sector of the population, noted by Schwartz and Mare. Among the educationally heterogamous couples in this age group, in 50.7% of the American Jewish couples the wife had a higher education than her husband, compared with 45% of the wives in the broader U.S. population (Schwartz and Mare, 2005: 631). So there is more similarity in education among American Jews than in the broader population, and when there is dissimilarity, it is evenly divided between husbands and wives having higher education, somewhat more egalitarian than in the broader population.

SUMMARY AND CONCLUSIONS

We have shown three main ways in which the family behavior of American Jews is distinct from that of the broader white population, even when education is controlled for: they marry later, they are less likely to divorce, and they have fewer children. Note that these are not unrelated phenomena: marrying later may decrease the likelihood of divorce, owing to greater maturity and financial stability; it may also decrease the number of children, owing to the fewer number of fertile years during which the woman is married (although for the most part American Jews do not seem to take advantage of most of those fertile years during married life to bear children). This distinctive family behavior characterizes both men and women.

However, once education is controlled for, Jewish women are not more likely to remain childless than are women in the broader population. This, their lower likelihood of divorce, and their longer first marriages compared with those of women in the broader population are all indicative of the greater "familism" that has been traditional among Jews.

We have also shown that educational homogamy tends to be greater among American Jews than in the broader white population, consonant with tendencies toward greater homogamy among more educated populations. We shall see how this relates to labor force and occupational comparisons of husbands and wives in the chapters to follow.

CHAPTER 4

Labor Force Participation and Occupational Achievement

According to the 1990 National Jewish Population Survey, not only are American Jewish women highly educated, they are (not surprisingly) active in the labor force and have high occupational achievement. These educational and economic characteristics grew out of a history of Jewish women being active in the labor force, reinforced by the tradition of supporting their families while their husbands engaged in religious study; by the immigrant experience, which pushed women to contribute to the household economy; and by active involvement in the contemporary women's movement, which emphasized women's equal participation in public roles. Such economic roles are facilitated by a relatively low rate of fertility, which reduces the familial obligations that constrain the pursuit of higher education and participation in the labor force. Despite their high level of education, labor force participation, and occupational status relative to other U.S. women, the 1990 NJPS data revealed a persistent gender gap in occupational achievement between Jewish women and Jewish men (Hartman and Hartman, 1996a).

One issue particularly of interest in the case of American Jews is how much gender equality they have achieved, a decade later, in labor force participation and occupational roles and rewards, given the high level of human resources both women and men have in terms of educational background. Do American Jewish women reach a plateau of labor force participation and a glass ceiling in terms of occupational achievement, despite their high educational level, or has economic parity been reached? Has the gender gap in occupational achievement narrowed since 1990? And what do we learn from the personal income data, which were not available in earlier studies of American Jews?

A second issue is how family roles affect the labor force participation of American Jewish women and men. Especially among Jewish women, family responsibilities have exerted a pull out of the labor force, at least temporarily or partially (to part-time employment), despite their high educational level and resultant opportunity costs for reducing their labor force involvement. Recent qualitative research suggests that this dynamic continues among American Jewish women, more so than among American Jewish men (who respond to familial responsibilities by a push to provide more adequately for the family) (Prell, 2007a). Of particular interest is whether American Jewish women continue to be more responsive to familial responsibilities than their counterparts in the broader population, as they have in the past (Chiswick, 1986) or whether increasingly delayed marriage and smaller family size translate into a greater compatibility between women's family roles and labor force involvement than was seen in the past, and hence less differentiation between American Jewish women and their highly educated counterparts in the broader population.

As we have already seen, American women in general have increased their participation in higher education, especially in completing undergraduate and graduate degrees (Chao and Utgoff, 2005). However, the rate of women's participation in the labor force has been relatively stable for about a decade, after having increased dramatically in the preceding few decades (Chao and Utgoff, 2005, p. 1). In fact, women's employment declined in the early 2000s as a result of general labor conditions (Boushey, 2005).

In this chapter, we first describe American Jewish women's contemporary economic roles and consider the differences between their labor force participation and that of American Jewish men. Second, we consider whether American Jews are maintaining their distinction from the rest of the U.S. population in terms of their economic roles and the gender differences within them. Third, we consider whether American Jews' economic roles have changed since 1990 and whether the differences between Jewish men and women in these respects have narrowed. Finally, we look at comparative rewards for labor force participation (annual earnings and occupational prestige) between Jewish men and women.

LABOR FORCE PARTICIPATION

According to the 2000–01 NJPS, 66.0% of American Jewish men and 54.1% of American Jewish women work in the paid labor force. Of those employed, most work full time (35 or more hours per week): 87.1% of men and 68.9% of women. As we show later, this is quite comparable to the percentages found in the broader U.S. population.

Labor force participation rates vary with age, as expected. Because most Jewish men and women go on to higher education, their entrance into the paid labor force is often delayed until their education is complete. Therefore,

Table 4.1 Percentage of American Jews in Labor Force and Percentage Employed Full Time, by Age and Gender

Age group	In labor force (%)				Employed full time (% of those in labor force)		
	Total	Men	Women	Female Rate/ Male Rate	Total	Men	Women
18–24	54.9	49.0	60.3	1.23	60.6	70.8	53.1
25–34	79.1	85.1	73.2	.86	86.8	89.1	84.1
35–44	85.2	92.2	78.8	.85	77.7	91.4	62.9
45–54	80.6	88.1	73.5	.83	82.6	91.7	72.0
55–64	66.9	79.0	56.7	.72	81.5	87.6	74.3
65+	13.2	16.8	10.3	.61	53.7	61.2	43.6
Total	59.7	66.0	54.1	.82	78.4	87.1	68.9
$(n)^a$	(4,050)	(1,792)	(2,266)		(3,490)	(1,220)	(1,270)

[a]Unweighted sample size in parentheses; calculations performed using person-weights provided with dataset.

only slightly more than half of 18- to 24-year-olds are in the labor force (Table 4.1). Labor force participation rates are higher among both men and women between the ages of 25 and 54, somewhat lower in the 55–64 age group, and dropping to less than 20% for those 65 and over, as they retire.

In the youngest age group, there is little difference between Jewish men and women's labor force participation rates, although a slightly higher proportion of women in this age group are in the labor force (perhaps because fewer of them continue on to graduate school). The differences are greater between the ages of 25 and 54, women's labor force participation rate hovering at about 85% that of men's. Apparently men retire later than women, as women's labor force participation rate is only 72% that of men's among those aged 55–64, and only 61% of men's among those 65 and older. This also reflects a cohort difference, as women's labor force participation has been steadily increasing over the past few decades, so for many of these older women, participating in the labor force was not the norm for women or, especially, married women.

At all ages, Jewish women are more likely to work part time than are men. The differences are especially noticeable among those between the ages of 35 and 54; more than 90% of employed men work 35 hours per week or more, compared with 70–75% of women. These are the ages when women's family roles (especially childrearing) are most demanding, which would explain the higher proportion of women employed part time. However, higher proportions of employed women also work part time in the younger age group (18–24); and more than half of those 65 and older work only part time when they are employed. During the younger years, when many men and women are continuing their education, almost 30% of the men work part time as well; and during the older years (65+), the proportion of men employed part time is also higher.

Educational Differences in Labor Force Participation

Labor force participation is higher for those with a higher education, as expected (Figure 4.1). Because most of those whose education ended with high school are 65 and older, and most of those who have not completed their education are under 24, we have confined our presentation to those between the ages of 25 and 64. About 60% of those with a high school education or less are employed, compared with about three-quarters of those with some college education, 80% of those with an undergraduate or master's degree, and more than 90% of those with a doctoral or professional degree. At all of these levels of education, a higher proportion of men are employed than are women, but the difference in labor force participation clearly is smaller at the higher educational levels. Among those with a high school education or less, about half of the women are employed, compared with 77% of the men; among those with some college education, women's labor force participation is close to 80% that of men's; and among those with doctoral and professional degrees, women's labor force participation rate is virtually the same as men's.

Education makes a bigger difference in the labor force participation rate of women than of men, which results in a smaller gender difference at

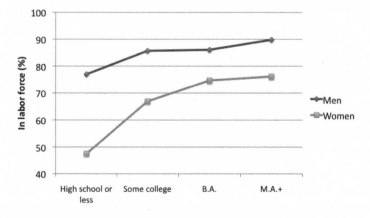

Figure 4.1. Percentage in labor force, by education and gender.

higher levels of education. Among those with a high school education or less, just half of the women are employed, compared with more than 90% of the women with doctoral or professional degrees. Among men, the variation is much smaller.

Family Roles and Labor Force Participation

Among American Jews, fewer married women are in the labor force than are non-married women (37.6% of the currently married, compared with 43.2% of the non-married). If we break down the non-married into never married, divorced or separated, and widowed, we find that more than half of the never married and divorced or separated are currently employed (58.3 and 53.6%, respectively), whereas only 11.4% of the widowed are. Most likely the percentage of the widowed who are employed is low because of their older ages.

   Thus, if we confine our analysis to women aged 25–64 again, reducing the effect of retirement and of delayed entrance into the labor force because of higher education, the differences between married and non-married women persist, but are considerably smaller. The main difference is between never-married women, who participate in the labor force at nearly the same rate as never-married men, and women who have been married at least once (Figure 4.2). Women currently in their first marriage have the lowest labor force participation rate and differ the most from men with the same marital status. In contrast, current marriage is associated with more labor force participation for men.

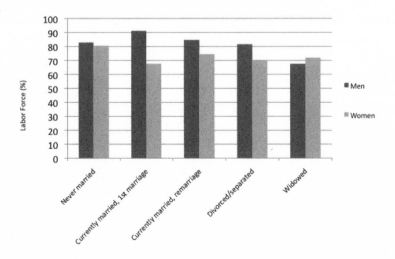

Figure 4.2. Percentage in labor force, by marital status and gender.

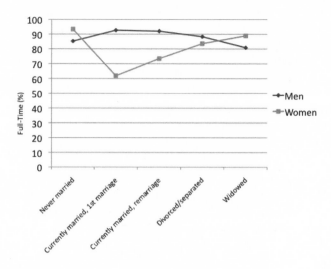

Figure 4.3. Percentage employed full time (35+ hours/week), by marital status and gender.

Married women are also more likely to be working part time when they work than are non-married women (Figure 4.3). More than 90% of never-married women who are employed work 35 hours per week or more, compared with 61.9% of women currently in first marriages and 73.5% of remarried women. There is no such relationship for men, whose full-time employment hovers around 90% for those of all marital statuses except the widowed. There are several possible explanations for this difference in the employment of married and non-married women. The major explanations are that married women's income may be considered supplemental to the household income, especially as most married men between the ages of 25 and 64 are employed (close to 90%), and married women are more likely to have children at home, which is more likely to negatively affect the labor force participation of mothers than that of fathers owing to traditional gender roles in the family, time, energy, and financial constraints of substitute childcare.[1]

Having children in the household is certainly related to lower labor force participation (Figure 4.4). With every additional child, employment rates are lower; lower labor force participation is found especially for those with three or more children. Furthermore, women with children at home are more likely to work part time than are women with no children at home. The majority of employed women with more than two children at home are employed part time (Figure 4.4).

Having children under 18 in the household does not have the same impact on labor force participation for men as it does for women. In fact, men

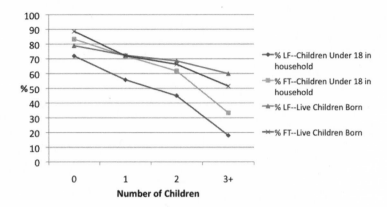

Figure 4.4. Percentage in labor force (LF) and percentage of those in LF employed full time (FT), by number of children (women ages 25–64).

are more likely to be employed in the labor force at a full-time job when they have children under 18 at home than when they do not have young children at home (Table 4.2) (again echoing the findings of Prell, 2007a, from her small qualitative sample). As a result, the gender gap in labor force participation and especially full-time employment is greater when there are children in the home than when there are not.

Table 4.2 Presence of Children Under 18 in Household by Labor Force Status, Gender, and Education[a]

Presence of children under 18 in household	In labor force (%)				Employed full time (%)			
	No children		1+ children		No children		1+ children	
Men	83.2	(771)	93.2	(422)	89.3	(636)	92.7	(396)
Women	72.0	(904)	70.0	(537)	82.2	(678)	58.1	(387)
Women's/men's rate of LFP[b]	86.5		75.1		92.0		62.9	
Less education than undergraduate degree								
Men	83.4	(212)	79.6	(109)	92.2	(173)	91.3	(93)
Women	60.4	(316)	59.5	(173)	74.8	(199)	61.8	(108)
Women's /men's rate of LFP	72.4		74.7		81.1		67.7	
Education B.A.+								
Men	83.1	(556)	98.6	(310)	88.1	(460)	92.7	(300)
Women	78.4	(586)	74.4	(359)	85.4	(477)	55.7	(274)
Women's/men's rate of LFP	94.3		75.5					

[a]Unweighted sample size in parentheses; calculations performed using person-weights provided with dataset.
[b]LFP denotes labor force participation.

When we consider the educational attainment of men and women in addition to the presence of children under 18 in the household, we see that having children changes women's labor force participation to only a small extent, whatever the woman's level of education. However, men's labor force participation is greater when they have children than when they do not (Table 4.2). As a result, among those with at least an undergraduate degree and no young children at home, women's labor force participation and full-time employment are nearly equal to that of men. However, among those with children under 18 at home, for every four men employed, only three women are. The number of children under 18 at home has an even greater impact on the full-time employment of women. The impact of having children under 18 at home is greater for women who have college degrees: when they do not have children of this age at home, their full-time employment is very similar to men's; when they do have children, the proportion employed full time is even lower than among women with less education. As a result, the gender difference in full-time employment is greatest for college-educated women with children under 18 at home (Table 4.2, Figure 4.5).

We considered the effect not only of "childcare burden," but also of indicators of "familism" or family roles that may have influenced more long-term choices made regarding women's participation in the labor force or a career. Although the presence of children under 18 in the household has an effect on women's labor force participation (see Figure 4.3), having more children (whatever their ages) also is related to lower labor force participation. Other "familistic" indicators include marrying at an early age and having children at a younger age. To see whether this assumption of family

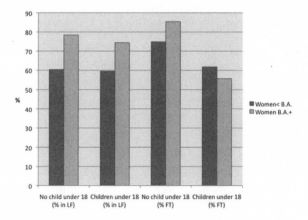

Figure 4.5. Percentage in labor force (LF) and percentage employed full time (FT), by education and presence of child under 18 in household.

roles at a younger age and having more children have an effect on women's labor force participation independent of the actual childcare "burden" of having children under 18 at home, we used a logistic regression analysis to predict women's participation in the labor force. The independent variables were the familistic indicators of age at marriage, age at first birth, and number of live births; and the current family role indicators of number of children under 18 at home, age of youngest child, and current marital status (married, 1; not married, 0). We also controlled for the woman's age and her highest educational attainment. Only women aged 25–64 are included in the analysis to minimize the effects of remaining in school to pursue a higher education and retiring from the labor force. The results are presented in Table 4.3.

Education is the factor most strongly related to a woman's labor force participation (the higher the education, the greater are the odds that she works in the labor force, no matter what her age or family situation), as indicated by the exponential coefficient of 1.492. Her current family situation is also related to her labor force participation: the more children under 18 in the household, the lower are the odds that she works in the labor force; the younger the youngest child, the lower are the odds of her working in the labor force. Current marital status is only weakly related to labor force participation ($p = 0.069$), reinforcing our findings that there is little "marriage penalty" on Jewish women with respect to their labor force participation. The indicators of prioritizing family roles (early age at marriage, early childbearing age) have little relationship to the odds of participating in the labor force once the presence and age of children in the household are controlled for. A woman's age

Table 4.3 Logistic Regression Analysis of Women's Labor Force Participation, by Current Family Status, Familistic Behavior, Education, and Age (Ages 25–64)

Independent variable	Unstandardized regression coefficient	Exponential coefficient
Education	0.400	1.492*
Age at first marriage	–.009	0.991
Age at birth of first child	–.009	0.991
Current marital status	–.376	0.687**
Age of youngest child	–.066	0.937*
Number of children under 18 in household	–.339	0.712*
Age	0.030	1.030
Nagelkerke R^2	0.113	—
(n)	(842)	—

* $p < 0.05$; ** $p < 0.10$.

Table 4.4 Multiple Regression Analysis of Women's Hours of Employment, by Current Family Status, Familistic Behavior, Education, and Age (Ages 25–64)

Independent variable	Unstandardized regression coefficient	Standardized coefficient (ß)
Education	.000	.000
Age at first marriage	.005	.049
Age at birth of first child	.004	.041
Current marital status	−.172	−.151*
Age of youngest child	.006	.139
Number of children under 18 in household	−.077	−.189*
Age	−.005	−.102
R	.298	
R²	.089	
(n)	(586)	

* $p < 0.05$.

is not related to her labor force participation once her current family status and past family behavior and education are controlled for.

A similar analysis of women's average weekly hours of employment shows that the only significant influences are current family situation: whether or not a woman is currently married and how many children under 18 are in the household. Even educational level does not have a significant relationship to hours of work, once current family status is taken into consideration (Table 4.4).

Comparison of Labor Force Participation with That of the Broader U.S. Population

The labor force participation of American Jews is quite similar to that of the broader U.S. population, among whom 70.0% of men and 57.5% of women were employed in 2000 (www.census.gov, Table QT-P24). Considering only the white U.S. population, there is an even greater similarity: 67.9% of men and 54.7% of women were employed in 2000 (www.census.gov, Table P150A). In terms of full- and part-time work, there is also great similarity. In the broader U.S. population, 86.0% of employed men and 71.0% of employed women worked 35 hours or more per week (www.census.gov, Table PCT82). Similarly, among the white population only, 86.1% of employed men and 69.5% of women worked 35 hours per week or more (Table PCT71A).

When we compare age groups, there is also great similarity, with two notable exceptions (Table 4.5). First, Jewish men aged 20–24 are much less likely to be in the labor force than are men in the broader U.S. population, owing to

Table 4.5 Percentage of American Jews and Non-Hispanic Whites in Labor Force, by Age and Gender[a]

Gender	Age group	American Jews		U.S. whites	
Total	20–24	59.8	(242)	71.0	(11,223)
	25–54	81.9	(1,661)	80.2	(79,741)
	55–64	66.6	(425)	61.0	(14,965)
	65+	12.9	(802)	14.1	(4,260)
Total		60.0	(3,235)	68.1	(110,200)
Men	20–24	52.8	(119)	75.1	(6,026)
	25–54	89.0	(812)	87.9	(43,724)
	55–64	78.4	(196)	67.3	(8,018)
	65+	16.1	(362)	18.5	(2,390)
Total		66.2	(1,536)	70.4	(62,159)
Women	20–24	66.5	(123)	66.8	(5,207)
	25–54	75.1	(850)	72.5	(36,016)
	55–64	56.5	(229)	55.0	(6,947)
	65+	10.4	(440)	10.8	(1,870)
Total		54.3	(1,698)	56.1	(50,041)
Female rate/male rate	20–24	1.3		.89	
	25–54	.84		.82	
	55–64	.72		.82	
	65+	.65		.58	
Total		.82		.80	

Data source for Jews: NJPS, 2000–01; for non-Hispanic whites: Chao and Utgoff, 2005, Table 3.
[a]*n* in parentheses in thousands; NJPS data weighted by person-weights provided with dataset.

the high proportion of Jewish men going on to higher education at those ages. Second, Jewish men have higher labor force participation rates at ages 55–64, probably also related to their higher education. Despite Jewish women's relatively higher level of education than that of women in the broader U.S. population, their labor force participation rates are very similar at all ages.

When we control for education, most of the differences between the Jewish and total U.S. population are eliminated (Table 4.6). The differences between men at any of the levels of education is minimal, and the main differences in labor force participation between Jewish and all women are in the lower education groups. Labor force participation rates among women who have earned college degrees (the majority of American Jewish women) are very similar.

Gender differences in labor force participation in both populations are smaller at higher levels of education. At lower levels of education, there are greater differences among American Jews than in the broader population. This is probably because most of the American Jews who discontinued their education after high school, or even after a few years of college, are on the average older than their counterparts in the broader population. Because older women were less likely to participate in the labor force, their participation rate is lowered by their age in addition to their lower level of education. This may be less true in the broader population, where there is a greater distribution of low through higher levels of education throughout the population.

Considering whether family roles have an impact on the labor force participation of Jewish women that is similar to their impact on women in the broader U.S. population (Table 4.7), we see similar rates of labor force participation among those who have never married and those currently in their first marriages. Among the currently remarried and the widowed, American Jewish women are more likely to be in the labor force than their

Table 4.6 Percentage of American Jews and Non-Hispanic Whites (Ages 25–64) in Labor Force, by Education and Gender[a]

Gender	Education	American Jews		U.S. whites	
Total	High school or less	61.7	(253)	68.4	(44,993)
	Some college	74.4	(404)	77.7	(31,899)
	B.A.	80.2	(726)	82.1	(24,758)
	M.A.+	85.8	(694)	85.7	(13,153)
Total		78.7	(2,077)	75.4	(114,803)
Men	High school or less	77.0	(122)	77.3	(25,599)
	Some college	85.7	(162)	83.6	(15,796)
	B.A.	86.1	(362)	88.9	(13,100)
	M.A.+	91.5	(368)	89.8	(7,146)
Total		86.9	(1,004)	82.6	(61,643)
Women	High school or less	47.5	(132)	59.3	(19,392)
	Some college	66.9	(242)	72.6	(16,103)
	B.A.	74.7	(374)	75.7	(11,659)
	M.A.+	79.3	(326)	81.3	(6,006)
Total		71.0	(1,073)	68.5	(53,160)
Female rate/male rate	High school or less	.62		.77	
	Some college	.78		.86	
	B.A.	.87		.85	
	M.A.+	.87		.91	
Total		.82		.83	

Data source for Jews: NJPS, 2000–01; for non-Hispanic whites: Chao and Utgoff, 2005, Table 8.

[a] *n* in parentheses in thousands; NJPS data weighted by person-weights provided with dataset.

Table 4.7 Percentage of American Jewish and U.S. Non-Hispanic White Women (Ages 25–64) in Labor Force, by Marital Status[a]

Marital status	Jewish women		Non-Hispanic white women	
Never married	80.6	(175)	80.7	(7,340)
Currently married, first marriage	67.6	(607)	68.7	(31,753)
Currently married, remarriage	74.5	(114)	70.3	(9,861)
Divorced/separated	70.0	(134)	77.5	(10,794)
Widowed	72.0	(25)	59.3	(2,277)

Data source for Jewish women: NJPS 2000–01; for non-Hispanic white women: SIPP, 2001.
[a]*n* in parentheses in thousands; NJPS data weighted by person-weights provided with dataset.

counterparts in the broader non-Hispanic white population. The main difference between widowed Jewish women and widowed women in the non-Hispanic white population is their level of education; that is, half of Jewish widows have at least an undergraduate degree, compared with only 13% of women in the broader population. This differential, however, exists in the other subgroups of women as well, though the differences are not as large. Jewish widows and widows in the broader population are of similar average age (55); it is possible that because college-educated women remain employed later in the life cycle, their higher education makes a greater difference among the widowed than in other groups.

The labor force participation of American Jewish women and the broader population of non-Hispanic white women is also quite similar when we control for number of children (Table 4.8). When we compare Jewish women to white women in the broader population with the same number of children, we see that education has a greater impact on Jewish women (Figure 4.6). It is especially interesting to note the extent to which educated Jewish women with four or more children (albeit a small number, unweighted *n* = 23) participate in the labor force compared with Jewish women with less education or white women, whatever their education. Most of the Jewish women with four or more children are Orthodox, and we shall see in Chapter 8 that this type of religious affiliation has a positive impact on labor force participation when there are large families.

Having children under 3 years of age at home results in lower labor force participation rates for Jewish women as well as for white women in the broader U.S. population; however, Jewish women's labor force participation is affected more by having such a young child at home (Table 4.9). The labor force participation rate of Jewish women with a child under the age of 3 at home is less than 70% of the labor force participation rate of mothers with a

Table 4.8 Percentage of American Jewish and Non-Hispanic White Women (Ages 25–64) in Labor Force, by Number of Live Births[a]

Number of live births	Jewish women		Non-Hispanic white women	
0	78.9	(356)	81.7	(13,119)
1	72.4	(170)	72.5	(10,202)
2	68.6	(319)	72.1	(20,229)
3	62.6	(138)	67.2	(11,476)
4+	56.3	(83)	56.6	(6,998)

Data source for Jewish women: NJPS, 2000–01; for non-Hispanic white women: SIPP, 2001.
[a] *n* in parentheses in thousands; NJPS data weighted by person-weights provided with dataset.

3- to 5-year-old at home; among the broader white population, the percentage is slightly less than 90%. One of the reasons for this difference is that Jewish women with 3- to 5-year-olds at home are more likely to be employed than are women with children of that age in the broader white population. Among mothers of older children, the labor force participation rates are more similar between Jewish and white mothers. These patterns are true for women with and without undergraduate degrees, although level of education appears to have a somewhat greater influence on labor force participation among Jewish mothers with children under 3 at home. It should also be noted that among women with no children under 18 at home and who do not have a college degree, the labor force participation of Jewish women is lower than for the broader white population; this is probably because of the relatively older age of Jewish women who have not earned undergraduate degrees.

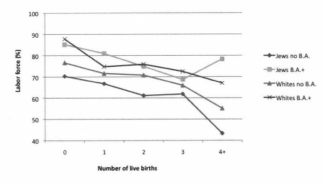

Figure 4.6. Percentage of American Jewish and non-Hispanic white women (ages 25–64) in labor force, by education and number of live births. *Data source* for Jewish women: NJPS, 2000–01; for non-Hispanic white women: SIPP, 2001.

Table 4.9 Percentage of American Jewish and Non-Hispanic White Women in Labor Force, by Age of Child under 18 in Household and Education[a]

	Education					
	Total		less than B.A.		B.A. or higher	
Age of youngest child in household	Jewish women	Non-Hispanic white women	Jewish women	Non-Hispanic white women	Jewish women	Non-Hispanic white women
Under 3	50.5	55.2	47.0	55.0	52.5	55.6
	(104)	(4,067)	(38)	(2,804)	(66)	(1,262)
3–5	74.5	63.8	67.3	62.1	76.5	68.7
	(63)	(3,955)	(14)	(2,927)	(49)	(1,028)
6–17	81.4	75.7	74.3	73.6	84.3	82.7
	(200)	(13,869)	(58)	(10,724)	(142)	(3,145)
None under 18	61.3	65.4	51.2	63.5	70.7	74.5
	(330)	(16,813)	(162)	(13,903)	(168)	(2,911)

[a]n in parentheses in thousands; NJPS data weighted by person-weights provided with dataset.
Data source for Jewish women: NJPS, 2000–01; for non-Hispanic white women: SIPP, 2001.

In conclusion, the labor force participation rates of American Jewish women are remarkably similar to those of women in the broader white population. The sensitivity of Jewish women's labor force participation to family roles, which has been noted in the past (Chiswick, 1986), appears to be confined, in 2000–01, to their greater tendency to curtail their labor force participation when they have a child under 3 at home. Other differences stem from the relatively older age of Jewish women who are widowed and who do not have undergraduate degrees, compared with their counterparts in the broader population, resulting in lower labor force participation rates of these groups of Jewish women.

Comparison of American Jewish Labor Force Participation in 2000–01 and 1990

Overall the labor force participation of American Jewish men and women is lower in 2000–01 than in 1990, which in large part is because the population is aging, so that a higher percentage are over 65. At almost every age except 18–24 and 65 and older, men's labor force participation rates are quite similar to what they were in 1990 (Figure 4.7). The lower rates among those 65 and older may be attributable to the aging population, as the average age of the 65+ age group is older in 2000–01 than it was in 1990. The higher labor force participation rate of men aged 18–24 may result from different patterns of work during college or the completion of college at an earlier age.

Women's labor force participation rates in 2000–01 are also quite similar to what they were in 1990, with a few notable exceptions. The labor force participation rate of women aged 18–24 is almost double what it was in 1990; men's also increased but not as dramatically. One result is that women aged 18–24 are employed at a considerably higher rate than are men in the same age range. Compared with 1990, in 2000–01 women in the 18–24 age group are less likely to have ever married and are less likely to have already had children, which probably explains their higher rate of labor force participation in 2000–01. Another change is slightly lower labor force participation rates among women aged 25–39, and because this is the period during which women are most likely to bear children, it may be that family roles are having a greater impact than they did in 1990. In the 40–44 age group, however, labor force participation rates are higher than they were in 1990.

The comparison between women's and men's labor force participation rates does not show a consistently increasing tendency toward equality (Figure 4.8). In a few age groups (18–24, 40–44, and 50–54) the labor force participation rates are more similar (or women's rates are higher than men's), but in most of the groups the rates are less similar than they were in 1990 or are about the same. It is possible, then, that women's labor force participation has reached a plateau rather than continuing to increase toward parity with men's labor force participation, at least among American Jews.[2]

Men and women with less than a high school education were more likely to be in the labor force in 1990 than in 2000–01 (Table 4.10)—a pattern especially noticeable for women. Men and women with more than a high school education, however, participated in the labor force at about the same rate in 1990 as in 2000–01. The labor force participation of women with

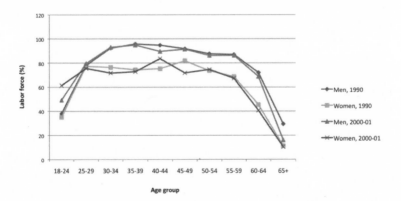

Figure 4.7. Percentage of American Jews in labor force, by age and gender, 1990 and 2000–01. *Data sources*: NJPS, 1990; 2000–01.

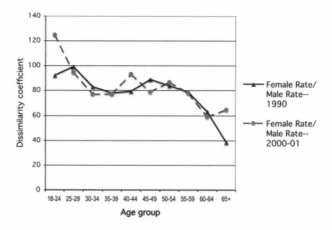

Figure 4.8. Dissimilarity of female to male labor-force participation rates by age, 1990 and 2000–01. *Data sources:* NJPS, 1990; 2000–01.

doctoral or professional degrees, however, has become more similar to that of men at the same educational level.

Women's marital status also seems to be related to their labor force participation somewhat differently in 2000–01 than in 1990 (Figure 4.9). First, the labor force participation of never-married women is higher in 2000–01 than it was in 1990: 68.2% of never-married women were employed in the labor force in 2000–01, compared with 57.6% in 1990. One of the reasons may be the increasing postponement of marriage, as we saw earlier; another may be the increasing postponement of birth of first child, which we also saw earlier. The delay of childbirth, in particular, may result in higher labor force participation of never-married women. On the other hand, divorced/

Table 4.10 Percentage of American Jews (Ages 25–64) in Labor Force, by Education and Gender, 1990 and 2000–01[a]

Highest educational attainment	1990				2000–01			
	Men		Women		Men		Women	
High school or less	81.8	(218)	61.5	(331)	77.0	(123)	47.5	(170)
Undergraduate college	86.6	(381)	70.7	(353)	86.0	(198)	71.6	(319)
M.A.	89.7	(155)	80.9	(174)	89.8	(437)	76.2	(488)
Doctoral, professional degree	94.0	(146)	87.0	(67)	94.6	(429)	91.3	(457)

Data sources: NJPS, 1990; 2000–01.

[a]*n* in parentheses in thousands; NJPS data weighted by person-weights provided with dataset.

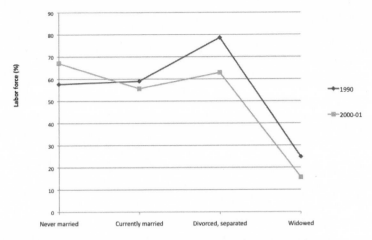

Figure 4.9. Percentage of American Jewish women in labor force, by marital status, 1990 and 2000–01. *Data sources*: NJPS, 1990; 2000–01.

separated and widowed women all participated more in the labor force in 1990 than in 2000–01. Especially striking are the differences among divorced and separated women, 78.6% of whom were employed in 1990, compared with 66.3% in 2000–01. Widowed women are less likely to be working as well, which may be a result of the aging population.

Women with no children or only one child were more likely to be employed in the labor force in 1990, but the rates are quite high for both time periods (hovering around 80% for women with no children and around 75% for women with only one child). Women with four or more children are more likely to be employed in 2000–01 than they were in 1990, perhaps reflecting the growth in childcare facilities and the norm for using them (Table 4.11). As a result, there has been a decline in the "child penalty" on labor force participation (the difference between the labor force participation rates of women with children and women with no children), from 17.0 in 1990 (calculated from Hartman and Hartman, 1996a, Table 3.9) to 11.5 in 2000–01. This reduction in "child penalty" mirrors a similar decrease in the broader U.S. population (Boushey, 2000).

When we compared the labor force participation rates of American Jews with those of the broader U.S. population in 1990, we found more differences than we found in 2000–01. In 1990, American Jewish women had higher labor force participation rates than many of their counterparts in the broader population, especially among women 45 and older; as a result, the gender differences between the labor force participation rates of Jewish men and women were smaller than they were in the broader U.S. population (Hartman and Hartman, 1996a, Table 3.1, p. 65). In 2000–01, American

Table 4.11 Percentage of American Jewish Women in Labor Force, by Number of Children, 1990 and 2000–01[a]

Number of children (live births)	1990		2000–01	
0	84.9	(366)	78.9	(356)
1	78.1	(935)	72.4	(170)
2	67.5	(209)	68.6	(319)
3	66.5	(411)	62.6	(138)
4+	46.8	(80)	56.3	(83)

Data sources: NJPS, 1990; Hartman and Hartman, 1996, Table 3.9; and NJPS, 2000–01.
[a]*n* in parentheses in thousands, weighted by person-weights provided with each dataset.

Jewish women's labor force participation was much more similar to that of the broader population, and gender differences were quite similar in both populations. In fact, in the 55–64 age group, men and women in the broader population were more similar in their labor force participation than were American Jews.

When education is controlled for, there seems to be more similarity between American Jews and the broader population in 2000–01 than we found in 1990 (Hartman and Hartman, 1996a, Table 3.6, p. 88). At that time, we found that Jewish labor force participation rates tended to be lower, especially among men, at every level of education; in 2000–01, labor force participation rates were quite similar at each level of education, with one exception: as in 1990, we found in 2000–01 that less educated women in the broader population were more likely to be employed in the labor force than were less educated American Jews; however, in the other education groups labor force participation rates are quite similar for both men and women.

Generally, then, comparing 1990 and 2000–01, we find increasing similarity between American Jewish labor force participation patterns and those of the broader population, especially when age, education, and family roles are controlled for. Given the similarity in labor force participation between American Jews and the broader population, might we also expect to find increasing similarity in their occupations? We shall see that the results differ when we compare the occupational niches of American Jews with those of the broader population.

OCCUPATIONAL ACHIEVEMENT

The distinctiveness of American Jewish occupations continued in 2000–01 as it had in previous decades (see also Chiswick, 1999; 2007). Jews are particularly concentrated in professional occupations, and are overrepresented in sales and managerial or executive occupations (Table 4.12). In contrast, they are underrepresented in service and blue-collar occupations and, particularly among women, in office or administrative support occupations.

Expressed as dissimilarity coefficients, more than 36% of the total Jewish population would have to change occupations to have a distribution similar to that of the broader non-Hispanic white population in 2000–01. Forty-one percent of the men would have to change occupations for the two distributions to be similar, and 31.7% of the women would have to do so. More than 42% of the American Jewish men have professional occupations, compared with less than 15% of the broader white population; 17.9% are in sales, compared with 10.6% of the broader white population; and only 6.2% are in blue-collar occupations, compared with 39% of the broader white population. Among women, the differences are similar, although they are somewhat smaller than among men: there is a much higher proportion of Jewish women with professional occupations and lower proportions with service and office or administrative support occupations compared with the broader white female population.

These differences are illustrated by a list of the top 10 occupations of American Jews and of the broader non-Hispanic white population (Table 4.13). Almost all of the 10 occupations employing the most Jewish men are in the managerial/executive, business/finance, or professional categories, with the exception of retail sales, in which 10.4% of Jewish men

Table 4.12 Occupations By Gender of American Jews and non-Hispanic Whites (Ages 25 and Over)

Occupation	American Jews (%)			U.S. non-Hispanic whites (%)		
	Total	Men	Women	Total	Men	Women
Managerial/executive	13.3	13.4	13.1	10.4	12.8	7.8
Business/finance	7.5	8.7	6.3	4.6	4.2	5.1
Professional	43.2	42.8	43.8	17.1	14.9	19.6
Technical	3.9	3.4	4.3	4.2	2.6	5.9
Service	3.9	4.5	4.2	12.6	9.7	15.8
Sales	15.3	17.9	12.4	11	10.6	11.5
Office/administrative support	8.7	4.0	13.6	15.2	6.2	25.3
Foreman, skilled, unskilled workers	4.2	6.2	2.1	24.8	39.0	9.1
Total	100.0	100.0	100.0	100.0	100.0	100.0
(n, thousands)[a]	(1,893)	(968)	(921)	(112,167)	(58,997)	(53,170)

Data sources: NJPS, 2000–01; U.S. Census, 2000.

[a]NJPS data weighted by person-weights provided with dataset.

Table 4.13 Ten Most Common Occupations of American Jews and Non-Hispanic Whites (Ages 25 and Over), by Gender[a]

American Jews			U.S. non-Hispanic whites		
Occupation	%	% Male[b]	Occupation	%	% Male[b]
Men					
Retail salespersons	10.4	44.7	Drivers/sales workers/truck drivers	4.4	93.5
Lawyers	5.4	71.9	First-line supervisors/managers of retail sales workers	2.5	57.2
Physicians and Surgeons	4.3	74.4	Managers, all other	2.1	65.8
Other teachers and Instructors	4.3	33.2	Carpenters	2.0	98.1
Managers, all other	4.1	65.8	Retail salespersons	2.0	44.7
Accountants and auditors	3.9	43.6	Janitors and building cleaners	1.8	68.1
Chief executives	3.6	81.3	Sales reps, wholesale and manufacturing	1.7	74.4
Engineers, all other	3.5	90.7	First-line supervisors/managers of production and operating workers	1.7	81.2
Management analysts	2.9	62.7	Laborers and freight, stock and material movers, hand	1.7	78.2
Computer programmers	2.4	72.6	Chief executives	1.6	81.3
Total/average	44.8	64.1	Total/average	21.5	74.2

Women

Occupation	%	% Female[b]	Occupation	%	% Female[b]
Retail salespersons	7.4	55.3	Secretaries and administrative assistants	6.8	97.1
Elementary and middle school teachers	6.0	79.4	Elementary and middle school teachers	3.1	91.2
Other teachers and instructors	5.3	66.8	Registered nurses	3.7	92.9
Managers, all other	4.4	34.2	Bookkeeping, accounting and auditing clerks	2.9	91.2
Secretaries and administrative assistants	3.7	97.1	Retail salespersons	2.7	55.3
Office clerks, general	3.4	87.0	Cashiers	2.4	82.5
Lodging managers	3.2	49.2	First-line supervisors/managers of office and administrative workers	2.0	68.8
Registered nurses	2.9	92.9	First-line supervisors/managers of retail sales workers	2.0	42.8
Social workers	2.8	79.7	Nursing, psychiatric, and home health aides	2.0	89.5
Lawyers	2.8	28.1	Customer service representatives	1.9	72.7
Total/average	41.9	67.0	Total/average	29.5	78.4

[a]Based on the most detailed level of occupations available in the 2000 U.S. Census (509 occupations).

[b]percentage male and percentage female calculated from U.S. Census, total population (ages 16 and over).

Data sources: U.S. Census, 2000; NJPS, 2000–01 .

are employed. In comparison, the 10 occupations employing the most men in the broader white population span most of the occupational categories of the labor force, from chief executives and managers to salespersons, drivers, carpenters, janitors, and laborers. However, no professional occupation is on this list, compared with 5 such occupations on the list for Jewish men. These 10 occupations account for 44.8% of the occupations of Jewish men, compared with 21.5% of the occupations of men in the broader white population. Three occupations are common to the lists for Jewish and white men: managers, all other; retail salespersons; and chief executives.

The 10 occupations employing the most Jewish women also contain 5 professional occupations (elementary and middle school teachers, other teachers and instructors, registered nurses, social workers, and lawyers), 2 managerial occupations (lodging managers and managers, all other), retail salespersons, secretaries/administrative assistants, and office clerks. These occupations account for more than 40% of the employment of Jewish women (comparable to the concentration of Jewish men in the top 10 occupations), compared with less than 30% for women in the broader white population (which is somewhat higher than the concentration of their male counterparts in the top 10 occupations). Four of these overlap with the list for the broader white population of women, and the other occupations listed are also in the broad categories of sales, managerial, or technical occupations. Thus, there is more overlap between the women's categories than between the men's.

Overall, Jewish men's and women's occupations are quite similar to each other; only 12.2% would have to change occupations to make the two distributions identical. In the top 10 lists of occupations, 4 are common to both Jewish men and women (retail salespersons; other teachers and instructors; managers, all other; and lawyers). (It is interesting, however, that whereas "lawyer" is one of the top 10 occupations for women, 73% of Jewish lawyers are men, compared with 70% in the broader population; a slightly lower percentage of Jewish doctors are men—67%—compared with 72% in the broader population.) In contrast, more than a third (34.5%) of the broader white population would have to change occupations to have identical distributions for men and women. Only 2 of the occupations overlap (retail salespersons and first-line supervisors of retail sales workers).

The greater similarity of Jewish men's and women's occupations is also reflected in the gender segregation of the occupations in which men and women are employed. Only 2 of the Jewish men's occupations employ more than 75% of men (chief executives and engineers), compared with 5 on the list of occupations for the broader white male population. On average,

Jewish men's occupations employ 62.9% of men, compared with 73.6% in the occupations of the broader population.

Jewish women are somewhat less likely to be employed in the traditional "female occupations" than are women in the broader white population, but even for Jewish women, 5 of their top 10 occupations employ more than 75% of women, compared with 6 of the broader female population's occupations. On average Jewish women's occupations employ 66.8% women, compared with 76.2% in the occupations of the broader population. Each of the top 10 lists for women reflect the concentration of women in typically "female" occupations, but overall there is less concentration of Jewish women in such occupations.

Compared with their occupational distribution in 1990, Jewish men and women seem to be similarly concentrated in a relatively small number of occupations. In 1990, the top 10 occupations of Jewish men employed 43% of Jewish men in the labor force (Hartman and Hartman, 1996a, Table 4.3, p. 121); in 2000–01, 44.8%. Half of Jewish women in the labor force were employed in the top 10 occupations; in 2000–01, 41.8%. Whether this represents a significant reduction in occupational segregation for Jewish women is a little difficult to determine, as the occupational classifications have changed considerably. What we can note is that among the top 10 occupations for women, in 2000–01 lawyers edged out the accountants and bookkeepers of 1990, reflecting Jewish (and other) women's inroads into formerly nontraditional occupations for women. Among men, changes in the top 10 occupations also reflect the changing times: in 2000–01, computer programmers and chief executives edged out the real estate and advertising agents of 1990.

Education and Occupation

Clearly, much of the dissimilarity between the Jewish and broader population can be linked to American Jews' high educational achievement. To determine how much of the dissimilarity is reduced when education is controlled for, we calculated dissimilarity coefficients at each of four levels of education (high school or less, some college, B.A., or M.A. or higher) (Tables 4.14–4.16). The occupational distributions on which these dissimilarity calculations are based are found in the Appendix, Table A-1.

Table 4.14 presents the dissimilarities in occupational distribution of Jews at different educational levels. Looking at the gender differences in occupational distributions at each level of education, we can see that there are much greater gender differences among the less educated than among the more highly educated. Among those with a high school education or less, nearly a third of the women (32.3%) would have to change occupation to have similar occupations as the men; among those with graduate degrees, only 13.5% would have to change their occupations to be similar to men at that level of education. Comparing the lower levels of education with the higher levels of education within gender, we can see that education makes a greater difference in the occupational distribution of Jewish women than in that of Jewish men. Comparing women with a high school education with women with graduate degrees, for example, we find a coefficient of dissimilarity of 67.2 (nearly two-thirds of the less educated women would have to change their occupations to make the distribution identical to that of women with graduate degrees); comparing similar levels of education among men, we find that the coefficient is 43.2. Similarly, the comparison of women with some college to women with graduate degrees shows a greater dissimilarity in occupations than among men. Comparing under-graduates with those with graduate degrees, however, we find that about a third of both men and women would have to change their occupations to be similar to each other. Thus, having a college degree makes an especially big difference in the occupations of women; once they have college degrees, be they undergraduate or graduate, education does not make a greater differ-ence in occupational distribution than it does for men.

Table 4.14 Dissimilarity Coefficients for Occupational Distributions of American Jews (Ages 25 and Over), by Years of Education and Gender[a]

Education	High school or less		Some college		B.A.		M.A.+	
	Men	Women	Men	Women	Men	Women	Men	Women
High school or less								
Men								
Women	32.3							
Some college								
Men	14.1	36.0						
Women	23.3	18.2	17.6					
B.A.								
Men	20.7	37.5	13.5	25.0				
Women	34.5	40.9	25.5	32.3	18.1			
M.A. +								
Men	43.2	55.6	36.9	48.5	30.4	21.9		
Women	51.3	67.6	46.8	57.5	41.9	34.4	13.5	

Data source: NJPS, 2000–01. See Appendix, Table A-1.
[a]Data are based on eight occupational categories.

Table 4.15 Dissimilarity Coefficients for Occupational Distributions of U.S. Non-Hispanic Whites (25 and Over), by Years of Education and Gender

Education	High school or less		Some college		B.A.		M.A.+	
	Men	Women	Men	Women	Men	Women	Men	Women
High school or less								
Men								
Women	48.0							
Some College								
Men	25.7	36.0						
Women	56.9	26.1	38.1					
B.A.								
Men	59.3	50.8	36.7	41.5				
Women	67.7	54.5	46.0	36.1	24.5			
M.A.+								
Men	73.4	67.6	57.9	57.0	28.5	25.2		
Women	75.5	73.8	59.5	57.7	39.0	26.0	15.1	

Data source: U.S. Census, 2000. See Appendix, Table A-1.
[a]Data are based on eight occupational categories.

Table 4.15 presents a similar analysis for the non-Hispanic white population in the United States. Here we find larger ranges in occupational distributions, especially for men. Less educated men in the broader population are much more likely to have blue-collar occupations than are Jewish men; as a result, the occupational dissimilarities between lower levels of education and higher levels of education are much greater for the broader population of men than for American Jews. Also, gender differences in occupational distribution in the broader population are much greater at lower levels of education than they are among American Jews.

Among men and women with master's degrees or higher, only around 10% of the men and women would have to change their occupations to have identical distributions between Jews and the broader white population—a remarkably small amount. A similar coefficient is found for women with bachelor's degrees, and a slightly higher coefficient (14.1%) for men with bachelor's degrees. Most of the dissimilarity is concentrated in the lower education categories (less than a college degree), especially among men (Table 4.16, Figure 4.10).

With respect to the distinctiveness of Jewish occupations, another question is whether level of education results in similar differences in occupational distributions among Jews as it does in the rest of the population, or

Table 4.16 Dissimilarity Coefficients for Occupational Distributions Between American Jews and Non-Hispanic Whites (Ages 25 And Over), by Gender and Level of Education

Education	Men	Women
High school or less	44.3	35.3
Some college	31.5	21.5
B.A.	14.1	8.9
M.A.+	10.8	9.0

Data sources: U.S. Census, 2000; NJPS, 2000–01. See Appendix, Table A-1.

whether there is a "Jewish" pattern of occupational distribution no matter what the educational level. We also consider whether level of education has a similar effect for Jews and the rest of the population on gender dissimilarity in occupations.

Educational level results in greater dissimilarities among men in the broader population than among American Jewish men (Table 4.17, Figure 4.11). For example, more than 70% of the men with graduate degrees in the broader population would have to change occupations to be like the men with high school degrees or less, compared with only 43% of the Jewish men with graduate degrees who would have to change occupations to be like Jewish men with high school degrees or less. Fifty-eight percent of the men in the broader population who have graduate degrees would have to change their occupations to be like men with some college education, compared with slightly more than a third of the Jewish men with comparable education. However, among men with graduate degrees, about 30% of the broader population and of the Jewish men would have to change occupations to be like men with undergraduate degrees. So, again, the biggest

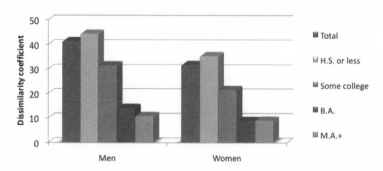

Figure 4.10. Occupational dissimilarity between American Jews and non-Hispanic whites, by gender and education, 2000. *Data sources*: NJPS, 2000–01; SIPP, 2001 (Wave 2).

Table 4.17 Dissimilarity Coefficients for Occupational Distributions of American Jews and Non-Hispanic Whites (Ages 25 and Over), with Different Levels of Education, by Gender

Education level A	Education level B	American Jews		Non-Hispanic whites	
		Men	Women	Men	Women
High school or less	Some college	14.1	18.2	25.7	26.1
	B.A.	20.7	40.9	59.3	54.5
	M.A.+	43.2	67.6	73.4	73.8
Some college	B.A.	13.5	32.3	36.7	36.1
	M.A.+	36.9	57.5	57.9	57.7
B.A.	M.A.+	30.4	34.4	28.5	26.0

Data sources: U.S. Census, 2000; NJPS, 2000–01. See Appendix, Table A-1.

differences are in comparison with the men with some college eduation or a high school degree or less, which can be explained by the high proportion of less educated men in the broader white population who have blue-collar occupations, compared with men with higher education level and Jewish men in general.

The findings are similar among women. Women in the broader population show greater dissimilarity in occupational distributions between educational levels than do Jewish women, especially in comparison with women with only a high school education. With a high school education or less, women in the broader population are more likely than Jewish women to have blue-collar occupations (17.6–3.1%) and service occupations (26–7.3%), while Jewish women are more likely to be in managerial positions (14.5–4.7%), business and finance, professional, sales, and office support (i.e., white-collar occupations). However, when we look at the differences

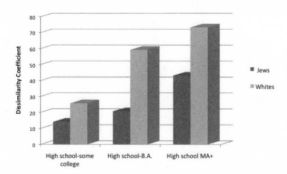

Figure 4.11. Occupational dissimilarity between education levels of American Jewish and non-Hispanic white men (ages 25 and over), 2000–01. *Data sources:* NJPS, 2000–01; SIPP, 2001 (Wave 2).

Table 4.18 Dissimilarity Coefficients Between American Jewish and Non-Hispanic White Men's and Women's Occupational Distributions by Level of Education, Ages 25 and Over

Education	American Jews	Non-Hispanic whites
High school or less	32.3	48.0
Some college	17.6	38.1
B.A.	18.1	24.5
M.A.+	13.5	15.1

Data sources: U.S. Census, 2000; NJPS, 2000–01. See Appendix, Table A-1.

between women with some college education, or with undergraduate or graduate degrees, these differences affect the broader population as much as they do Jewish women.

It should also be noted that in comparison with Jewish men, there is a greater dissimilarity between Jewish women with graduate or undergraduate degrees and women with a lower level of education than there is for Jewish men at similar educational levels. This is probably because of the higher concentration of Jewish women with college degrees in professional occupations, whereas the men with college degrees are spread over a greater range of occupations.

Among both Jews and the broader population, gender dissimilarity is lower for higher levels of education (Table 4.18, Figure 4.12). Gender differences are greater at each level of education for the broader population than for Jews, and the greater gender dissimilarity is especially apparent for those who have some college, or high school or less education. This is also probably

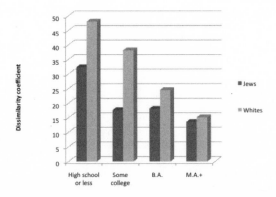

Figure 4.12. Gender dissimilarity in occupations of American Jews and non-Hispanic whites (ages 25 and over), by education, 2000–01. *Data sources:* NJPS, 2000–01; SIPP, 2001 (Wave 2).

a result of the higher proportion of men in the broader population who, with a lower level of education, have blue-collar jobs (62.9% of those with a high school education or less, compared with only 20.6% of Jewish men with a comparable education). Jewish men with less education are still concentrated in sales or—even with a low level of education—professional occupations. As a result, level of education makes a greater difference in gender dissimilarity of occupations for the broader population than for American Jews.

To sum up this section, education accounts for many of the differences in occupational distribution between Jews and the broader population in the United States—but not all. Large differences remain between Jewish men and men in the broader white population at lower levels of education, mainly because less educated men in the broader white population are much more likely to be employed in blue-collar occupations than are Jewish men at any level of education. This probably also explains why there is greater gender dissimilarity in occupational distribution in the broader population at lower levels of education than between American Jewish men and women. It also accounts for the greater effect of education on occupational dissimilarity among men in the broader population than among Jewish men. Similarly, the higher proportion of less educated women in the broader population employed in blue-collar and service occupations may account for the greater effect of education on occupational dissimilarity among women in the broader population than among Jewish women.

Given that the proportion of the population with a high school education or less is declining (NCES, 2007), it might be expected that occupational dissimilarity between American Jews and the broader population will also decline, but it is not clear that it will disappear completely.

Age Cohort and Occupation

The labor force has been undergoing a trend toward greater white-collar employment (Wyatt and Hecker, 2006), precisely the occupations in which Jews have been disproportionately employed, and toward less blue-collar and agricultural employment, the occupations in which Jews are least well represented. It would be expected, therefore, that dissimilarity between Jews and the broader population would be diminishing over time. The first way we examined this was to look at cohort differences in dissimilarity between the occupations of Jews and the broader white population by gender (Table 4.19). (The occupational distributions on which these dissimilarity calculations are based are found in the Appendix, Table A-2.) We can see that among both men and women, dissimilarity between Jews and the

Table 4.19 Dissimilarity Coefficients for Occupational Distributions between American Jews and Non-Hispanic Whites, by Gender, Age, and Education

Age cohort	Total		B.A.+	
	Men	Women	Men	Women
25–34	44.0	33.8	12.3	12.9
35–44	41.1	34.1	18.8	8.6
45–64	40.6	31.0	17.9	9.9
65+	41.7	31.7	21.3	14.4

Data sources: U.S. Census, 2000; NJPS, 2000–01. See Appendix, Tables A-2, A-3.

broader population does not really vary by age cohort, and the differences in dissimilarity by gender also remain constant over these cohorts.

When our analysis is confined to those with undergraduate or higher degrees, the dissimilarity is greatly reduced in each cohort, as expected (dissimilarity calculations are based on the occupational distributions in the Appendix, Table A-3). Among men, there is somewhat greater dissimilarity in the oldest cohort (65+) and somewhat less among men in the youngest cohort (25–34), which may reflect changes in the occupational structure which make more common the kinds of occupations Jews have been employed in, as already mentioned. Among women, a note of caution is in order: the variations in dissimilarity may result from the small number of Jewish women 65 and older who were in the labor force with undergraduate degrees or higher ($n = 15$). Among the younger cohort, ages 25–34, the somewhat higher occupational dissimilarity between Jewish women and women in the broader white population may be related to the higher educational achievement of Jewish women: nearly half of the 25- to 34-year-old Jewish women in the labor force had college degrees, graduate degrees, or professional degrees, compared with about a quarter of the women in the broader population.

In summary, cohort analysis provides little support for the expectation that dissimilarity between Jews and the broader white population is decreasing, for men or for women. It does make a case for the continuing distinctiveness of American Jewish occupations.

Occupation and Family Roles

We also considered whether family roles are at all related to occupational achievement. Some occupations might be more compatible with family roles, such as marriage and childrearing, than others, in that they are more flexible with respect to part-time employment or actual hours of work, delayed entry, and reentry (Glass and Camarigg, 1992; Rosenfeld and Spenner, 1992). Other occupations might depend on a spouse to help out with "backstage" obligations, including social functions and service support, such as laundry and meals, more often fulfilled by wives than husbands (Hochschild, 1989). In 1990, we found that family roles were related to the types of occupations of American Jewish women and men, but in different ways:

> Men in professional, technical, academic, and managerial occupations are more likely to be married, but they will have married at an older age, presumably after completing higher education. Although being married is not related to the occupations women are in, the age at which family roles have been entered is. Women in professional, technical, academic and managerial occupations had children later, and have fewer children than women in clerical, sales, blue-collar and service occupations. This lends support to the human capital theory, which suggests that women who have invested more in family roles would have less time and resources to invest in the labor force and hence would attain different occupations than women who invest more in the labor force and relatively less in family roles. Unlike women, men's human capital may be raised by being married because of the support provided by the family, and therefore married men are also more successful in the labor force. (Hartman and Hartman, 1996a, p. 137)

We looked at the relationship between family roles and occupational achievement for women and men ages 35–64 in 2000–01 (Table 4.20). We limited the analysis to these ages to cover the ages at which most first marriages had already occurred, most college education had been completed, and retirement was not yet entered. Looking first at men, we see that men in business/finance and sales occupations are the most likely to be currently married; these occupations are often enhanced by the "backstage wealth" families provide. It is interesting that men in management/executive positions were not the most likely to be married, as we would have expected, although a higher proportion of them had been married at least once in the past. Those in technical, service, office/administrative support, and blue-collar occupations were least likely to be married. The latter occupations appear often to be used as temporary positions for Jewish men; for example, a relatively low proportion of men are employed full time in office/administrative support jobs. Furthermore, in service, office/administrative support, and blue-collar jobs, men are the least educated (lowest proportions with college degrees). Those in technical and blue-collar occupations are the least likely to have ever been married. Age at marriage varies little from occupation to occupation, hovering on average around age 27; those in service occupations married somewhat later, suggesting that it was more difficult for them to find a compatible spouse. Divorce rates are highest among those with management/executive, service, sales, office/administrative support, and blue-collar occupations: the former, perhaps because of the demand on spouses to help out with the occupation; the latter, perhaps because of the low monetary returns from these occupations, as discussed later. Men in business/finance occupations had the lowest rate of divorce.

Among women, family roles are mildly related to occupation. Women in business/finance and in service occupations are the least likely to have ever been married, and women in service and sales occupations are the most likely to have divorced. Without more detailed information on the timing of occupational history and its overlap with marital history, it is difficult to determine why. Perhaps it is easier for women to enter these occupations when their family status changes. Women in business/finance, service, and office/administrative support occupations are the least likely to be currently married, the former perhaps because of the demanding nature of the job (this is the occupation with the highest proportion of women working full time). Age at marriage hovers around 25 for most of the women, with minor variation by occupation. Age at first birth hovers around 27 for women in most of the occupations, somewhat lower for those in office/administrative support, somewhat higher for women in business/finance and professional, the occupations for which women have the longest preparation (the highest proportion with college degrees). It is difficult to explain the slight variation in the number of children by occupational status—women in business/finance, professional, and sales occupations have the most children, whereas women in management/executive, technical, and service occupations have the fewest.

Perhaps comparing these patterns (Table 4.20) with those in the broader white population (Table 4.21) will clarify the distinctiveness of the relationship between Jewish family characteristics and occupation. Compared with men in the broader white population, Jewish men apparently are much more likely to enter blue-collar, office/administrative support, and technical occupations as temporary and even, in the case of office jobs, part-time positions before marriage, but once married, they are more likely to assume other occupations. Jewish men in management/executive positions are less likely to be currently married than men in the broader white population, and a relatively large proportion of them are divorced, compared with those in other professions; this is not seen in the broader population. The proportion of those who have ever divorced is highest for Jewish men in sales, perhaps reflecting the strain that traveling sales jobs puts on marriages, as well as in lower-paying jobs such as blue-collar and service jobs.

Table 4.20 Family Characteristics, Education, and Percentage Employed Full Time of American Jews (Ages 35–64), by Occupation and Gender[a]

	Married (%)	Ever married (%)	Ever divorced (%)	Mean age at marriage	Childless (%)	Mean age at birth of first child	Mean number of children	Employed full time (%)	College degree (%)	n
Men										
Management/executive	69.5	87.5	27.5	26.1				94.3	70.8	(121)
Business/finance	82.6	87.8	11.4	26.8				94.2	87.2	(69)
Professional	71.1	85.5	24.5	27.3				89.3	84.1	(261)
Technical	57.4	74.9	22.8	29.0				89.5	71.6	(25)
Service	64.0	86.5	28.9	28.6				94.7	33.5	(26)
Sales	75.9	89.1	37.5	26.9				90.9	62.5	(142)
Office/administrative support	56.5	72.0	27.5	24.2				59.5	58.5	(20)
Blue collar	63.2	78.8	30.1	25.8				91.2	36.5	(49)
Women										
Management/executive	69.9	87.5	30.2	24.4	28.9	26.3	1.5	76.6	64.6	(119)
Business/finance	66.6	79.9	22.6	23.8	25.6	27.2	1.8	56.9	75.8	(60)
Professional	71.6	91.0	28.3	25.1	19.8	28.7	1.7	69.1	88.0	(392)
Technical	61.7	81.8	26.8	24.0	37.2	25.2	1.4	62.9	60.6	(40)
Service	59.8	76.2	35.2	24.7	36.4	26.7	1.4	76.2	40.5	(40)
Sales	67.2	90.4	32.2	23.0	30.7	25.7	1.8	71.5	38.9	(120)
Office/administrative support	61.8	80.7	22.7	22.7	26.2	25.7	1.6	68.5	34.3	(107)
Blue collar	—	—	—	—	—	—	—	—	—	(14)

[a]Unweighted *n* in parentheses; calculations performed using person-weights provided with dataset.

Large proportions of men in these occupations in the broader population are divorced. Office and blue-collar jobs are also characterized by somewhat lower ages of first marriage for Jewish men; these are occupations, along with service occupations, in which there is a lower proportion of college-educated men. In all occupations, though, Jewish men are more likely to have college degrees than are men in the broader population. In the latter population, there is a much larger variation in the proportion that are college-educated: in management/executive, business/finance, professional, and technical occupations, more than half of the men have college degrees; while less than 20% of those employed in service, sales, office/administrative support, and blue collar occupations have college degrees.

Among women, there is less variation in marital status by occupation than among men. However, some occupations, including service and sales jobs, have higher proportions of divorced women; these occupations may have been easier to reenter when marital status changed and a job became necessary. In the broader white population, service, office, and blue-collar jobs have especially high proportions of divorced women. There is a little variation in age at marriage according to the extent of education common in an occupation (e.g., earlier ages of marriage for office and sales job), but the variation is not great for Jewish or white women. Among Jewish women, age at birth of first child is around 26 or 27, with little variation by occupation; in the broader population, there is a greater difference between occupations requiring more education (management/executive, professional, technical) and occupations requiring less (service, sales, blue-collar, and office/administrative support). Accordingly, the number of children born to women in service, sales, and blue-collar occupations is greater in the broader population. The pattern is not as clear for Jewish women. Finally, all women in the broader population are more likely to be working full time in most of the occupations, compared with Jewish women, with the exception of sales and service jobs.

Among Jewish women, the relationship between occupation and family roles is not as clear as it is among women in the broader white population, for whom occupational patterns suggest that certain occupations are more compatible with certain family statuses than others. Among Jewish women, variations in occupation seem to be related more to educational attainment than to family status. The next analysis confirms this conclusion. The results of a logistic regression predicting the odds of being in a high-status profession (managerial, business/finance, or professional) are presented in Table 4.22. Only education has a statistically significant effect on whether a woman is in a high-status profession; none of the current family roles (marital status, age of youngest child) have a statistically significant effect, nor do

Table 4.21 Family Characteristics, Education, and Percentage Employed Full Time of U.S. Non-Hispanic Whites (Ages 35–64), by Occupation and Gender[a]

	Married (%)	Ever married (%)	Ever divorced (%)	Mean age at marriage	Childless (%)	Mean age at birth of first child	Mean number of children	Employed full time (%)	College degree (%)	n
Men										
Management/executive	78.4	92.8	29.5	22.9				98.1	57.2	(1,361)
Business/finance	80.5	92.0	26.7	23.3				98.4	66.3	(579)
Professional	73.9	87.1	30.6	22.5				95.5	49.2	(917)
Technical	74.8	88.6	30.2	22.3				96.7	62.0	(558)
Service	65.4	85.3	23.4	21.9				93.0	16.9	(921)
Sales	65.9	85.3	23.4	21.9				88.6	8.3	(205)
Office/administrative support	68.5	89.5	35.1	22.2	—	—	—	97.0	44	(1,060)
Blue collar	69.8	90.3	37.7	21.8	—	—	—	96.2	5.7	(1,963)
Women										
Management/executive	66.8	91.1	39.4	20.4	22.8	25.0	1.7	90.7	36.6	(1,364)
Business/finance	67.9	88.3	35.1	21.5	21.1	26.1	1.9	82.4	50.9	(460)
Professional	65.1	91.2	38.0	20.3	18.9	24.6	1.9	80.2	26.3	(1,848)
Technical	72.3	92.8	33.5	20.8	17.6	25.7	1.9	85.2	54.2	(1,019)
Service	61.5	91.9	40.9	19.9	14.7	23.6	2.1	77.0	10.6	(1,719)
Sales	69.8	88.5	26.2	20.8	17.8	23.0	2.2	67.8	7.7	(71)
Office/administrative support	60.1	91.3	51.8	19.2	15.3	22.3	1.8	93.6	18.3	(43)
Blue collar	60.7	91.8	45.7	19.7	11.4	22.7	2.2	85.8	3.1	(721)

Data source: SIPP, 2001.

[a] *n* in thousands.

Table 4.22 Logistic Regression for Predictors of High-Status Professions[a] for Women (Ages 25–64), Employed Full Time

Independent variable	Jews		Non-Hispanic whites	
	Unstandardized coefficient	Exp (ß)	Unstandardized coefficient	Exp (ß)
Education	.923	(2.517)*	.535	(1.707)*
Age	−.065	(0.937)	.030	(1.030)
Age at first marriage	−.060	(0.942)	.014	(1.014)
Age at birth of first child	.080	(1.083)	−.021	(0.979)
Number of live births	.055	(1.056)	−.186	(0.830)*
Current marital status (not married/married)	.190	(1.210)	.169	(1.185)
Age of youngest child	.048	(1.050)	−.019	(0.981)
Nagelkerke R^2	.259		.075	
(Unweighted n)	(384)		(1,196)	

[a]High-status profession = managerial/business/finance/professional occupation.
*Statistically significant at $p < 0.001$.

the more long-term indicators of familistic tendencies (age at marriage, age at birth of first child, number of live births). Age does not change the odds of being in such a profession. Jewish women do not appear to suffer from a "marriage penalty" (or advantage) or a "child penalty" in terms of occupational achievement. In the next chapter, when we look at Jewish couples, we will explore this further. Among the broader white population of women, however, although education has the most important influence on occupational attainment, number of children also has a statistically significant negative relationship with occupational attainment, showing that family roles are more closely related to occupational achievement than among Jewish women.

Occupational Rewards

Finally, we consider the rewards that Jewish men and women receive from their economic roles. We use two indicators of such rewards: annual earnings and occupational prestige. Note that each has some limitations. Many respondents are reluctant to report what their annual earnings are, not only on the NJPS but on surveys in general. An analysis of the response patterns for the 2000–01 NJPS has shown that the non-response is biased toward higher-income earners, at least among men (Chiswick and Huang, 2008). There is no reason to expect that this pattern differs for women. We suggest that rather than level of income, the main interest in what we present lies in the relationship between men's and women's earnings.

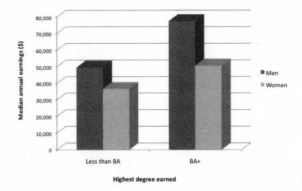

Figure 4.13. Median annual earnings, by gender and education (employed full time, ages 25–64).

Income. Jewish women earn only about 56% of what Jewish men earn. Confining our comparison to men and women employed full time does not change this differential appreciably. Among those employed full time with college degrees, the differential persists. Among those employed full time who do not have a college degree, women earn about 73% of what men earn annually (Figure 4.13). One reason that there is a greater gender differential between those with college degrees and those without is that women's earnings do not increase as much with education as men's do (Figure 4.14).

When we compare earnings within the same broad occupational group, we see that the greatest differentials are in occupations that confer the highest status (managerial/executive, business/finance, and professional; Table 4.23). This is true for the broader U.S. population, there being a wider

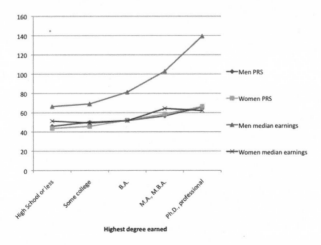

Figure 4.14. Median annual earnings (in thousands) and mean occupational prestige score (PRS), by gender and education (employed full time, ages 25–64).

gender gap in earnings in the highest-status occupations (Weinberg, 2004). Because so many Jewish men and women are in such occupations, the overall gender gap in occupational earnings is greater for the Jewish population than for the broader population. In technical and service occupations, Jewish men and women earn practically the same amount on average, but this is not true for the broader population, in which women employed full time earn about 76% of what men earn. In the broader population, the smallest gender gap in earnings is found in office/administrative jobs, but this contrasts with the Jewish population.

One of the reasons for the greater gender gap among Jews might be the actual distribution of men and women among detailed occupations. Looking again at the 10 most common occupations of Jewish men and women, we can see that in several of the common occupations of men, women on average make less than two-thirds of what men make (Table 4.24). In the most common occupation of women (retail salesperson), women make only two-thirds of what men make (in the broader population). Note that we could not go into this detail using the comparison of Jewish men's and women's earnings because of the relatively small number of respondents in each detailed occupation.

Family characteristics may also be related to the gender gap in occupations. Investing in family roles, especially at early ages, may interrupt

Table 4.23 Gender Gap In Median Annual Earnings of American Jews and Non-Hispanic Whites (Ages 25 and Over), Employed Full Time, by Occupation

Occupation	Ratio of Women's to Men's Earnings			
	Jews		Non-Hispanic whites[a]	
Management/executive	61.3	(249)[b]	71.7	(10,221)[c]
Business/finance	60.3	(127)	74.1	(4,558)
Professional	67.6	(678)	73.1	(21,371)
Technical	96.9	(63)	76.1	(4,680)
Service	94.2	(57)	78.6	(13,763)
Sales	71.8	(256)	62.1	(9,984)
Office and administrative support	71.8	(95)	88.9	(14,966)
Blue collar	81.1	(60)	72.4	(11,280)
Total	66.8	(1,698)	80.4	(101,224)

[a]Chao and Utgoff (2005, Table 18). Median usual weekly earnings of full-time wage and salary workers, 2004 annual averages; *n* in thousands.
[b]Unweighted sample size in parentheses; calculations performed using person-weights provided with dataset.
[c]*n* in thousands.

Table 4.24 Gender Gap in Median Annual Earnings in the Ten Most Common Occupations of Jewish Men and Women

Men

Occupation	Jewish men in occupation (%)	Ratio of women's to men's earnings in U.S.[a]
Retail salespersons	10.4	64.7
Lawyers	5.4	73.4
Physicians and surgeons	4.3	52.2
Other teachers and instructors	4.3	74.9
Managers, all other	4.1	—
Accountants and auditors	3.9	74.5
Chief executives	3.6	69.9
Engineers, all other	3.5	77.3[b]
Management analysts	2.9	75.9
Computer programmers	2.4	87.4

Women

Occupation	Jewish women in occupation (%)	Ratio of women's to men's earnings in U.S.[a]
Retail salespersons	7.4	64.7
Elementary and middle school teachers	6.0	84.6
Other teachers and instructors	5.3	74.9
Managers, all other	4.4	—
Secretaries and administrative assistants	3.7	92.0
Office clerks, general	3.4	95.4
Lodging managers	3.2	84.7
Registered nurses	2.9	86.8
Social workers	2.8	95.7
Lawyers	2.8	73.4

[a]Chao & Utgoff, 2005, Table 18. Median usual weekly earnings of full-time wage and salary workers, 2004 annual averages.
[b]Ratio for all engineers (breakdown not available).

women's careers or reduce the amount of time and energy that can be devoted to them. To test the extent to which family roles are related to women's earnings, we used a multiple regression of annual earnings. We included their pattern of investment in family roles by controlling for age at marriage, age at birth of first child, or number of children, as well as their current family roles (current marital status and age of youngest child). We controlled for age, education, and hours of work (analyzing the earnings of full-time-employed women only; Table 4.25). Among women employed full

Table 4.25 Multiple Regression Analysis of Median Annual Earnings for Women (Ages 25–64), Employed Full Time

Dependent variable	Standardized coefficient (ß)	Unstandardized coefficient
Education	.349	1.756*
Age	.091	0.056
Age at marriage	−.005	−0.006
Age at birth of first child	.024	0.026
Age of youngest child	−.097	−0.051
Number of live births	.084	0.464
Current marital status	.081	0.959
R	.363	0.390
R^2	.132	0.152
(Unweighted n)	(219)	

*Statistically significant at $p < 0.05$.

time, earnings are most strongly related to their education, rather than to their familistic characteristics or current family roles. None of the family characteristics or age have statistically significant relationships with median annual earnings (Table 4.25). Note, however, that only 15.2% of the variance is explained by these variables (R^2 = 0.152), so clearly there are other factors at work in predicting earnings, such as length and stability of career pattern, husband's education and earnings, size and type of employer. What is notable is that, again, there appears to be no "marriage penalty" or "child penalty" with respect to Jewish women's earnings.

Occupational Prestige. A second measure of occupational rewards is the occupational prestige score, a ranking of the "social desirability" of an occupation. Measured by how individuals in the general population rank occupations, occupational prestige is related to the ability and skills perceived to be necessary for an occupation as well as the material and other rewards associated with it (Wegener, 1992). The occupational prestige scores that we use are adapted from those developed for the 1980 Census categories of occupation and adapted to the 1990 Census categories (Nakao and Treas, 1994). Since then, a new study of occupational prestige has not been undertaken, but the scores have been adapted to the 2000 Census categories of occupation.[3] No new prestige scores have been collected in the United States since 1989, but their stability, both over time and between genders, is fairly well established (as summarized in Hauser and Warren, 1997). Again, we suggest emphasizing the comparison of men's and women's occupational prestige scores, with the expectation that any bias that may be present would affect men's and women's scores similarly.

For each detailed occupation, a prestige score was assigned on the basis of adaptation for the 2000 Census categories, as already mentioned. The mean prestige score reported for men in professional occupations (Table 4.26), for example, is an average of all of the detailed occupations that Jewish men hold in the broader professional category.

What is perhaps most striking is the similarity of Jewish men's and women's occupational prestige scores. Despite the differences in the occupations that Jewish men and women hold in each of the broader occupational groups, as we discussed earlier, their mean occupational prestige scores in each broad occupational group are very similar. This mirrors the lack of gender difference in occupational prestige ratings for men and women found in the broader U.S. population (Fox and Suschnigg, 1989; Nakao and Treas, 1994). While we note some changes in the mean occupational scores according to these broader categories between 1990 (Hartman and Hartman, 1996a, Table 4, p. 14) and 2000–01, we caution against drawing any conclusions from this comparison, because the composition of the broader categories changed considerably between the 1990 and 2000 Censuses. However, it should be noted that in 1990 there was a considerable gender gap in occupational prestige favoring men over women, which could be explained by differential education, age (which can be interpreted as a proxy for years in the labor force), hours of work per week, and marital status (Hartman and Hartman, 1996a, pp. 153–62).

Table 4.26 Mean Occupational Prestige Scores for American Jews (Ages 25–64) by Occupation and Gender, 2000–01

Occupation	Total (n)[a]		Men (n)[a]		Women (n)[a]	
Managerial/executive	52.6	(361)	52.6	(173)	52.6	(188)
Business/finance	57.8	(206)	59.8	(111)	53.7	(95)
Professional	64.9	(1,121)	66.3	(522)	63.3	(599)
Technical	48.9	(117)	49.0	(53)	48.8	(64)
Sales	36.8	(126)	36.9	(51)	36.6	(75)
Office/administrative support	41.3	(436)	41.5	(231)	41.2	(205)
Service	39.3	(254)	39.2	(61)	39.3	(193)
Blue collar	37.0	(105)	36.5	(83)	38.3	(22)
Total	53.7	(2,726)	54.1	(1,285)	53.1	(1,441)

[a]Unweighted n in parentheses; calculations performed using person-weights provided with dataset.

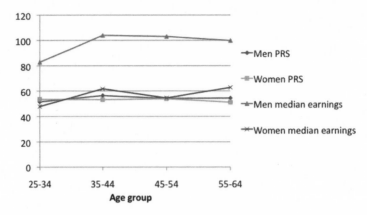

Figure 4.15. Median annual earnings (in thousands) and mean occupational prestige score (PRS), by gender and age (employed full time, ages 25–64).

This similarity in occupational prestige scores is found in all age cohorts from ages 25 to 64. Just as constant is the gap in earnings between men and women in all age cohorts (Figure 4.15). Here we have controlled for full-time employment in order to eliminate the possibility that the gender gap arises from unequal hours of work.

In the next chapter we will see how these patterns of gender similarity and difference play out for married couples.

SUMMARY AND CONCLUSIONS

In this chapter, we have looked at the labor force participation and occupational patterns of American Jewish women and men, as well as the role that education plays in these patterns, and have compared them to patterns in the broader U.S. population. Once we controlled for education, we found remarkable similarity between American Jews and the broader population in terms of labor force participation. Women's labor force participation is affected by their marital status, in that women in first marriages are less likely to be working in the labor force and less likely to have full-time jobs when they do. However, remarried women are more likely than women in first marriages to be in the labor force and to be working full time. As a result, there is greater similarity between men and women in remarriages than in first marriages. Women's labor force participation depends noticeably on whether there is a child under the age of 3 at home; however, this sensitivity, though greater than that found in the broader population, indicates a greater similarity between Jewish women and women in the broader population than has been found in the past. Furthermore, the "child penalty" on labor force participation of women is smaller than it was in 1990.

Both Jewish men and women differ in their occupational patterns from the broader population in that a higher proportion are in professional occupations and a lower proportion are in blue-collar or service occupations. As a result, occupations vary less by level of education among American Jews than they do in the broader population; and there is greater similarity in the occupations of American Jewish men and women than in those of men and women in the broader population. American Jewish women and men also have very similar occupational prestige. However, there is a large gender gap in income among American Jews, consonant with the wider gaps in income found among the educated in the broader population.

The higher level of education of Jewish women thus does not translate into income rewards, although it does bring about greater similarity in labor force participation patterns, especially when there are no young children at home, and greater similarity in occupational achievement and prestige.

CHAPTER 5

Dual-Earning Patterns of American Jews

Given the high labor force participation rates of both Jewish men and women, it is expected that in a high proportion of American Jewish couples, both spouses will be working in the labor force, that is, as dual-earner couples. The main purpose of this chapter is to explore the patterns of dual earning among American Jews.

As we have seen in earlier chapters, both American Jewish men and women are highly educated and highly represented in occupations characterized by high income and occupational prestige, even in comparison with those of similar educational achievement. Because both women and men share this high achievement relative to the broader population, there is an expectation of gender equality between Jewish women and men in this respect, and presumably between spouses. Relations between spouses often reflect status in the broader society (Hout, 1982), which makes gender relations between spouses of even greater interest. However, spousal relations often reflect tensions in the broader society as well, and certainly gender equality has been a focus of tension as gender roles have shifted and varied in the past few decades. How this affects Jewish men and women was explored in Prell's *Fighting to Become Americans* (1999), which shows that the tensions in gender role transitions played out not only in intimate relations between Jewish men and women, but also in terms of their status vis-à-vis the broader society. Gender equality in secular achievement can therefore not be assumed between Jewish spouses and is the subtext of this chapter.

Dual-earning patterns can vary in at least three ways. First, they vary in terms of the work hours involved—the husband's work hours, the wife's work hours, the combined work hours, and the husband's work hours in comparison with the wife's (e.g., Bielby and Bielby, 1989; Chenu and Robinson, 2002; Gilbert, 2005). A related issue is whether the wife is in the position of "secondary earner," with fewer work hours and more flexible adjustments to family demands (Becker and Moen, 1999; Gershuny, Bitt-man, and Brice, et. al., 2005).

Second, dual-earning patterns vary in terms of the educational and occu-pational equality between husbands and wives in dual-earner couples (e.g., Schwartz and Mare, 2005). As we have already shown, there appears to be a tendency toward increased educational homogamy among American Jew-ish married couples as well as among couples in the broader population (Schwartz and Mare, 2005) . There also appears to be increasing occupa-tional homogamy among contemporary couples (Kalmijn, 1994), which would not be an unexpected tendency among American Jews. The transfor-mation of American Jewry into a social and ethnic network, maintained to a great extent by similar social class, educational venues, and occupations (Goldscheider and Zuckerman, 1984), leads one to expect occupational and status homogamy among married Jewish couples.

In addition to the increased odds of meeting a marriageable partner of similar social status, there is also a possibility that, once married, spouses influence each other's achievement. There are three prevailing theories about the effects spouses have on each other's occupational achievement (Robert and Bukodi, 2002). (1) *Advantage redistribution among households* sug-gests that the husband's advantages in the labor market will depress the wife's occupational achievements, because her efforts will be more highly valued within the home than will his; this implies that even if the status of the husband and that of his wife are similar at the time of marriage, over time a traditional gender gap will develop, with the husband achieving an occupation that provides a higher income and more prestige than his wife. (2) *Advantage accumulation within households* suggests that households ben-efit from and therefore facilitate wives' work, and that shared economic, so-cial, and cultural resources enhance the achievement of each spouse (Ber-nasco, 1994, cited in Smits, Ultee, and Lammers, 1996). (3) *Status similarity within households* suggests increased occupational similarity because of the similar backgrounds of the spouses. At the same time, empirical research shows some anomalies: among academic couples, occupational homogamy was found to have no effect on the achievement of spouses (Ferber and Hoff-man 1997), and in some studies, husbands with working wives were found to be less successful in their careers than were husbands whose wives did not participate in the labor force (Bellas, 1992; Stanley, Hunt, and Hunt, 1986). In a cross-cultural comparative study, the husband's occupation was shown to produce both a ceiling effect and a facilitating effect on the wife's occupational achievement, the strength of which differed between countries (or cultural contexts) (Smits, Ultee, and Lammers, 1996). Our focus on Jew-ish dual earners will shed light on this controversy.

Third, dual-earning patterns vary in terms of gender equality in rewards from the labor force, including occupational prestige and earnings. Critical to understanding dual-earner couples is how much the wife contributes to the joint income (e.g., Raley, Mattingly, and Bianchi, 2006; Winkler, 1998; Winkler, McBride, and Andrews, 2005; Winslow-Bowe, 2006). Even when there is occupational homogamy, it may not imply gender equality in terms of these rewards, for a number of reasons. Men and women have different occupations within broad occupational classifications, as we have already seen. Income disparity between men and women appears to be greatest for most occupations that require the highest education and that yield higher incomes, as we showed in Chapter 4 and as Huffman (2004) has shown for dual-earner couples in the broader population, so that having the same occupation may not result in income homogamy. Also, women may take advantage of their husband's earnings to not work full time, which may in turn decrease both their earnings (both in the short term and as an accumulative disadvantage) and occupational prestige relative to their husband's (men are less likely to opt for such an arrangement).

Furthermore, intimate gender relationships often mirror tensions in the broader society, be it that of American Jews or, more generally, U.S. society (Prell, 1999). American Jewish women, having been at the forefront of the (third-wave) feminist movement, might be expected to display achievement equal to that of their husbands in their private lives. However, inasmuch as such equality might be threatening in intimate relationships, it is possible that family life is structured in such a way that it maintains some traditional status differences; indeed, some research has shown that marriages characterized by nontraditional status differences (where women earn a higher income or their occupation confers higher status than does that of their husband) are more vulnerable to dissolution (Gelissen, 2004).

For all these reasons, we are skeptical that, despite having strong human resources in their résumés, American Jewish wives will translate this into equal economic status with their husbands.

Most of the variation in dual-earning patterns has been related to husbands' and wives' educational levels, respective occupations, need for and desired income, and family roles (Winslow-Bowe, 2006). Husbands' and wives' relative education levels, occupations, and incomes have also been related to the likelihood and persistence of the wife's contributions to the family income (Raley et. al., 2006; Winkler, 1998; Winkler et. al., 2005). Sociocultural influences have also been explored, but primarily in terms of race or ethnicity (Winslow-Bowe, 2006) or other religions, usually Christian denominations (Heineck, 2004; Lehrer, 1995). Ammerman and Roof (1995) and Demmitt (1992) have explored how particular forms of religiosity among conservative Protestants are related to dual-earning patterns; and Hertel (1995) and Edgell (2006) have explored whether wives' employment has affected their religiosity, but the samples are primarily Christian. Because American Jewish attitudes toward women's employment differ from those of Protestant and Catholic women (see, e.g., Harville and Rienzi, 2000), and because of Jewish women's relatively high level of education and tradition of labor force involvement, research on the relationship between Jewish involvement in the labor force and dual-earning patterns need not follow those of the broader U.S. population.

Expectations about Jewish dual earning stem from Jews' high level of education, occupation, and income status relative to those of the broader population, which leads us to expect a higher proportion of dual earners, with long working hours. That the Jewish tradition has never opposed, and has even encouraged, the idea of women contributing to the family economy by working for pay outside the home (Baskin, 1991; Fishman, 1993; Wegner, 1988) adds to this expectation. At the same time, the family is central to Jewish life, and women are expected to take on major domestic responsibilities, which often curtail or interrupt labor force participation and achievement. Many highly educated Jewish women want both careers and families, in contrast to the feminist ethos, which in the past has pressured women to put careers first (Fishman, 1993). Some have suggested that the separate roles for men and women according to traditional Judaism might be expressed in traditional patterns of gender inequity with respect to education, hours of work, occupation, and earnings within Jewish couples, but Jewish tradition does not actually suggest that women need to be or should be inferior to their husbands in terms of secular education and occupational achievement, even if separate roles and obligations were condoned for domestic life (see also Wegner, 1988). Our previous research did not support the notion that traditional Judaism brought with it gender inequality within couples (Hartman and Hartman, 1996a).

Another factor to consider is marital status. Some research has suggested that second marriages differ from first marriages in terms of homogamy (Gelissen, 2004). The two prevailing theories are (1) that people learn from their first marriages that homogamy is desirable (*learning theory*), and therefore their second marriages are more homogamous than their first marriages; and (2) that remarriages are less homogamous because there is less selection in the marriage market (*marriage market theory*). Jewish intermarriage supports the second theory: 43% of remarriages are intermarriages, compared with 25% of first marriages. The figures are similar for both men and women. Kalmijn (1994) found, however, that economic homogamy is more important than cultural homogamy when couples enter into marriage when they are older. Because remarriage takes place between people who are older than those marrying for the first time, marriage when one is older may be related to increased occupational homogamy in remarriage even as cultural homogamy (represented by religious identification) decreases. This may be a variant of "trading up" in remarriage—that is, giving up cultural homogamy for economic homogamy. However, there is no guarantee that the economic status (even if more homogamous) will be higher in remarriage. The last section of the chapter addresses this issue, and we explore its interaction with intermarriage in Chapter 10.

Previous research about American Jewish dual earners showed that in the past the proportion of dual earners among American Jews lagged behind that of the broader U.S. population. As immigrants, in 1911, only 8% of Jewish women were employed outside their homes (Fishman, 1993, p. 69), although they were often involved in moneymaking activities from their homes (Hyman, Baum, and Michel, 1976; Glenn, 1990; Weinberg, 1988). Even as they became more highly educated than most women in the United States, a large proportion of Jewish women did not participate in the labor force once they became pregnant or mothers, even through the 1960s (Fishman, 1993, p. 72). It was in a relatively short time, therefore, that the majority of Jewish families became dual earners: according to the 1990 NJPS, 55% of Jewish couples were dual earners (Hartman and Hartman, 1996a, Table 5.6, p. 180), quite comparable to the national U.S. proportion of dual-earner families (52.1%) at the time.

However, the patterns of Jewish dual-earner couples in 1990 were somewhat different than patterns found among dual-earner couples in the broader U.S. population (Hartman and Hartman, 1996a). For example, there was less occupational similarity between the spouses than expected. Unlike the pattern of dual earners in the broader population, in which husbands' and wives' employment seemed to be modified by each other's characteristics, Jewish wives' labor force participation and occupational prestige were related more to their own education and number of children than to their spouse's characteristics. Jewish wives were more likely than wives in the broader U.S. population to have the same level of education as, or a higher level than, their husbands. We also found that more than half of the women in dual-earner couples had the same or higher occupational prestige as, or higher prestige than, their husbands, another unusual pattern, and that the proportion of "cross-class" couples was particularly large among American Jews (Hartman and Hartman, 1996a). Data on individual husbands' and wives' income were not available to make that comparison. Thus, it is with considerable interest that we turn to analyzing this subject among American Jews with the data available from the 2000–01 National Jewish Population Survey.

Using the 2000–01 NJPS, we include in our sample the 1,415 Jewish respondents who were currently married (and not separated). We excluded
non-married "partners," who would have introduced extraneous variations
into the analysis, would have reduced comparability with other studies, and
would have added fewer than 53 couples to the analysis (of whom 31 were
same-sex couples, which would have introduced another set of variations
into the analysis).

Dual-earner couples are designated as married couples in which the husband and the wife are both currently in the labor force. *Hours of work* are
considered part time if they are employed 34 hours or fewer in a typical
week; hours of work are considered full time if they are employed 35 hours
or more per week. In the data set, actual hours worked were recorded in
groups of work hours; the midpoint of the group was used in our analyses.
For the spouse, the actual hours were given (and used for analysis).

Occupation is coded according to the 2000 Census codes, as in the preceding chapter. *Occupational prestige* is also coded as explained in the preceding chapter. *Income* was reported as annual earnings (before taxes) for
respondent and spouse. *Household income* was reported as pre-tax household income for 1999.

DUAL-EARNING PATTERNS

Dual earners comprised 45% of Jewish couples in 2000–01 (down from
54.8% in the 1990 NJPS). This is lower than the proportion of dual-earner
couples in the broader U.S. population (57.0% in 2000, 59.3% in 2001;
based on the Current Population Survey Annual Social and Economic Supplement, 1968–2005, Table 23). This is even less in line with expectations,
given American Jews' high educational level, than was found in 1990,
when the proportion of dual earners among American Jews was very similar to that found in the broader U.S. population (Hartman and Hartman,
1996a, Table 5.6, p. 180).

Because at least one of the spouses in younger couples may be pursuing
higher education, and one of the spouses in older couples may be retired,
we looked at the incidence of dual-earner families by respondents' age and
found that, indeed, a higher proportion of couples, around 74%, were dual
earners in the 25–64 age groups (Table 5.1), more comparable to the
broader population.[1] The low proportion of dual earners among those 65
and older, and the relatively older age of the 65+ age group among American Jews brings the overall proportion to the lower level reported above.

Husbands and wives in single-earner families are significantly older
than husbands and wives in dual-earner couples, presumably because one

Table 5.1 Percentage of Dual-earner Couples for American Jews, by Age Group

Age group of respondent	% Dual earner
18–24	54.5
25–44	75.3
45–64	73.1
65+	27.6
Total	68.8
(*n*)[a]	(1,415)

[a]Unweighted *n* in parentheses; calculations performed using person-weights provided with dataset.

of the spouses in older couples has retired while the other spouse continues to work. Among single-earner couples, 31.9% of the husbands and 22.2% of the wives are 65 or over, whereas among dual-earner couples, only 9.1% of the husbands and 4.1% of the wives are 65 or over. As a result, the mean age of husbands and wives in single-earner couples is greater than the mean age of their counterparts in dual-earner couples.

In both single-earner and dual-earner couples, there is the traditional age difference, with most husbands being older than their wives by 2–3 years. In about 16% of the couples, wives are older than their husbands, but in less than 2% of the couples does this difference exceed 5 years. The mean age difference between husbands and wives is smaller among couples whose husband is under 65 (3–3.4 years) than among couples in which the husband is 65 or over (5.8 years).

Among dual-earner couples in which the husband is 65 or over, the age difference is particularly large (7.1), suggesting that in these couples it is probably the wife who has continued to work full time after the husband semi-retires. As Table 5.2 shows, the dominant pattern of dual earners in all age groups is that the husband and wife both work full time, but the older the husband is, the lower the proportion of dual-earner couples in which both spouses work full time, the lower the percentage of husbands working full time while the wife works part time, and the higher the percentage of both husband and wife working part time and the wife working full time with the husband working part time.

Like their counterparts in the broader U.S. population, Jewish dual-earner couples work long hours, 43.6% working a combined total of 80 or more hours per week. This is quite comparable to the average of 82 hours per week of the dual-earner couples in the broader population (NSCW, 2002).

Table 5.2 Full-time and Part-time Employment by Husband's Age, for American Jewish Couples

Husband's age	25–44	45–64	65+
Both husband and wife employed full time (%)	58.0	65.1	36.5
Husband employed full time, wife employed part time (%)	36.4	27.2	20.2
Wife employed full time, husband employed part time (%)	2.9	3.9	12.5
Both husband and wife employed part time (%)	2.7	3.8	30.8
Total (%) (n)[a]	100.0 (355)	100.0 (499)	100.0 (56)

[a]Unweighted n in parentheses; calculations performed using person-weights provided with dataset.

Jewish men in the labor force are more likely to be working full time than are women (Table 5.3), with an average work week of about 46 hours. As a result, there is a traditional difference in that husbands worked longer hours than wives in the majority of Jewish dual-earner couples (58.8%). In 27% of dual-earner couples, husbands and wives worked the same number of hours; and in 14.2%, wives worked longer hours than their husbands. As mentioned earlier, this is more likely to be the case for couples in which the respondent is over 65.

Husband's hours of work are not significantly different in single-earner and dual-earner couples (46.2 vs. 45.3%). However, wives in dual-earner couples are almost twice as likely to be working full time than are working

Table 5.3 Hours of Employment in American Jewish Single- and Dual-Earner Couples (Ages 25–64)

	Dual-earner couples	Single-earner couples
Husband employed full time (%)	92.9	93.4
Husband's mean hours of employment per week	46.1	47.6
Wife employed full time (%)	65.6	67.0
Wife's mean hours of employment per week	36.8	37.1
(n)[a]	(955)	(216)

[a]Unweighted n in parentheses; calculations performed using person-weights provided with dataset.

wives in single-earner couples (presumably because they are older). On average, wives in dual-earner couples work significantly more hours (34.9) than wives in single-earner couples (31.2%, t-test significant at $p = 0.063$). When we confine our analysis to the main labor force participation ages of the respondent (25–64), these differences disappear (Table 5.3).

Educational homogamy is the same for Jewish dual-earner couples and single-earner couples (38.4% in each group). However, there is a much higher proportion of husbands with a higher education than their wives among single-earner couples than among dual-earner couples, as might be expected. In more than 70% of educationally heterogamous single-earner couples, husbands have more education than their wives, compared with 56% of dual-earner couples. This is a result of wives in dual-earner couples having higher educational attainment: more than 40% of dual-earner wives have graduate degrees, compared with 24.9% of single-earner wives; conversely, 21.5% of single-earner wives have no college education, compared with less than 10% of dual-earner wives. The higher education of dual-earner wives leads to considerable occupational and income similarity among American Jewish spouses, as we shall see later.

In terms of the broad occupational categories, there is a similarity in the occupations of Jewish dual-earner husbands and wives (Table 5.4). More than one-third of husbands and wives have occupations in the same general category, with an especially high proportion of couples (22.4%) in which both husband and wife have professional occupations. Almost half of wives and 41% of husbands have professional occupations; somewhat

Table 5.4 Occupations of American Jewish Dual-Earner Couples

Occupation	Husband (%)	Wife (%)	Both (%)
Management/executive	13.3	11.3	2.5
Business/finance	8.5	6.5	1.3
Professional	41.2	44.5	22.4
Technical	2.1	4.2	0.3
Service	3.4	4.3	0.6
Sales	15.3	11.2	3.3
Office/administrative support	2.8	10.8	0.8
Foreman, skilled/unskilled	6.9	2.2	0.8
Other	6.5	5.0	1.0
Total	100.0	100.0	33.0
$(n)^a$			(1,191)

[a]Unweighted n in parentheses; calculations performed using person-weights provided with dataset.

higher proportions of husbands than wives are in management/executive, business/finance, sales, and blue-collar occupations; and somewhat higher proportions of wives have technical, service, and office/administrative support occupations. This distribution follows the traditional pattern of "female" and "male" occupations, but is less differentiated than in the past. In 1990, using similar classifications of occupations, we found that more than 20% of wives would have to change occupations to have the same occupational distribution as their husbands (Hartman and Hartman, 1996a, p. 188). In 2000–01, this percentage decreased to 16.5%.

Collapsing these categories to upper-/upper-middle-class (professional, managerial/executive, and business/finance); middle-class (sales, office/administrative support, technical); and lower-/lower-middle-class (blue-collar, service) occupations, we find that more than half (52%) of husbands and wives have occupations in a similar class, whereas 47% are in "cross-class" marriages, a percentage somewhat higher than that in 1990, when we found that about 41% of dual-earner couples were "cross-class" and 58% were in a similar occupational class. In 1990 we found an unusual pattern in that that these cross-class couples among American Jews were disproportionately ones in which the wife's occupation was in a higher class than her husband's. In 2000–01, this pattern shifted, so that in about half of cross-class couples, the wives had higher-status occupations than their husbands, and in the other half, the husbands had higher-status occupations than their wives.

Table 5.5 Occupations of American Jewish Dual-Earner Couples, 1990 and 2000–01

	1990		2000–01	
Occupation	Husbands (%)	Wives (%)	Husbands (%)	Wives (%)
Professional, technical, academic	44.5 (328)	48.4 (357)	43.8 (516)	51.7 (580)
Managerial, administrative	17.9 (132)	15.0 (111)	22.6 (259)	16.8 212)
Sales, clerical	17.3 (128)	27.9 (206)	19.5 (215)	21.5 (262)
Blue collar, service	20.3 (150)	8.7 (206)	7.3 (123)	4.5 (99)

Data sources: NJPS, 1990 and 2000–01; Hartman & Hartman, 1996a, Table 5.10.
[a]Unweighted *n* in parentheses; calculations performed using person-weights provided with datasets.

One of the reasons for this is that the occupational distributions have become less "traditional": wives' occupations have become more similar to their husbands,' with a higher proportion of women (as well as men) now in professional, management/executive, and business/finance positions than in 1990, and with fewer spouses in blue-collar or service occupations, especially men (Table 5.5; see also Chiswick and Huang, 2006). (Keep in mind that the occupational classification changed from 1990 to 2000, so that several categories of occupations are collapsed for comparability.)

Another way of comparing occupational attainment of husbands and wives is to look at occupational prestige scores. For both husbands and wives, these scores are slightly higher in dual-earner than in single-earner couples (Table 5.6). There is considerable similarity between the prestige scores of husbands and wives, whether they are in single-earner or dual-earner families. Indeed, in 48.4% of dual-earner couples, the husband's occupational prestige score is higher than the wife's; yet in 41.2% of couples, the wife's occupational prestige score is higher than the husband's. In 10.5%, the occupational prestige score of the husband is equal to that of the wife.

These results are very consistent with those obtained in 1990, when we found that in 51% of dual-earner couples, wives had the same occupational prestige or higher prestige than their husbands (Hartman and Hartman, 1996a, p. 191).

As might be expected, dual-earner couples have slightly higher household incomes than single-earner couples (but the t-test was *not* significant at $p < 0.05$; Figure 5.1).

One reason that the difference in household income is not greater between single- and dual-earner couples is that the husband's income is significantly higher in single-earner couples (mean \$125,586 vs. \$95,678; t-test = 0.024).[2] In contrast, the wife's income is significantly higher in dual-earner couples (\$40,000 vs. \$56,304; t-test = 0.004).

In two-thirds of dual-earner couples (on which we have income data for both husband and wife; $n = 311$), husbands earned more than wives; in 15%

Table 5.6 Mean Occupational Prestige of American Jews in Single-Earner and Dual-Earner Couples

	Single-earner couples	Dual-earner couples
Husband	54.3	56.8
Wife	52.3	53.9
$(n)^a$	(316)	(955)

[a]Unweighted n in parentheses; calculations performed using person-weights provided with dataset.

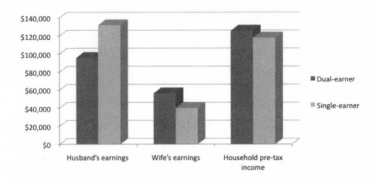

Figure 5.1. Mean annual earnings for single-earner and dual-earner couples.

of couples, wives earned the same as their husbands; and in 17%, wives earned more than their husbands. This is a somewhat lower proportion of wives earning more than their husbands than in the greater U.S. population, in which 24.1% of wives in dual-earner families earned more than their husbands (U.S. Bureau of the Census, 2003a). Other research has found this proportion to vary between 20% and 30% (Tichenor, 1999; Winslow-Bowe, 2006; Winkler, 1998). One reason may be that wives are more likely to earn more than their husbands when their husbands earn lower incomes, which is less likely among Jewish men than in the broader population (see discussion in Winslow-Bowe, 2006).

Another way of looking at the couple's income is to consider what proportion of the couple's dual income comes from the wife. Among American Jews, the average of 38.7% contribution is quite comparable to the estimate of the National Study of the Changing Workforce, according to which women in dual-earner families contribute on average an estimated 40% of family earnings (Bond, 2002, p. 9). Among full-time workers, the average contribution of wives among American Jews is 43.8%; among part-time workers, it is 30.5%. In about one-third of the couples, the wife contributes 50% or more to the couple's income. Among wives employed full time, the percentage of those contributing 50% or more to the couple's annual income is even higher, 42.7%.

Nock (2001) defines "marriages of equally dependent spouses" as those in which wives contribute 40–59% of the family income; among American Jews, nearly half (46.3%) of dual-earner couples fall in this category (not considering non-earnings income), compared with 30% of dual-earner couples in the broader U.S. population (Nock, 2001). Raley et al. (2006) found that in 12% of all couples, wives earned at least 60% of the total income; among American Jews, more than 16% of wives earned at least 60%

Table 5.7 Multiple Regression Analysis of Wife's Income Advantage (Husband's Age <65)

Independent variable	Standardized coefficient (ß)	Unstandardized coefficient	Significance
Wife's age	.016	0.000	.715
Husband's age	.034	0.000	.421
Number of children under 18 in household	.038	−0.005	.396
Wife's education	.046	0.006	.368
Wife's educational advantage over husband	.117	0.024	.004
Wife's weekly work hours	.192	0.002	.000
Wife working more hours than husband	.187	0.033	.000
Wife's occupational prestige	.042	0.001	.361
Husband's occupational prestige	−.007	−0.000	.868
Husband's annual earnings	−.398	−0.000	.000
Multiple R	.612		
R^2	.375		
(Unweighted n)	(364)		

of the dual income. So American Jewish wives in dual-earner couples appear to contribute a higher proportion of the earnings than do wives in the broader U.S. population.

Given the relatively high proportion of American Jewish wives earning nearly the same as or more than their husbands, our data allow us to test some of the explanations for the growing phenomenon of wives' income advantage. The prevailing (and competing) explanations are (1) that differences in economic resources and investments between husband and wife predict whether or not a wife will have an income advantage over her husband; and (2) a life course perspective, which suggests that life-cycle stage, age, and presence of children predict whether or not a wife will have an income advantage over her husband (there is also a sociodemographic explanation, which is not addressed here because we are using data from a fairly homogeneous sociodemographic group) (Winslow-Bowe, 2006).

We use a multiple regression analysis with the wife's percentage of the dual income as the dependent variable (Table 5.7). The independent variables indicating the life-cycle stage are the wife's age, husband's age, and number of children under 18 in the household. We limit the analysis to husbands who are under 65, so that we are not confounding the analysis with husbands being semi-retired and therefore earning less money. The independent variables indicating the human capital investments and economic resources are the wife's education, whether she has more education than her husband, the wife's hours of work, whether she works more hours than her husband, her occupational prestige, her husband's occupational prestige, and the husband's income.

We find that the wife's income advantage increases when she has a higher education than her husband, she works more hours, and her husband has a lower income. Her income advantage is not significantly related to her age, her husband's age, her level of education (only her education relative to her husband's education), her occupational prestige or her occupational prestige relative to that of her husband, the number of hours the wife works relative to her husband, or the presence at home of children under 18. These results lend considerable support to the explanations of wives' income advantage that are related to human capital and employment, because the main explanations for the wife's income advantage in this population are her hours of work, her educational advantage over that of her husband, and her husband's lower earning power. However, that neither her level of education nor her occupational prestige is related to her income advantage suggests that this may be a transitory phenomena related to her husband's (possibly temporary) lower earnings, as has been suggested in studies of the broader population (Winkler et al., 2005; Winslow-Bowe, 2006).

Among Jewish couples with children under 18 in at home (531 couples), 72.3% are dual earners. The proportion of dual earners is lower for those with no children under 18 at home, probably related to their older age, and for those with more than four children at home (Table 5.8). But the proportion of dual earners among those with one to three children at home is 73–75%, well above the proportion for the general U.S. population, 67% in 2002 (Bond, 2002, p. 4).

Table 5.8 Percentage of Dual-earner Couples for American Jews, by Number of Children Under 18 in Household

Number of children under 18 in household	Single earner	Dual earner	Total $(n)^a$
0	36.7	63.3	100.0 (490)
1	27.2	72.8	100.0 (184)
2	25.3	74.7	100.0 (166)
3	27.4	72.6	100.0 (62)
4 or more	41.0	59.0	100.0 (39)

[a]Unweighted *n* in parentheses; calculations performed using person-weights provided with dataset.

Number of children decreased slightly in younger cohorts of American Jews from 1990 to 2000–01 (possibly because couples were waiting longer to have their first child), but this tendency is found mainly among single-earner couples, not dual-earner couples (Table 5.9). In fact, as we have already seen, having up to three children at home does not deter both parents from working.

The work hours of couples with children has been of major concern, because long work hours reduce the amount of time parents have for family life, and their children in particular. Among American Jewish dual-earner couples with children at home, the average combined hours of work are 79 per week. In the broader U.S. population, however, the average work hours of a couple with children at home is considerably higher, 91 per week (Bond, 2002, Figure 9, p. 4). Whether the lower figure for American Jews reflects a conscious effort of parents to spend more time at home, possibly related to the age of the children at home, and/or reflects the higher average incomes of American Jews than those of the broader population, awaits further research (with more data than are available in the NJPS). What we analyze here is how hours spent with the family and income are related to the number of children of married couples.

Research shows that families strategize ways to maximize time spent with children within their working schedules, including "scaling back" on work hours (Becker and Moen, 1999). It is clear that, in American Jewish couples, it is the wife's hours of work that fluctuate with number of children rather than the husband's (Table 5.10), consistent with the notion of wives as "secondary earners," whose labor force commitments are manipulated to balance role conflicts and overloads accompanying multiple family and career demands.

Table 5.9 Mean Number of Children for Single-earner and Dual-earner American Jewish Couples, by Husband's Age, 1990 and 2000–01

	1990				2000–01			
Husband's age	Single earner (male breadwinner)		Dual Earner		Single Earner		Dual Earner	
18–34	1.9	(77)	0.9	(180)	1.7	(165)	0.8	(88)
35–44	2.2	(130)	1.6	(303)	2.4	(53)	1.9	(133)
45–64	2.4	(115)	2.0	(260)	2.2	(141)	2.0	(285)
65+	2.2	(51)	2.1	(31)	2.1	(244)	1.7	(35)

Data source: NJPS, 1990 and 2000–01.
[a]Unweighted *n* in parentheses; calculations performed using person-weights provided with dataset.

Table 5.10 Mean Hours of Employment in Single-Earner and Dual-Earner Couples, by Number of Children under 18 in Household[a]

	Number of children under 18 in household				
	0	1	2	3	4+
Husband's mean hours of work					
Single-earner	42.9 (118)	49.0 (78)	47.8 (83)	51.0 (20)	48.6 (14)
Dual-earner	44.0 (469)	45.5 (204)	48.0 (198)	46.1 (61)	45.6 (23)
Wife's mean hours of work					
Single-earner	30.8 (97)	33.7 (27)	35.3 (15)	—[b]	—[b]
Dual-earner	37.9 (470)	35.7 (206)	30.7 (194)	28.0 (61)	25.9 (24)
Couple's combined mean					
hours of work	81.9 (456)	81.2 (201)	78.7 (191)	74.2 (60)	71.5 (22)
Husband employed full time (%)					
Single-earner	38.9	78.0	78.6	82.4	87.5
Dual-earner	86.8	91.0	94.4	91.1	82.6
Wife employed full time (%)					
Single-earner	13.3	55.9	64.7	—[b]	—[b]
Dual-earner	71.3	66.4	50.0	33.3	21.7

[a]Unweighted *n* in parentheses; calculations performed using person-weights provided with dataset.
[b]Fewer than 10 cases of wives participating in the labor force.

When the husband is the single earner in the family, his work hours hardly fluctuate with the number of children at home. Those with no children at home are less likely to be working full time and thus have fewer work hours on average; these are probably either young husbands, balancing education with work, or older husbands who are semi-retired. Among husbands with one to four or more children, however, the percentage of those who work full time increases with the number of children, and work hours hover around 50 per week on average. Similarly, among dual-earner families, more than 90% of husbands with one to three children are working full time, and their work hours hover around 46 hours per week. While a slightly lower percentage of husbands with four or more children are employed full time, their work hours are still about 46 hours per week. So generally men's work hours do not fluctuate according to number of children at home.

Wives' work hours, on the other hand, clearly respond to the number of children. So few wives are the single earner of a married couple with young children at home that we could not analyze their work hours. But among dual earners, the proportion of wives working full time is lower with each additional child at home, dropping from 71.3% when there are no children at home to 21.7% when there are four or more children at home. Work hours fluctuate accordingly, from an average of 37.9 among dual-earner wives with no children at home to 25.9 among dual-earner wives with four or more children at home. Accordingly, the combined work hours of the couple are 81.9 on average among those with no children or one child at home, and drop to 71.5 among those with four or more children at home. Still, this is a large workload and is far from the optimal 60-hour work week advocated by some (Browning, Miller-McLemore, Couture, Lyon, and Franklin, 2000; Hill et al., 2006).

To get a better idea of the influences on the wife's hours of work, the main variation among dual earner's hours of work, we performed a multiple regression analysis with the wife's hours of work as the dependent variable; the independent variables were her age and education, her husband's age and education, the number of children under 18 at home, and the husband's hours of work (Table 5.11). We found that the number of children at home has the strongest relation to the wife's hours of work, significantly lowering the number of hours she works . The lower the husband's educational level, the greater the number of hours the wife works, and the higher the wife's educational level, the more hours she works. Husband's hours of work, his age, and her age were not related significantly to the wife's hours of work. Thus, her hours of work appear to respond clearly to the number of children at home, but also to the need for her income (as indicated by the husband's educational level) and her ability to bring in income (as indicated by her educational level).

Table 5.11 Multiple Regression Analysis of American Jewish Wives' Mean Hours in the Labor Force, Among Couples in Which Husband Is Employed

Independent variable	Unstandardized coefficient	Standardized coefficient (ß)
Wife's age	0.005	.004
Husband's age	–.097	–.084
Wife's education	1.372	.110*
Husband's education	–1.770	–.158*
Number of children under 18 at home	–3.287	–.290
Husband's hours of work	0.085	.074
Multiple R	0.316	
R^2	0.100	
(Unweighted n)	(607)	

*Statistically significant at $p < 0.05$.

The relationship between number of children and earnings is not as simple as the relationship between number of children and hours of work. On average, husbands with children earn more than husbands without children, whether or not they are in dual-earner couples. Dual-earner husbands earn less on average than single-earner husbands, generally (as we saw earlier) and comparing single-earner and dual-earner husbands with the same number of children (Table 5.12). Thus, when there are no children at home, husbands in single-earner households earn more than husbands in dual-earner households, and the same is true for households in which there are one to four or more children at home. Furthermore, husbands' earnings in single-earner households appear to be greater the more children they have—up to four or more children, when income is lower than it is among those with three children. Among dual earners, earnings are also greater the more children they have, up to a point; with four or more children, however, dual-earner husbands' income is lower even than that of dual earners with one child at home. Among wives, however, earnings are affected to a much lesser degree by number of children at home than are hours of work. Only in households in which there are four or more children is the wife's income considerably lower than in other households. The proportion of earnings the wife contributes decreases slightly with each successive child, but remains at 32% even with four or more children. As a result, the combined income of the couple is greater with each additional child up to four or more children and is lower in households with four or more children than in households with fewer children.

Table 5.12 Earnings in Single-Earner and Dual-Earner American Jewish Couples (Ages 25–64), by Number of Children under 18 in Household[a]

Number of children under 18 in household	Single-earner		Dual-earner			
	Husband's mean annual earnings ($)	Wife's mean annual earnings ($)	Husband's mean annual earnings ($)	Wife's mean annual earnings ($)	Couple's mean annual earnings ($)	Wife's earnings as percentage of couple's earnings
0	106,250	42,065	83,224	54,349	139,493	41.1
	(37)	(38)	(240)	(250)	(227)	(227)
1	131,250	67,812	99,578	64,223	168,021	39.1
	(51)	(16)	(128)	(125)	(120)	(120)
2	117,596	—[b]	107,250	51,500	159,067	36.8
	(48)		(111)	(109)	(104)	(104)
3	173,125	—[b]	125,916	63,750	182,000	33.3
	(13)		(44)	(39)	(39)	(39)
4+	133,409	—[b]	83,250	45,250	131,111	32.0
	(11)		(12)	(11)	(10)	(10)

[a]Unweighted *n* in parentheses; calculations performed using person-weights provided with dataset.
[b]Less than 10 unweighted cases in cell.

Occupational Combinations

The top 10 pairings of occupations of husbands and wives, which are shown in Table 5.13, are either egalitarian or traditional: it is most common by far for both husband and wife to be professionals. In 6 out of 10 of the most common combinations (more than 40% of the sample), both husband and wife are in professional, managerial/executive, and/or business/finance professions. In 2 of the top 10 pairings of occupations (about 7% of the sample), we find the traditional combination of the husband being in a professional occupation and the wife in sales or office/administrative support. In only one combination (5% of the sample) is the wife a professional and the husband in sales. Together, these top 10 combinations account for more than half of the occupational combinations; all other combinations account for less than 2% each (or less than 30 unweighted cases).

Even when men and women have the same occupation, let alone are in the same broad occupational classification, traditional gender patterns may be preserved, with husbands earning more than their wives, working more hours, and having higher occupational prestige. With the high qualifications of American Jewish women (like those of men), however, there is a greater possibility of parity between the spouses. With the high proportion of both husbands and wives in management/executive, business/finance, and professional occupations, it is also possible that occupational homogamy may enhance each spouse's achievement. We therefore looked at the median income, mean occupational prestige, and mean hours of work of husbands and wives in each of these occupational combinations (Table 5.14).

The first observation to be made is that in all occupational pairings, except when both spouses are in managerial or executive occupations, husbands earn more than their wives annually. However, the wife's occupational prestige is either similar to or higher than that of the husband in 7 of the 10 combinations; it is lower than the husband's when the husband has a professional occupation, while the wife is in office/administrative support, sales, and business/finance. We can also see that, in all of the pairings, husbands work longer hours than wives; the gap is narrower when both spouses are employed in management/executive positions or in sales positions. The fact that the wife is in the same occupational group as the husband does not seem to influence the income gap, the occupational prestige gap, or the hours gap, as the two summary measures at the end of the table show; however, spouses who are in the same occupational group tend to earn more and have higher occupational prestige than spouses in different occupational groups. This suggests that being in the same occupational group as one's spouse confers some advantage in terms of occupational achievement and rewards.

Table 5.13 Ten Most Common Combinations of Occupations among Currently Married American Jewish Couples

Husband's occupation	Wife's occupation	Total (%)	$(n)^a$
Professional	Professional	22.4	(267)
Management/executive	Professional	6.0	(71)
Sales	Professional	5.1	(61)
Professional	Sales	3.8	(45)
Business/finance	Professional	3.7	(44)
Professional	Management/executive	3.6	(43)
Professional	Office/administrative support	3.4	(41)
Sales	Sales	3.3	(39)
Professional	Business/finance	2.6	(31)
Management/executive	Management/executive	2.5	(30)
Total		56.4	(672)

^{a}Unweighted n in parentheses; calculations performed using person-weights provided with dataset.

Table 5.14 Income, Occupational Prestige (PRS), and Hours of Employment for Top 10 Occupational Combinations in American Jewish Couples

Husband's occupation	Wife's occupation	Wife's income as percentage of husband's income	Husband's PRS	Wife's PRS	Husband's weekly hours of employment (mean)	Wife's weekly hours of employment (mean)	Combined couple weekly hours of employment (mean)	(n)[a]
Management/executive	Management/executive	—[b]	51.3	51.4	45.9	42.8	87.0	(30)
Professional	Professional	65.5	62.9	60.0	45.9	35.1	81.5	(267)
Sales	Sales	81.8	44.9	42.7	46.0	40.2	88.0	(39)
Management/executive	Professional	52.4	52.1	59.9	47.3	36.1	83.4	(71)
Business/finance	Professional	84.0	54.4	58.6	46.9	34.2	80.4	(44)
Professional	Management/executive	64.7	59.7	53.8	47.6	40.2	87.2	(43)
Professional	Office/administrative support	52.0	61.5	43.2	42.8	28.0	68.9	(41)
Professional	Business/finance	51.5	63.0	54.3	52.4	34.4	85.6	(31)
Professional	Sales	55.6	57.6	40.2	44.4	37.9	81.4	(43)
Sales	Professional	53.8	45.8	57.3	43.5	36.3	81.9	(61)
Spouses in same broad occupational group (summary)		79.1	58.3	56.6	45.6	35.2	82.2	(392)
Spouses in different broad occupational groups (summary)		78.0	51.2	51.3	45.7	35.8	81.3	(795)

[a] Unweighted n in parentheses; calculations performed using person-weights provided with dataset.
[b] Less than 10 cases in unweighted sample.

Since some of the gap in wages may also be a result of the wife's fewer hours of work, Table 5.15 presents data confined to couples in which both the husband and wife work full time (i.e., 35 hours per week or more). However, the number of cases in each group is, of course, reduced when we impose this condition, and in some of the groups there are 10 or fewer cases to analyze, so we collapsed the occupational pairs, classifying husband's and wife's occupations as managerial/executive, business/finance, professional, or other.

Where both spouses are in managerial/business/professional occupations, the wife's income is 67.7% that of the husband's, their occupational prestige scores are equal, and they work nearly the same number of hours per week on average. As a point of comparison, women working full time in management, professional, and related occupations in the broader U.S. workforce made 71.0% of men's earnings in 2004 (Chao and Utgoff, 2005, Table 18, p. 50), a percentage not very different from that of Jewish women's earnings in relation to men's.

When both spouses are in other occupations, such as sales, service, office support, or blue collar, the women make only 56.5% of the husband's salary on average, despite having higher occupational prestige and working nearly as many hours. This suggests greater parity among those couples in which both have greater human resources, and a wider gender gap among those in less prestigious and less well paid occupations. Thus, the wider disparities in income in high-status occupations found in the overall distributions of men's and women's income (shown in the preceding chapter) are not replicated within married couples.

When only one spouse is in a managerial/business/professional occupation, the relative contributions of each spouse to the couple's income are commensurate with their occupational status. That is, when the husband has a managerial/business/professional occupation and the wife does not, she makes only 58.6% of his earnings and contributes only 37% to the couple's income; her occupational prestige is nine points lower than his; and she works four fewer hours per week than he does. When the situation is reversed and it is the wife who has the manager/business/professional occupation and the husband does not, the wife makes 123.5% of the husband's earnings and has higher occupational prestige than he does, although on average she still works somewhat fewer hours per week than he does. Because of women's disproportionate representation in the professional occupations, there are more of the latter than the former among spouses with occupations in different broad occupational groups.

It is interesting that, when we compare the mean incomes of husbands and wives in couples with the same or different occupations, husbands who

Table 5.15 Income, Occupational Prestige (PRS), and Hours of Employment for Top 10 Occupational Combinations in American Jewish Couples (in which Both Spouses Are Employed Full Time)

Husband's occupation	Wife's occupation	Wife's income as percentage of husband's income	Husband's PRS (mean)	Wife's PRS (mean)	Husband's weekly hours of employment (mean)	Wife's weekly hours of employment (mean)	Combined couple weekly hours of employment (mean)	(n)[a]
Spouses in same broad occupational group (total)		71.4	57.1	57.1	48.0	44.2	92.1	(338)
Mgr/Bus/Prof[b]	Mgr/Bus/Prof[b]	67.7	58.2	58.2	47.7	44.2	91.9	(250)
Other	Other	56.5	42.1	45.5	47.5	46.6	94.2	(88)
Spouses in different broad occupational groups (total)		81.0	49.6	51.8	46.8	44.3	91.1	(198)
Mgr/Bus/Prof[b]	Other	58.6	55.5	46.4	46.5	42.7	89.2	(86)
Other	Mgr/Bus/Prof[b]	123.5	44.3	53.9	46.3	43.8	90.1	(112)

[a] Unweighted n in parentheses; calculations performed using person-weights provided with dataset.
[b] Mgr/Bus/Prof denotes managerial/executive, business/financial, professional occupation.

have managerial/business/professional occupations earn 7% more when their wife is in a similar occupation than they do when she is in a different occupation (data not presented). This is also true for men in other occupations whose wives are in other occupations; they make on average 35% more when their spouse is in a similar occupation. However, this is not true for wives; the median income of wives in managerial/business/professional occupations is the same whether or not their husband is in the same occupational group; wives in other occupations, when their husband is in a similar occupation, make on average 30% *less* than wives whose spouses are in managerial/business/professional occupations. This suggests that wives add more to their husbands' "backstage wealth" when they have the same occupation as their husbands but that husbands do not provide a similar advantage for their wives.

In summary, despite considerable occupational homogamy, the traditional pattern of gender difference within marriages is prevalent among Jewish couples, with husbands earning more and working more hours than their wives. Also along traditional lines, occupational homogamy appears to contribute to the income achievement of husbands, but not to that of wives. Occupational prestige of spouses, however, is much closer to being equal than is income, and in some occupational combinations, the parity of both prestige and income is greater than in other occupational combinations.

REMARRIAGE AND OCCUPATIONAL PATTERNS
Considering remarriages in comparison with first marriages among Jews, there is no difference in terms of occupational homogamy. However, when we compare husbands' remarriages to husbands' first marriages, and wives' remarriages to wives' first marriages, we find a significant relationship between occupational homogamy and remarriage for women, but not for men. That is, there is more occupational homogamy in couples when the wife has remarried than when she is in her first marriage, but the couple's occupational homogamy does not vary according to whether the husband is in his first or later marriage.

One possible explanation for this, as already suggested, is that women's high-status occupations make them more vulnerable to marital dissolution, because marriages in which women have the same status as, or higher status than, their husbands are at greater risk for marital dissolution (Kalmijn, Loeve, and Manting, 2007), and this is a more likely scenario for women in high-status occupations than for women in lower-status occupations. This would make women whose status is similar to or higher than that of their husband less likely to be or stay in first marriages. At the same time, women's higher economic status may make them more attractive in the (re)marriage market, so they are more likely to remarry. To reinforce this explanation, there is some evidence that women's economic status is increasingly considered an advantage in marriage markets in the broader population (Sweeney, 2002).

To explore this in our sample, we compared husband's and wife's occupational groups, educational attainment, income, and occupational prestige in first marriages and remarriages for both men and women (Table 5.16). We found that in men's remarriages, there are fewer spouses in the same occupation than in men's first marriages; among women, however, there is a higher proportion of spouses in the same occupation among the remarried than among those in first marriages. Among both men and women, there is a higher proportion of wives with a higher education, income, and occupational prestige than their husbands in remarriages than in first marriages. The differences in income are small but in the same direction.

These findings suggest that, indeed, higher-status women are more likely to remarry but that the marriage market for remarriage is such that it may be more difficult for men seeking remarriage to find occupationally homogamous partners.

If the percentage of remarried women who have a higher status than their husbands tends to be greater than that of women in first marriages, what can we say about them in comparison with women who never married

Table 5.16 Occupation, Education, Income, and Occupational Prestige in First Marriages and Remarriages of American Jews

	Men		Women	
	In first marriage	Remarried	In first marriage	Remarried
Husband and wife in same occupational group (%)	34.5	27.5	28.9	35.1
Wife's education > husband's education (%)	18.5	31.7	32.4	38.3
Wife's median income > husband's median income (%)	14.0	15.2	25.3	28.3
Wife's occupational prestige > husband's occupational prestige (%)	40.9	51.3	59.8	77.5
(n)[a]	(322)	(100)	(478)	(113)

[a]Unweighted n in parentheses; calculations performed using person-weights provided with dataset.

Table 5.17 Occupation, Education, Occupational Prestige, Income, and Age of American Jewish Men and Women (Ages 25 and Over), Employed Full Time, by Marital Status

	In first marriage	Remarried	Divorced, not currently married	Never married
Women				
Mgr/Exec/Bus/finance/ professional (%)	63.6	65.5	60.7	55.7
B.A. or higher (%)	74.7	70.3	68.0	59.3
Mean occupational prestige	53.47	53.78	53.08	49.35
Median annual income ($)	47,500	52,500	42,500	42,500
Mean age	44.9	49.1	49.8	37.5
$(n)^a$	(478)	(113)	(106)	(217)
Men				
Mgr/Exec/Bus/finance/ professional (%)	64.8	51.4	61.2	57.1
B.A. or higher (%)	77.7	60.2	59.4	70.2
Mean occupational prestige	54.94	53.36	52.61	53.22
Median annual income ($)	77,500	72,500	77,500	52,500
Mean age	46.1	50.2	48.6	37.7
$(n)^a$	(322)	(100)	(135)	(204)

[a]Unweighted *n* in parentheses; calculations performed using person-weights provided with dataset.

or divorcees who have not remarried? Does remarriage boost women's achievement in comparison with that of other women who used to be married and have not remarried or women who never married? In the top half of Table 5.17 we present the proportion in managerial/executive, business/ finance, and professional occupations, proportion with bachelor's degrees or higher, median annual income, mean occupational prestige of women in first marriages, remarried women, divorcees not currently married, and never-married women; in the bottom half of the table we present the same data for men. For a point of reference, we also present the mean age in each group.

Comparing currently married women who are in first marriages as opposed to remarriages, we see little difference. That is, remarried women may have a higher status than their husbands, but not because they have a higher status than women in their first marriages. Remarried women earn a somewhat higher median annual income, but they are comparable in occupation, education, and occupational prestige to women in first marriages. What is much more striking is the comparison between men in first marriages and remarriages: men who have remarried are less likely to be in managerial/executive, business/finance, or professional occupations; have a lower educational level; have slightly lower occupational prestige; and earn slightly lower annual incomes.

Divorced women who have not remarried are less likely to be in managerial/executive, business/finance, or professional occupations, have a somewhat lower educational level, and have a lower median income than women currently married. Divorced men who are not currently married have a lower educational level than men in first marriages (though it is comparable to that of men who have remarried), have higher occupational attainment than remarried men (but lower than that of men in first marriages), have lower occupational prestige than currently married men, and earn an income comparable to that of men in first marriages. Never-married men and women have educational levels that are comparable to those of men and women in first marriages, but lower occupational attainment, income, and occupational prestige; however, they are considerably younger, even when we restrict the analysis to those 25 and older.

To minimize the effect of age on these findings, we limited our comparison to women and men aged 45–64, who had had time to complete their education and to achieve career stability (Table 5.18). Among women, those currently in their first marriage stand out in that there is a somewhat higher percentage who have earned college degrees, but those who have never married stand out in that they have non-managerial/business/professional occupations and lower occupational prestige. Non-remarried divorcees stand out in that they earn a somewhat lower income. Among men, we see that divorcees, whether currently married or not, have the lowest educational level and occupational prestige; remarried men have the lowest proportion of managerial/business/professional occupations; and never-married men have the lowest income. These findings appear to corroborate the notions that (1) stable marriages reinforce human capital (echoing the argument put forth in Waite and Gallagher, 2000)—or that higher economic status of men and women matters a lot in the Jewish marriage market—and (2) divorced men have lower educational and occupational achievement (possibly a precursor to divorce). We see little evidence of a marriage penalty for women or a "ceiling" effect for the occupational achievement of married women. Divorcees and single women do not have higher educational or occupational achievement than married women.

One conclusion from the comparison between unmarried divorcees and currently married women in first marriages and remarriages is that marriage does not appear to dampen Jewish women's occupational achievement and/or that their economic characteristics are indeed considered a plus by their marriage partners. A second conclusion is that it is not that remarried

Table 5.18 Occupation, Education, Occupational Prestige, Income and Age of American Jewish Men and Women (Ages 45–64), Employed Full Time, by Marital Status

	In first marriage	Remarried	Divorced, not currently married	Never married
Women				
B.A. or higher (%)	62.3	53.3	57.1	53.4
Mgr/Exec/Bus/finance/ professional (%)	64.3	65.2	66.9	39.0
Mean occupational prestige	53.91	54.29	53.54	48.05
Median annual income ($)	52,500	52,500	47,500	52,500
(*n*)[a]	(382)	(118)	(160)	(92)
Men				
B.A. or higher(%)	79.7	63.3	59.3	73.2
Mgr/Exec/Bus/finance/ professional (%)	64.9	48.5	60.4	60.3
Mean occupational prestige	54.58	53.53	52.72	54.88
Median annual income ($)	82,500	72,500	77,500	52,500
(*n*)[a]	(301)	(127)	(112)	(75)

[a]Unweighted *n* in parentheses; calculations performed using person-weights provided with dataset.

women differ so much from women in first marriages, as that remarried men differ from men in current marriages and from women who have remarried. Men who have remarried tend to have lower educational and occupational achievement relative not only to their wives (as we saw earlier) but also to currently married men in first marriages and to divorced men who have not remarried.

SUMMARY AND CONCLUSIONS

We began this chapter by investigating to what extent American Jews are distinct from the broader population in terms of dual earning. Comparison with the broader population shows that married Jewish couples are more likely to be dual earners than are couples in the broader population and face problems of long work hours similar to those of couples in the broader population. In comparison with 1990, the proportion of dual earners among American Jews has increased (as it has in the broader population). Today few are working at what has been deemed an optimal combined work week of 60 hours, something that communal agencies might note.

When they have children, however, Jewish dual earners work on average fewer hours than do parents in the broader population, and this is accomplished mainly by the wife adjusting her work hours so that she is working part time. In contrast, men's work hours show very little correlation to the number of children at home; if anything, husbands work more hours when there are more children at home. This indicates that the typical working married Jewish mother acts as a secondary earner whose employment and hours can be manipulated to meet the family's needs or demands, which are indicated in our data by such variables as number of children at home, husband's income, and occupational prestige.

This pattern of the wife being a secondary earner, adjusting her work hours according to the family's needs, may allow Jews to preserve the familism that has long been central to Jewish culture, and it may be facilitated by the relatively high social status that Jews enjoy. It may be that this pattern is more common among Jews because they are able to manage with a single earner who is making a good salary, often a better one than single earners in the broader population. Certainly we see that, among our Jewish couples, the lower the husband's income, the longer the wife's hours of employment, no matter how many children under 18 they have at home.

American Jews are also characterized by relatively higher educational and occupational homogamy than the broader population, although as in the broader population, when the educational levels of the couple are not equal, it is usually the husband who has a higher education. Although there was somewhat less educational homogamy among American Jewish married couples in 2000–01 than among Jews in 1990, both husbands' and wives' education increased. There was more occupational similarity between spouses in 2000–01 than there was in 1990, and the pattern of a high proportion of wives having higher occupational prestige than their husbands continued from 1990 to 2000–01.There was a slightly lower proportion having similar incomes, which may be related to the fact that greater income similarity in the broader population is characteristic of lower-income families. Jewish wives make larger contributions to the joint household earnings than wives in the broader population of dual earners.

American Jewish couples have a relatively high incidence of occupational homogamy, especially when both spouses are in professional occupations. Nevertheless, even when spouses have similar occupations, similar educational levels, and similar hours of work, traditional patterns of achievement are the most common, with husbands having higher annual earnings and occupational prestige than wives. Furthermore, occupational homogamy results in higher income for husbands but not for wives, suggesting that wives facilitate husbands' achievements when they share the social capital of occupations, but not vice versa. We do find greater parity among husband's and wife's achievements when both are in managerial/

executive, business/finance, or professional occupations as compared with other occupational combinations.

Alternative theories abound in this field of inquiry about the interplay between husbands' and wives' occupational status, and its interaction with remarriage and cultural homogamy. Our analysis of occupational achievement and homogamy of husbands and wives among American Jews, married and remarried, offers some insight into the contradictions. First, our data show that the dynamics are different for husbands and wives and, second, that it is important to take into account wives' economic status. How economic homogamy interacts with cultural homogamy or intermarriage will be explored in Chapter 10.

Occupational homogamy is more common among women who have remarried than among women who have remained in their first marriages. Remarried women are also more likely to be in marriages where they earn more than their husbands, have higher occupational prestige, and have higher educational attainment than their husbands than are women in their first marriages. This suggests that the relatively high economic status of Jewish women makes them more likely to succeed in the (re)marriage market. On the other hand, Jewish men who are divorced (whether or not they have remarried) tend to have lower occupational achievement than their counterparts in first marriages, which is one reason that women in second or later marriages are more likely to have a higher status than their husbands.

Comparing the married with the non-married (whether divorced or never married) shows that marriage is related to higher educational and occupational achievement for both men and women. It does not appear to result in a "marriage penalty" or "ceiling" effect dampening women's achievement in this subcultural U.S. context. The findings reinforce Waite and Gallagher's (2000) contention that marriage is good for economic status; but they could equally reinforce the importance of economic status in the Jewish marriage market.

PART II

Ways of Being Jewish and the Distinctive Secular

Roles of American Jewish Women and Men

CHAPTER 6

Gendered Patterns of Jewishness

So far we have considered the Jewishness of the gendered patterns of family and labor force behavior and achievements by comparing American Jews with the broader population and, to some extent, examining the changes in this comparison (at least since 1990). In the second part of the book, we consider Jewishness in terms of the strength of various expressions of Jewish identity, and look at the relationships between Jewishness, family behavior, and labor force behavior and achievements. In this chapter we present our conceptualization of Jewishness and the gender differences in this respect.

In order to consider the relationship between secular behavior and achievement and Jewishness, we need to devise a measure of "Jewishness"—not a simple task. One can express one's "Jewishness" in multiple ways—simply by being identified as a Jew (e.g., by being born to a Jewish mother and/or father, depending on who is doing the identifying), by identifying oneself as a Jew, by affiliating with other Jews in an organized setting (synagogue, voluntary organization, community center, youth group, etc.), by exhibiting ethnic and/or religious behaviors that are Jewish in nature (the identification of which is itself controversial), by holding beliefs or attitudes that are considered Jewish, or by any combination of these. The possible ways of defining "Jewishness" multiply and stimulate discussion and a variety of opinions. The 2000–01 National Jewish Population Survey attempted to incorporate a wide array of indicators of Jewish identity, so that multiple ways of defining or expressing "Jewishness" could be developed and examined. We used many of these indicators as we developed measures of Jewishness, which are presented in this chapter. This chapter also presents gender differences in Jewishness, as measured in a variety of ways. We begin the chapter with some background to our expectations of gender differences in Jewishness and then discuss our measures of Jewishness. We then present our findings of gender similarity and difference with respect to Jewishness, and relate them to denominational preference and to formal Jewish educational background.

Much attention has been given to the gender inequality of women in public religious positions of power, to their implied secondary status as expressed in theology, ideology, and language used in religion, and to their relegation to secondary domestic status in contemporary religions. All of these lead us to expect gender inequality in public expressions at least of religious identity. Nevertheless, women have traditionally been more strongly identified with religion than have men. This anomaly has sometimes been attributed to the fact that women are underprivileged (Weber's, 1963 [1922], explanation, supported by Mueller and Johnson, 1975, and more recently by Hertel, 1995) or "socially vulnerable" (Walter and Davie, 1998) and thus, like other disadvantaged people, turn to religion as a compensation. Stark (2002) reviews how religious movements have historically recruited women more successfully than men, and how women outnumber men both in conventional and in new religious movements in the United States. (He suggests that risk aversion may be an explanation, although Schumm, 2004, debates this.) Rayburn (2004) confirms that women see themselves as more religious and more spiritual than men, and also as more spiritual even if they do not consider themselves religious. Ozorark (1996) suggests that women are more likely than men to belong to religions for social and emotional support, following their "ethic of connection" (Walter and Davie, 1998).

Woolever, Bruce, Keith, and Smith-Williams (2006), analyzing data from 18 countries, found that women reported greater feelings of spiritual connection and faith than men, even when education was controlled for. Lefkovitz and Shapiro (2005) suggest that books and educational material that can be obtained on the Internet has increased their availability to groups previously denied access to them, reinforcing women's involvement in religion.

All of these studies support the expectation that American Jewish women will express stronger Jewish religious identities than men. It has also been suggested that because women are less immersed structurally in secular roles (such as careers) than are men, they maintain a connection to religion that men may lose (de Vaus and McAllister, 1987). This is reinforced by historical research, which suggests that Jewish women have played a greater role than men in the transmission of Jewish culture and identity, as men have focused their energy on acculturating themselves to the workforce and general public sphere, and women have maintained religious standards and customs in the home (Hyman, 1995; Kaplan, 1991). Continuing along these lines, Prell (1999) has analyzed how the American Jewish immigrant experience transferred much of the role of perpetuating Judaism to the intimate relations of family and the public relations of community and institution building, rather than to prayer or individual observance. In fact, Heschel (2004) suggests that women's role in perpetuating Judaism through the home and social institutions paved the way for men to be less observant (as she puts it, using a quote from Hull, 1996, p. 411, "Her unfreedom created his freedom"). This leads us to expect that American Jewish women will also express stronger ethnic Jewish identities than men.

In terms of empirical gender differences in contemporary Jewish identity, analysis of the 1990 NJPS revealed that Jewish women fit the pattern just described, with significantly stronger Jewish identity in terms of the collective rituals and involvement in formally organized Jewish associations, even when age and marital status were controlled for (Hartman and Hartman, 1996a). Women were more involved in informal Jewish circles also, but the gender difference was not statistically significant once age and marital status were controlled for. Women showed weaker observance of the traditional rituals, but the difference was not statistically significant once age and marital status were controlled for. Women did have a significantly weaker background in Jewish education than men, but this did not seem to weaken their Jewish identity (Hartman and Hartman, 2003b).

According to the "structural location" interpretation of gender differences in religious commitment, since women's full-time employment has increased, and women have come closer to parity with men in terms of status-conferring occupations and income, it has been expected that the traditional gender gap in religious involvement would decrease. Because Jewish women are at the forefront of such changes in labor force participation and occupational achievement, it would be expected that any such changes would certainly show up among Jews. However, Becker and Hofmeister (2001), in their research using a national sample of around 1,000, found that not only is women's religious involvement lower when they are employed full time, but so is their spouse's, suggesting that something else is going on. Becker and Hofmeister discuss the possibility that women's employment is accompanied by a greater individualism and a decreased willingness to assume the traditionally gendered roles that are historically associated with religious institutions, echoing some of the suggestions made by Walter and Davie (1998). Therefore, another reason to look at gender differences in Jewish identity is to note the relative parity of secular positions and then to explore how this affects gender differences in Jewish identity.

In our analysis of the 1990 data for both men and women, higher secular academic achievement was associated with greater involvement in the various aspects of Jewish identity (except for the most traditional rituals; Hartman and Hartman, 1996a). For men, greater labor force participation was also associated with greater involvement in organized Jewish associations and in collective rituals. However, for women, there was a negative relationship between labor force participation and the various aspects of Jewish identity. Controlling for marital status and number of children explained most of this negative relationship, from which we concluded that the connection between Jewishness and labor force participation for women occurred primarily through traditional familistic roles rather than directly through Jewish identity.

Thus, our results did not exactly reinforce the structural location interpretation that focuses on labor force participation, because we found that familism rather than labor force participation was the mitigating variable in variations in women's Jewish identity. Walter and Davie (1998) offer an explanation for the relationship between family roles and greater commitment to religion. However, they suggest that this relationship might lose power with in modern culture. This research, therefore, leads us to expect a greater trend toward equality in expressions of Jewish identity rather than in gender differentiation, and a greater trend toward equality between men and women.

DENOMINATIONAL DIFFERENCES IN JEWISH IDENTITY

Another complexity is introduced by the comparison of Jewish denominations and gender differences within them. In several ways, Jewish identity is expected to vary among denominations and has been shown to do so in the past. Denominations differ in their emphasis on religion and ethnicity, in their emphasis on traditional ritual, and in their attachment to Israel (Hartman and Hartman, 2001). On the other hand, all denominations stress organized and public activities (Woocher, 1986). An initial analysis of the 2000–01 NJPS showed that contemporary Orthodox Jews are more likely than other denominational groups to go to synagogue on a regular basis, to be synagogue members, and to observe most of the traditional rituals, collective or personal (Ament, 2005). They also express stronger subjective identification as Jews, are more strongly attached to Israel, are more likely to have contributed to a Jewish charity, and are more likely to belong to a formal Jewish organization. Those classified as "just Jewish" exhibit the weakest Jewish identity on the same measures. There does not seem to be evidence of a particularly strong ethnic identity compensating for a lack of religious affiliation or of spirituality in place of organized rituals (see also Klaff, 2006). This is a repetition of the pattern found in the 1990 NJPS and the 1991 New York Jewish Population Survey, with Orthodox Jews expressing stronger Jewish identity on all of the various dimensions of Jewish identity, and unaffiliated, and sometimes Reform Jews, the weakest.

Not as clear may be the variation by denomination of gender differences in Jewish identity. Some reasons to expect difference are that the Reform and Conservative denominations have granted women a public religious role equivalent to the more traditional public religious roles of men, suggesting that there may be a greater trend toward gender equality in Jewish identity in these denominations. Also, as we've already seen, the Orthodox tend to marry younger and have larger families, indicating more traditional familism, which might increase gender differences in many respects. However, some members of the Orthodox denomination have also integrated the feminist claims for gender equality into some of their rituals (see, e.g., Fishman's [2007] description of modern Orthodox Jews). Furthermore, the 1990 NJPS showed more gender similarity in Jewish identity among the Orthodox than expected (Hartman and Hartman, 1996a), so we do not expect a simple relationship between denomination and gender differences in Jewish identity.

GENDER AND JEWISH EDUCATION

Formal Jewish education is associated with stronger Jewish identity, no matter how it is measured (Cohen, 2004), although formal Jewish education is not the only influence on Jewish identity (Cohen, 2007; Hartman and Hartman, 2003b). Formal Jewish education is also associated with stronger "Jewish social capital," that is, networking and associations with other Jews (Hurst and Mott, 2006). Therefore, the relationship between gender and Jewish education is certainly an important one to consider. We do so in this chapter as part of our introduction to the "Jewishness resources" that respondents carry and that we consider in later chapters as they relate to family behavior and roles, secular education, labor force participation, and occupational achievement.

INDICATORS
Jewish Identity

There are two major dimensions along which Jewish identity varies: (1) the religious–ethnic dimension, which differentiates Jewish identity both from other religious identities and from other ethnic identities (Herman, 1977; Himmelfarb, 1982; Phillips, 1991; Sharot, 1991), and (2) the public–private dimension of expressing Jewish identity, a dimension that has gained increasing importance with a more general privatization of contemporary religion (Casanova, 1992; see overview of this trend in religion in McGuire, 2001).

Jewish identity has long been recognized as multidimensional, involving both ethnic and religious dimensions, whose balance fluctuates with historical context and ideology of the particular Jewish movement or denomination in focus. Sharot (1997) documents Jewish movements that are completely religious, which combine ethnicity and religion, and that are completely secular (ethnic). More recently, Gitelman (2003) has documented the primarily ethnic identification of Jews from the former Soviet Union. American Jewish identity has fluctuated in its balance of religious and ethnic identity, both historically and across denominations, as has been reviewed in previous publications (e.g., Diner, 2003–4; Dollinger, 2003–4; Hartman and Hartman, 2001).

The second dimension along which identity varies is whether it is expressed privately, as internal feelings or within the privacy of one's home or close circle of friends and family, or expressed publicly and collectively. The debate over secularization has been centered largely on the declining influence of religion in the public arena, while the evidence of the persistence of personal faith has undermined the prediction that religion would disappear. Rather, the balance of how publicly or privately it is expressed seems to fluctuate over time.

These two dimensions emerged empirically from an analysis of the Jewish identity indicators in the 1990 NJPS (Hartman and Hartman, 2001). The two dimensions divide Jewish identity into four components: (1) the public religious component, composed of religious behaviors performed in public settings such as synagogues; (2) the private religious component, composed of personal or private expressions of religious ritual performed individually or in a private home, or consisting of personal beliefs about religion; (3) the public ethnic component, composed of public activities organized around ethnic themes of peoplehood or nationhood, for example; and (4) the private ethnic component of Jewish identity, comprising personal beliefs about Jewish ethnicity or behaviors performed in private or in a home, such as subscribing to a Jewish magazine.

Recent attention in the sociology of religion has been devoted to the concept of "spirituality," roughly conceived of as personal faith or an expression of personal religious identity. Spirituality has traditionally been studied with regard to non-Jewish religions; its study has been neglected in many studies of Jewish religiosity because the Jewish religion has been characterized more commonly by action than by faith. Perhaps as a result of U.S. society being predominantly Christian, and certainly as both religion and ethnicity become more voluntary constructs for all contemporary groups, studies of Judaism in the United States have recently included more measures of spirituality to complement indicators of religious practice. Greeley and Hout (2001) show that Jews, like other U.S. religious groups, have increased their expression of spiritual beliefs in the past few decades and that this is not just a spill-over from exposure to other religions but something internal to the evolution of American Judaism itself.

Other researchers have noted the important function of community and communal solidarity within contemporary religion and ethnicity (e.g., Johnson, 2003); that is, public ethnic or religious expressions of identity (depending on whether the community in question is primarily ethnic or religious).

Gender differences in Jewish identity are one of the social issues that can benefit from an analysis of Jewish identity using these two dimensions (religious–ethnic; public–private) and various combinations. Women's Jewish identity has often been described in terms of private, home-based actions and orientations, both religious and ethnic (Davidman and Tenenbaum, 1994; Sered, 1994). Traditionally men have dominated public religious roles in Judaism, but among the major trends in the past few decades have been the inroads women have made into these roles and their legitimization in them by Reform and Conservative denominations. On the other hand, because of the difficulties of entering such public roles, some women may have become disenchanted with public expressions of religiosity and have made their religiosity private or turned to public ethnic roles, if these offer greater opportunities for their participation. We cannot assume that men and women construct their Jewish identity in the same way, in any of the denominations. Thus, looking at these two dimensions, and their respective emphases in the Jewish identity of men and women in different denominations, can be very instructive for our investigation of gender differences in Jewish identity.

It should be noted that we are examining here the main aspects of Jewish identity as measured in the NJPS survey rather than derived from a comprehensive model of Jewish identity. That is, our analytical results emerge from the data gathered, using a survey which seems to have been somewhat haphazardly developed to test a wide range of Jewish behaviors and attitudes, rather than to test a particular theoretical model (see the critique in Hartman and Hartman, 2003c). If we omit an aspect that others might think is central to Jewish identity, it is probably because it was not systematically operationalized in the survey questionnaire (that is, the survey questions did not adequately measure it).

Let us now proceed to describe the analysis of the variables that were available. The 2000–01 NJPS makes it possible to explore these four components of Jewish identity much more thoroughly than did earlier NJPS surveys. Extensive questions appear to probe both religious and ethnic orientations to respondents' Jewishness, on both public and private levels. In addition to questions about the observance of Jewish rituals that were also asked in previous national and many local Jewish population surveys, the 2000–01 NJPS includes questions about cultural practices related to being Jewish (such as reading books with Jewish content or traveling to Jewish places of interest), as well as questions about spirituality (such as praying in one's own words and belief in God), subjective feelings about being Jewish, and comfort during services of various denominations. More than 90 indicators dealt with the respondent's "Jewish identity" in some way.

In using these data to study Jewish identity, some researchers have selected what seems to them to represent the main aspects of Jewish identity (e.g., Ament, 2005). Some researchers have used an a priori approach, deciding in advance which variables belong to a particular category such as religion or ethnicity (e.g., Klaff, 2006). Others have confined their studies to variables used in a comparable data set (e.g., Rebhun and Levy, 2006). In contrast, we used an empirical approach to construct indices of Jewish identity, using as many of the variables as possible. That is, we used indices that arose from the data rather than superimposing our own theoretical expectations on the data. Thus, we did not arbitrarily classify the questions as religious or ethnic, subjective or objective, public or private. Such classification often means that the researcher is imposing his/her own expectations on the data, rather than allowing the data to express the way the respondents see the issues. For example, is attending synagogue perceived to be primarily a religious act? Or is its ethnic dimension, expressing solidarity with other Jewish people, as important or more so? Is attachment to Israel a religious or ethnic quality or both? Do respondents make the distinction between "public" (such as attending synagogue) and "private" (such as lighting candles at home) acts, or is this a construct that is meaningful mainly to sociologists of religion? Rather than make assumptions a priori, we used factor analysis to show what indices should be constructed from the data, that is, how variables clustered together according to the responses given.[1] We then interpreted the results of the factor analysis. The advantage of such a method is that it makes use of all of the available indicators and uncovers the construct of identity in the respondents' minds, rather than superimposing a priori expectations. That in many instances the results validated our previous understanding reinforces the theoretical dimensions we have come to understand as Jewish identity; when the results did not, they indicated where the theoretical model needed modification.

Measurement of Jewish Identity (Identity Factors)

We began with the approximately 90 questions in the survey that in some way touched on the respondent's current Jewish identity. We eliminated questions referring to the respondent's childhood or high school years. We eliminated questions that were not asked of a substantial portion of the sample, such as those asked only of respondents who had children, or had been to college, or who said they kept kosher. Even when there was some logic to not asking all those in the sample these questions, we could not assume a priori what their answers would have been. As it was, we still had more than 80 questions.

A factor analysis indicated that five of these questions should be eliminated because they did not have enough commonality with the other variables.[2] More than half of the variance in the questions could be explained by an 11-factor solution, which is what we use here. We concentrate primarily on the factors explaining most of the variance.

Factor 1 expresses what "being Jewish" means to the respondent. This factor measures the extent to which the respondent agrees that being Jewish is about celebrating Jewish holidays, being part of the Jewish community, attending synagogue, observing *halacha*, having a rich spiritual life, supporting Jewish organizations, learning about Jewish history and culture, remembering the Holocaust, connecting to family heritage, leading an ethical and moral life, making the world a better place, caring about Israel, and countering anti-Semitism. Further analysis of this factor (i.e., a factor analysis of these variables alone) showed that two subfactors were involved: (a) those aspects of being Jewish that reflect involvement in the contemporary Jewish community, including being part of the Jewish community, attending synagogue, celebrating Jewish holidays, observing *halacha*, having a rich spiritual life, learning about Jewish history and culture, and caring about Israel; we call this "Activity"; and (b) those aspects that reflect the ways that being Jewish expresses morals, ethics, and heritage, including leading an ethical and moral life, making the world a better place, connecting to family heritage, remembering the Holocaust, and countering anti-Semitism. This second factor recalls what Heilman (2003–4, p. 59) has termed the connection to a Jewish "moral community": "For some Jews—particularly those who understand their Jewish identity essentially as a matter of vague 'heritage,' are not looking for something that requires too much in the way of activity and concrete commitments, and who are satisfied with symbolic attachments—the Jewish community constitutes above all else a kind of 'moral community'. . . a set of moral codes and certainties that offer guidance as to what is the right way to act or believe."[3] We call this "Universal Morality."

Factor 2 pertains to the performance of Jewish rituals and includes a general question about how much the respondent observes or practices Jewish rituals, as well as more specific indicators: attending a Passover *seder*, lighting Shabbat candles, fasting on Yom Kippur, lighting Chanukah candles, having a *mezuzah* on any door of the home, belonging to a synagogue, attending synagogue, keeping kosher at home,[4] and feeling comfortable attending Orthodox services. Further analysis of this factor showed that it could also be broken down into two subfactors: (a) the more commonly observed rituals or Jewish practices such as belonging to and going to synagogue, attending a *seder*, lighting Chanukah candles—what has been referred to as collective "ceremony" in earlier studies ("affirming membership in the social and cosmological order"; Alexander, 1987, p. 124) (what we here call "Ceremony")—and (b) those indicators of stricter daily and personal commitment to ritual, such as keeping kosher at home, lighting Shabbat candles every week, fasting on Yom Kippur, feeling comfortable at Orthodox services, and self-description as more observant (what we here call "Ritual").

Factor 3 expresses a sense of Jewish "tribalism"—a sense of belonging and commitment to a cohesive ancestral group of people with particular customs, traditions, and values (Lipset and Raab, 1995, p. 8) and to its continuity. It includes the importance of a child's spouse being Jewish (or converting to Judaism), of grandchildren being raised Jewish, of having and considering it important to have Jewish friends, and of having an understanding that Jews in the United States are distinctive as a cultural, ethnic, religious group or worldwide people. Further analysis (a factor analysis of these variables alone) showed that it too could be subdivided into two components: (a) indicators of personal commitment to Jewish continuity and cohesiveness ("Tribalism") and (b) indicators of the extent to which the respondent characterized Jews in the United States as a distinctive or exceptional group ("Exceptionalism").

Factor 4 reflects personal attachment to cultural aspects of Jewish identity. Variables with high loading on this factor include reading books with Jewish content, listening to audio media with Jewish content, reading Jewish print media, seeing a movie or video because of its Jewish content, ability to read Hebrew, participation in adult Jewish education, and looking for Jewish places of interest when traveling.[5] None of these explicitly indicate religious content, although they may include it. We termed this "Culture."

Factor 5 reflects personal attachment to religious belief or spirituality, and we call it "Belief." It includes questions about specific Jewish and religious beliefs as well as the importance attached to Judaism and religion in general. The variables with high loading on this factor included belief in God, understanding being Jewish as believing in God, the importance of religion in one's life today, the extent to which Judaism guides one in making important life decisions, the extent to which one characterizes oneself as personally religious, and whether one ever prays in one's own words.

Factor 6 reflects involvement with formal Jewish organizations (other than synagogues), which we call "Organizations." This includes attending a Jewish Community Center (JCC) or Young Men's/Young Women's Hebrew Association (YM/YWHA) program, paying dues to a JCC or YM/YWHA, paying dues to any other Jewish organization (except a synagogue or JCC or YM/YWHA), making a contribution to the Jewish Federation (or its local equivalent), and observing a Jewish mourning or memorial ritual (which necessitates participating in an organized group of Jews).

Factor 7 reflects attachment to Israel. It includes familiarity with the social and political situation in Israel, visiting Israel, having family and friends in Israel, being emotionally attached to Israel, seeing Israel as the spiritual center of Jews, believing that Jews in the United States have a common destiny with Jews in Israel and elsewhere in the world, and believing that Israel needs the financial support of American Jews. Further analysis (performing a factor analysis of these variables alone) showed that there were two subfactors: (a) one related to familiarity with the situation in Israel, having traveled there, having relatives and friends there, and personally being emotionally attached to Israel, which we call "Attachment to Israel," and (b) one related to a more abstract understanding of the centrality of the role of Israel for American and world Jews, which we call "Israel's Role Central."

Relating these factors to earlier theoretical understandings of Jewish identity, we certainly can see that the main dimensions of ethnicity and religion are represented (Table 6.1): factors 2 and 5, reflecting aspects of religious identity; and factors 3, 4, 6, and 7, reflecting aspects of ethnic or nationalistic identity. The distinction between public and private is also evident (factor 5, reflecting private beliefs; factor 6, reflecting public involvement in organizations; and the subfactors of 1, 2, 3, and 7, reflecting the subdivision of the factors into personal and public aspects). This supports our earlier analysis of Jewish identity (as expressed in the 1990 NJPS and the 1991 New York JPS) but should not be seen as a real test of the theory, because the questions were not designed explicitly to test it.[6] Furthermore, the first set of factors actually spans ethnic and religious aspects, and they are the strongest factors in the analysis.

We created factor scores for each of the factors and subfactors just described, by performing a secondary factor analysis on the variables with a

Table 6.1 Two Dimensions Of Variation In Jewish Identity Factors

	Public	Private
Mixed	Factor 1b—Universal Morality	1a—Activity
Religious	Factor 2a—Ceremony	2b—Ritual
		5—Belief
Ethnic	Factor 3b—Exceptionalism	3a—Tribalism
	Factor 6—Organizations	4—Culture
	Factor 7b—Israel's Role Central	7a—Attachment to Israel

Source: Hartman and Hartman, 2006. Questions with high loading on each factor are presented in the Appendix, Table A-4.

high loading on each of the factors. The scores resulting from these secondary factor analyses were used as scores for the Jewish identity indicators. The loadings of the individual variables on each factor can be found in the Appendix, Table A-4. Because the scores are normalized, the mean for each factor for the entire sample is 0.000. Lower scores indicate higher Jewish identity on that factor; higher scores indicate lower Jewish identity on that factor.

Denomination

The 2000–01 NJPS asks respondents for both their denominational preference and their denominational membership, recognizing that, while there is considerable overlap between them, they are in fact two distinct concepts. According to Klaff's (2006) analysis of the 2000–01 NJPS, only a little more than a third of the sample both self-identifies and claims membership (through a synagogue) in one of the major American Jewish denominations (Orthodox, Conservative, and Reform), and another 22% do not self-identify or claim membership in one of these denominations' synagogues. This leaves almost half of the sample who self-identify with one denomination but belong to another denomination's synagogue (or none at all). There are a variety of reasons for such disjunction, including such factors as geographical proximity to a synagogue in the denomination one prefers, family pressures, or financial considerations, among others. Klaff (2006) has analyzed some of the implications for Jewish identity of consonant or disjointed patterns.

For the purposes of our analysis, we use denominational identification rather than membership or formal affiliation. Respondents were asked, "Thinking about Jewish religious denominations, [what] do you consider yourself to be?" Respondents were grouped according to their first response to this question (multiple responses were allowed) into the four main American Jewish denominations (Orthodox, Conservative, Reform, or Reconstructionist) and those who did not identify with these or any particular denomination (which we refer to as "unaffiliated").

Jewish Education

Formal Jewish education has many forms. Adults take occasional classes or participate in ongoing programs of study; children may go to a private Jewish day school in lieu of a public elementary, middle, or high school. Many synagogues and some community centers have supplementary classes on weekday afternoons and/or Sunday, and some have "Sunday School" once a week. The content varies in terms of history, explanations of and celebrations of holiday rituals, learning Hebrew, and learning the prayers and prayer structure. Before a Bar or Bat Mitzvah, children usually learn the weekly portion they will recite, often in Hebrew and often including the liturgical trope they will use to chant it. Traditionally this training has been most common for boys, who are called up to the Torah in each of the denominations; in the past 20 or 30 years, it has become more common for girls to be called up to the Torah as well, at least in the Reform and Conservative traditions. Many of the gender differences in formal Jewish education can be traced to the Bar or Bat Mitzvah event. Fewer adolescents continue on with formal Jewish training, but some do, as we will see later.

To study the extent and kinds of contemporary formal Jewish education, respondents were asked whether they had ever received formal Jewish education, and if so, what kind (day school, supplementary school more than one day a week, supplementary school only one day a week—Sunday School—private tutoring, or something else), and for how many years during grades 1–8 and grades 9–12.

GENDER DIFFERENCES ON JEWISH IDENTITY FACTORS

Comparing men and women's scores on the Jewish identity factors, we find that women express stronger Jewish identity than do men on all but two of the factors (Figure 6.1). This is true for their concept of what being Jewish means, collective rituals, tribalism (personal or with regard to Jews in the United States), attachment to culture or to formal Jewish organizations, religious belief, and opinions about Israel's role for world and American Jewry. In the case of the more Orthodox rituals and practices, the gender difference is in the opposite direction but is not statistically significant, and in the case of personal attachment to Israel, men indicate stronger attachment than women. The latter result, the only statistically significant finding

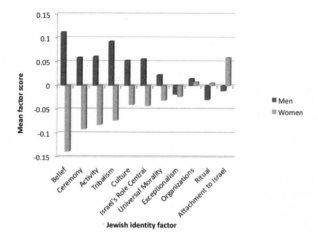

Figure 6.1. Mean scores on Jewish identity factors, by gender.

in which men express stronger Jewish identity than women, stems from men's greater familiarity with the current political and social situation in Israel; there are no gender differences with respect to the other three questions making up the index (level of emotional attachment to Israel, having close friends or relatives living in Israel, or number of visits to Israel).

These results thus reinforce conclusions based on previous studies of other religions, that women are more religious or spiritual, more involved in religion (in various ways), and more engaged culturally and socially as well. Their connection to the Jewish people, whether expressed by what they think being Jewish means, their perception of American Jewish exceptionalism or tribalism, their personal connection to being Jewish, and their own participation in collective rituals and formal organizations, is stronger than that of Jewish men. The gender differences are strongest for some of the private (Belief) and public (Ceremony) religious expressions of Jewish identity, and weaker for some of the ethnic expressions of Jewish identity (Israel's Role Central, Organizations).

DENOMINATION AND JEWISH IDENTITY

There are basically three patterns of denominational difference in Jewish identity, which apply to both men and women. On eight of the factors, the Orthodox express the strongest identity, including the belief that being Jewish means involvement in the current Jewish community and practices; practice of the stricter rituals; personal "tribalistic" attachment to the Jewish people; attachment to Jewish culture; religious belief; participation in formal Jewish organizations; and attachment to Israel. On some of these factors, Orthodox Jews are very different from the other groups, as in, for example, their stricter observance of rituals; on others, there is a less dramatic difference, as in personal attachment to the Jewish people. On most of these factors, Conservative Jews have the next strongest identity, Reform Jews the third strongest, and the unaffiliated the weakest. On the halachic rituals, however, the unaffiliated scores indicate stronger identity than the Reform scores, which probably reflects the upbringing of the currently unaffiliated, many of whom were raised Conservative or Orthodox; however, the difference between the Orthodox and the other denominations in this respect is especially large. For an example of this pattern, see Figure 6.2 (note that lower scores indicate stronger identity).

On a few factors, the expressions of Jewish identity of the Orthodox are not significantly different from the Conservative, and sometimes not from the Reform either. In terms of the more common ceremonial rituals and practice, analysis of variance shows us that there is no significant difference between the Orthodox and Conservative groups, and there is only a weak difference between them and the Reform denomination (Figure 6.3). All three are significantly different from the unaffiliated, however. In terms of feeling that Jews in United States are a distinct group, there are no significant differences between the Orthodox and the other denominational groups; however, the unaffiliated score significantly lower than the Conservative or Reform groups on this. The Orthodox and the Conservative denominations do not differ significantly in terms of their participation in formal Jewish organizational life, nor do they differ in terms of attaching importance to Israel's role for worldwide and U.S. Jewry. Both see Israel's

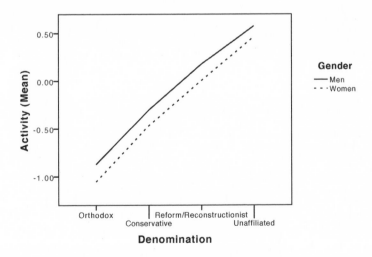

Figure 6.2. Mean scores on Activity factor, by denomination and gender.

role more centrally than do the Reform groups or unaffiliated. In terms of personal attachment to Israel, the Orthodox have significantly stronger attachment than all of the other groups, the Conservatives express the next strongest attachment, and the Reform and unaffiliated are lowest in attachment and not significantly different from each other.

It is interesting that on two of the factors the Orthodox are quite low in comparison with the Reform and Conservative denominational groups: in terms of expressing being Jewish as a universalistic kind of ethics or family heritage (Universal Morality), the Orthodox are much lower than the Conservative or Reform groups (who are not significantly different from each other) (Figure 6.4). This factor expresses almost the opposite of a particularistic identification, defining being Jewish in a way that does not differentiate it from affiliation with other U.S. religions or ethnicities except that it includes countering anti-Semitism. This, too, is a resistance to particularism. The Orthodox, however, do not fight particularism and therefore would be less likely to define being Jewish in this way.

The second factor demonstrating this pattern is that of belief in Jewish American exceptionalism, perhaps because the Orthodox are less likely to

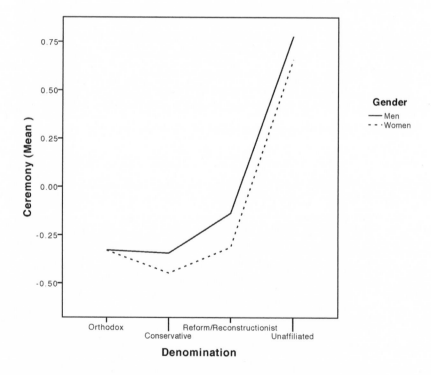

Figure 6.3. Mean scores on Ceremony factor, by denomination and gender.

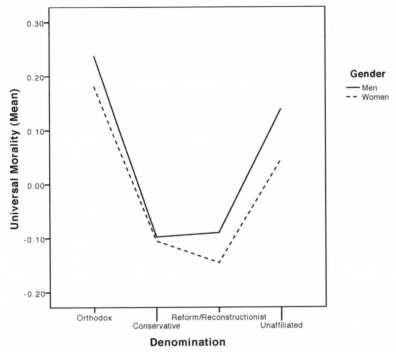

Figure 6.4. Mean scores on Universal Morality factor, by denomination and gender.

characterize American Jews as a cultural or ethnic group rather than a religious group.

These denominational patterns are the same for men and women, analyzed separately, with little variation, with one exception. On the factor Exceptionalism, Orthodox women are much more likely to express this attitude than are Orthodox men, Conservative women are somewhat less likely to express it than Conservative men, and Reform and Reconstructionist women are somewhat more likely to express it than Reform and Reconstructionist men. As a result, we get a curvilinear pattern among men but not among women. All of the affiliated women express this type of Jewish identity more strongly than unaffiliated women, with Reform and Reconstructionist women expressing it most strongly among women.

Gender Differences in Jewish Identity by Denomination

With respect to gender differences by denomination, one expectation was that there would be a greater gender difference among the Orthodox than among the other denominations, whose allocation of public religious roles primarily to men and greater familism suggested greater gender differentiation; however, our findings from 1990 did not suggest this pattern.

In the 2000–01 NJPS data, there is only one factor on which the Orthodox groups show a significant gender difference from the other denominations: the practice of halachic rituals (Table 6.2). This is in accordance with the expectations of gender difference with respect to ritual performance. However, the differences between Orthodox women and women in the other denominations, like the differences between Orthodox men and men in the other denominations, far outweigh any gender difference within the Orthodox group. It is interesting that, with respect to the collective and more commonly practiced rituals and celebrations, among the Orthodox there is no significant gender difference, but among the other denominations women are more active than men.

Significant gender differences, with women expressing stronger Jewish identity than men, remain for three factors in all denominations: women express stronger religious beliefs than men, stronger (tribalistic) attachment to the Jewish people than men, and a greater tendency than men to express "being Jewish" as being active in the current Jewish community and practices. These consistent gender differences across all denominations reinforce expectations based on previous studies that women are personally more involved and committed to being Jewish with respect to both religion and ethnicity than are men.

For attachment to Jewish culture or participation in formal Jewish organizations, the gender difference is not statistically significant when denomination is controlled for. In terms of attachment to Israel, gender differences among the Reform groups are statistically significant, and they show that although women have greater personal attachment to Israel than men, men are more likely to consider Israel's role important. This suggests that women keep up the personal connections that allow Israel to have the central role men think is important. In the other denominational groups, the pattern is similar, but statistically the significance is either very weak ($p < 0.1$) or not significant.

Gender, Denomination, Education, Age, and Jewish Identity

Now we add the variation in Jewish identity introduced by (secular) education and age or birth cohort. Education can be seen as an indicator for "structural immersion," or investment in secular roles; such investment, usually greater for men, has been suggested as an explanation for the fact that men are less invested in religious identity than women. In terms of age, the older generation supposedly had more traditional ways of "being

Table 6.2 Jewish Identity Factor Scores (Means), by Denomination and Gender

Jewish identity factor	Type of identity factor[a]	Orthodox		Conservative		Reform/ Reconstructionist		Unaffiliated	
		Men	Women	Men	Women	Men	Women	Men	Women
Activity	Priv (mixed)	-0.873	-1.054*	-0.303	-0.468*	0.177	0.005*	0.576	0.463
Ritual	Priv religious	-1.551	-1.772*	-0.274	-0.187	0.380	0.417	0.300	0.284
Belief	Priv religious	-0.847	-1.057*	-0.340	-0.453*	0.184	-0.114*	0.764	0.459*
Tribalism	Priv ethnic	-0.852	-1.105*	-0.349	-0.458*	0.210	-0.014*	0.516	0.573*
Culture	Priv ethnic	-0.944	-1.049	-0.284	-0.360	0.208	0.070*	0.491	0.451
Attachment to Israel	Priv ethnic	-0.953	-0.787	-0.198	-0.127	0.192	0.279*	0.218	0.204
Universal Morality	Pub (mixed)	0.238	0.181	-0.097	-0.105	-0.090	-0.145	0.139	0.046
Ceremony	Pub religious	-0.329	-0.330	-0.344	-0.447*	-0.137	-0.314*	0.779	0.658*
Exceptionalism	Pub ethnic	0.084	-0.044	-0.113	-0.025	-0.069	-0.110	0.071	0.084
Organizations	Pub ethnic								
Israel's Role Central	Pub ethnic	-0.315	-0.464	-0.256	-0.264	0.049	-0.069*	0.434	0.324
(n)[b]		(199)	(210)	(446)	(613)	(619)	(841)	(527)	(609)

[a] *Pub* denotes public; *Priv*, private.

[b] Unweighted *n* in parentheses; calculations performed using person-weights provided with dataset.

*T-test between men and women within the denomination statistically significant at $p < .05$.

Jewish," which may be changing among younger cohorts. This cohort difference may, however, be confounded by life-cycle differences: younger people have a less established family situation, less money, and are more involved in career building; older people may be more emotionally attached but may have less stamina and fewer resources for active participation in the community. So age may reflect cohort differences in identity orientation or life-cycle changes in identity involvement. In a previous analysis (Hartman and Hartman, 2006), we showed that there are significant differences in the scores of different age groups on almost all of the Jewish identity factors. The exceptions are the first factor expressing that being Jewish is involvement in the contemporary Jewish community and the factor expressing religious belief. For all of the other factors, an analysis of variance shows statistically significant variation by age. The pattern of variation, however, is complex.

On several of the factors, the older age groups express stronger Jewish identity than the younger age groups. For example, those aged 45 or older express more strongly than those under 45 the viewpoint that being Jewish means following universal moral guidelines and heritage. It is possible that this reflects the "baby boomer idealist" mentality.[7] Older cohorts also express greater involvement in collective rituals, a greater personal "tribalistic" connection to the Jewish people, greater attachment to Jewish culture, greater involvement in Jewish organizations, and greater personal attachment to Israel. Some of these, such as greater involvement in Jewish organizations and greater personal attachment to Israel, may certainly be related to life-cycle differences—older people having more opportunity to become personally acquainted with Israel, for example, and more time to devote to Jewish cultural and organizational pursuits.

Younger cohorts, on the other hand, tend to be more involved in stricter rituals (which may reflect the resurgence of Orthodoxy among the younger cohorts); the youngest cohort is also quite involved in more common ceremonial and collective rituals, and they tend to have a clearer sense of the distinctiveness of Jews in the United States. Both young and old are more supportive of Israel's role for world Jewry than the baby boomer generation.

Because these patterns may differ by gender and education, and because there is a larger proportion of women among the oldest cohort (women tend to outlive men), we thought it important to look at gender differences in Jewish identity controlling for both age and education. Because of the differences in Jewish identity by denomination, we also thought it important to control for denomination. To determine whether there are significant gender differences in the various expressions of Jewish identity once age and denomination have been controlled for, we used an analysis of variance for each Jewish identity factor, with gender, age, education, and denomination being the independent variables. Using an analysis of variance allows us to look at the variation introduced by each category of the independent variables—for gender and for denomination, Orthodox, Conservative, Reform/Reconstructionist, each of which is contrasted with the unaffiliated denominational group. Age and education are introduced as continuous covariates. The unstandardized effects are presented, along with whether or not they are statistically significant (at a $p < 0.05$ level). The magnitude of the effect for each variable is determined after the other variables in the model have been controlled for (Table 6.3). In Figure 6.5 we present the adjusted mean scores of men and women for the Jewish identity factors, after the analysis of variance controls for age, education, and denomination.

The results show that women have significantly stronger Jewish identity in almost of its expressions even when age, education, and denomination are controlled for. Thus, the suggestion that gender differences are a result of "structural immersion" (in secular roles) is not supported by this analysis, as gender differences remain significant even after education is controlled for. Similarly, the suggestion that women are more strongly identified with the various expressions of Jewishness because they are older is not supported, as gender differences remain significant even when age is controlled for. Furthermore, controlling for denomination does not undermine most of the gender differences just described.

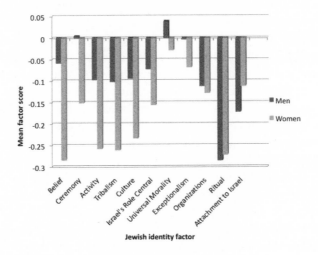

Figure 6.5. Mean scores on Jewish identity factors, by gender (controlling through analysis of variance for age, education, and denomination).

Comparing the unstandardized coefficients across factors allows us to see where the gender differences are the greatest. The biggest differences between men and women's Jewish identity are with respect to the factor Belief, a private religious expression of Jewish identity. This factor reflects spirituality, and the results are consistent with the aforementioned research by Rayburn (2004) and Woolever et al. (2006). Jewish women's expressions of spirituality are more highly differentiated from those of men than are their more behavioral expressions of private religiosity measured in the factor Ritual, perhaps because women traditionally have been excused from some of the behavioral obligations expressing religiosity. Compared with men, women also are more likely to understand Jewish identity as involvement in activities of the current Jewish community, have a stronger ethnic connection to the Jewish "tribe" (Tribalism) and culture (Culture). They also express more involvement in the public celebrations of Jewish identity (Ceremony). Gender differences in other expressions of Jewish identity are smaller, but in the same direction seen for women expressing stronger Jewish identity than men.

The analysis presented in Table 6.3 also shows that the Orthodox are differentiated from the other denominations primarily in terms of the private expressions of Jewish identity, as the unstandardized parameter estimates for being Orthodox are greater for the private expressions of Jewish identity (in the top half of the table) than for the public expressions of Jewish identity (in the bottom half). Self-identification as Conservative or Reform/Reconstructionist is also related to stronger Jewish identity on almost all factors, but the differences between public and private expressions of Jewish identity are much smaller for these denominations.

A higher level of education is related to weaker expressions of private religious Jewish identity and an understanding of being Jewish as being active in the current Jewish community, but with stronger expressions of Jewish identity in terms of the public religious and ethnic factors. Age has a weak but significant effect on some of the Jewish identity factors, indicating stronger Jewish identity among older Jews, independent of the fact that more older Jews are women and older Jews tend to be less educated than younger Jews. But the effect of age is quite small and not statistically significant in almost half of the expressions of Jewish identity.

In summary, women express stronger Jewish identity than do Jewish men, independent of their denomination, education, and age; Jews identifying with a denomination express stronger Jewish identity than Jews who do not, independent of gender, education, and age; and education is related to the ways in which Jews express their Jewish identity, independent of gender, denomination, and age.

Table 6.3 Multivariate Analysis of Variance of Jewish Identity Factors, by Denomination, Gender, Education and Age

Jewish Identity Factor	Type of identity factor[a]	Gender	Orthodox	Conservative	Reform/ Reconstructionist	Education	Age	R^2
Activity	Priv (mixed)	0.172*	−1.527*	−0.934*	−0.494*	0.026*	0.000	.252
Ritual	Priv religious	−0.013	−1.872*	−0.525*	0.095*	0.035*	0.003**	.372
Belief	Priv religious	0.226*	−1.489*	−1.008*	−0.573*	0.068*	0.001	.254
Tribalism	Priv ethnic	0.159*	−1.638*	−0.979*	−0.518*	−0.021	−0.009*	.273
Culture	Priv ethnic	0.139*	−1.496*	−0.774*	−0.310*	−0.136*	−0.003*	.209
Attachment to Israel	Priv ethnic	−0.060**	−1.183*	−0.346*	0.041	−0.164*	−0.006*	.163
Universal	Pub (mixed)	0.067*	0.098**	−0.171*	−0.183*	−0.063*	−0.003*	.252
Ceremony	Pub religious	0.155*	−1.070*	−1.133*	−0.950*	−0.067*	−0.002	.233
Exceptionalism	Pub ethnic	0.065**	−0.058	−0.136*	−0.119*	−0.155*	0.010*	.076
Organizations	Pub ethnic	0.016	−0.625*	−0.548*	−0.292*	−0.062*	−0.010*	.145
Israel's Role	Pub ethnic	0.085*	−0.776*	−0.667*	−0.403*	057*	0.000	.091
(Unweighted n)								(2580)

[a] *Pub* denotes public; *Priv*, private.

*Significant at $p < 0.05$; **Significant at $p < 0.10$.

In this section we explore gender differences in formal Jewish education, and relate these to Jewish identity differences shown in the preceding section. According to the 2000–01 NJPS, more than three-quarters of American Jews report having received Jewish education between the ages of 6 and 17.[8] There is a clear gender difference, with more than 80% of men and slightly more than 70% of women reporting having had some formal Jewish education. Most of this education took place before the ninth grade for both men and women, and there is a gender gap at both younger and older levels of Jewish education (Table 6.4). One reason for this gap is most likely that more men received at least some formal Jewish education leading up to their Bar Mitzvah, and because fewer women had a Bat Mitzvah than men had a Bar Mitzvah, there was more impetus for men to receive a Jewish education than women.[9]

Among those who had some formal Jewish education, men were slightly more likely to have gone to Hebrew school (55.1% compared with 46.5% of women), whereas women were more likely to have attended Sunday School (35.4% compared with 24.0% of men). This may also be because more boys need to learn Hebrew for their Bar Mitzvah.

It is interesting that among those with some formal Jewish education, there is no gender difference in the number of years of education they received (an average of 6.5 years for both men and women; last two rows of Table 6.4). In terms of informal education, men appear to have experienced more sleep-away Jewish camp experience than women, although almost half of both men and women went to a Jewish day camp.[10]

When we look at gender differences in Jewish education by denomination, we see that there is no gender difference among the Orthodox—about 90% of both men and women received formal Jewish education (Table 6.4). But among the Conservative, Reform/Reconstructionist, and unaffiliated, more men received formal Jewish education than women. There is a greater gender difference among the unaffiliated than the Reform/Reconstructionist groups, a greater gender difference among the Reform/Reconstructionist than the Conservative groups, and a greater gender difference among the Conservative than the Orthodox groups. This is reflected by (or stems from) the larger difference by denomination among women than among men. Perhaps the need for training for Bar Mitzvah, more common among boys, narrows the differences between denominations for boys more than for girls.

Among those who had some formal education, there is little gender difference in the length of formal education within any of the denominations. The length of education for both men and women varies by denomination:

Table 6.4 Jewish Education of American Jews, by Gender and Denomination

Denomination	Formal Jewish education, grades 1–12 (%)	Mean years of Jewish education, grades 1–8	Mean years of Jewish education, grades 9–12	Mean years of Jewish education, grades 1–12	(n)[a]
Orthodox					
Men	91.4	6.4	3.6	9.0	(199)
Women	89.1	6.3	3.9	9.1	(210)
Conservative					
Men	92.3	5.5	2.8	6.9	(446)
Women	79.7	5.5	2.9	6.7	(613)
Reform/ Reconstructionist					
Men	89.3	5.1	2.7	6.0	(619)
Women	73.6	5.2	2.9	6.2	(841)
Unaffiliated					
Men	66.4	4.6	2.6	6.5	(527)
Women	51.7	4.5	2.9	5.1	(609)
Total					
Men	83.8	5.3	2.9	6.5	(1,791)
Women	77.0	5.3	3.0	6.5	(2,273)

[a]Unweighted n in parentheses; calculations performed using person-weights provided with dataset.

among the Orthodox, the average length of formal Jewish education is about 9 years; among the Conservative, about 6.8; among Reform/Reconstructionist, 6.1 years; and among the unaffiliated, about 5.9 years.

Jewish education is more common among the younger generations. A gender difference persists but is smaller among the younger than the older (Figure 6.6). Among those 65 and over, 84% of men and 63% of women had some formal Jewish education; among those 18–24, 88% of men and 79% of women had some formal Jewish education. The differences by age cohort are greater for women, which accounts for the narrowing gender gap. The length of formal Jewish education is also longer for younger cohorts, probably because of a proliferation of Jewish day schools (Cohen, 2004), but there are few gender differences in the length of education within each age group (as we saw for the total and for each denomination).

We can see from Figure 6.7 that even though there is variation between the age cohorts in each denomination, both denominational and gender differences persist at every age. Thus, in the oldest group shown (55+), there are gender differences in formal Jewish education—some of them much wider than among the younger generation—in every denomination, but especially among the unaffiliated. Gender differences are narrower in the 45–54 age group in all denominations and have almost disappeared in the youngest age group (18–44) for Orthodox and Conservative. Denominational differences are greater among the women than the men in each group, including the youngest; and the unaffiliated are more differentiated from the rest of the denominational groups in the younger cohort, in terms of having had some formal Jewish education.

In sum, gender differences are apparent in whether respondents received formal Jewish education and what kind of Jewish education they had, but among those who had some formal Jewish education, there is little difference in length of education by gender. The gender gap in formal Jewish education is smallest for the Orthodox and greatest for the unaffiliated (perhaps because denomination makes a bigger difference for women than for men and perhaps because of the widespread celebration of Bar Mitzvah by men, which necessitates a modicum of formal Jewish education). We also find a narrowing of the gender gap in formal Jewish education among the younger age groups, owing primarily to the increasing preponderance of formal Jewish education, especially for women.

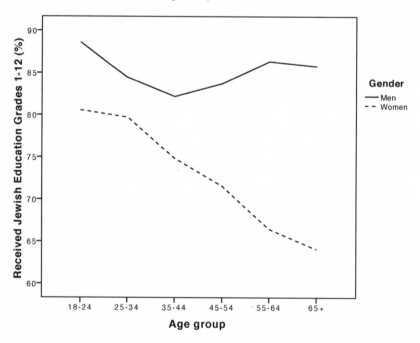

Figure 6.6. Percentage receiving Jewish education, by age group and gender.

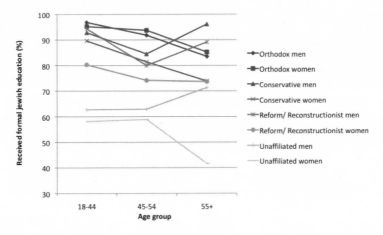

Figure 6.7. Percentage receiving Jewish education, by age group, denomination, and gender.

Jewish Education and Jewish Identity

Both the amount and type of formal Jewish education have been shown to be related to stronger Jewish identity, as measured by intermarriage, percentage of closest friends who are Jewish, ritual observance, membership in a synagogue, feeling that being Jewish is very important, and attachment to Israel (Cohen, 2007; Cohen and Kotler-Berkowitz, 2004). We have shown that men are more likely to have received formal Jewish education than women, especially among the Reform/Reconstructionist groups and those who do not identify with any denomination. Yet women tend to have a stronger Jewish identity on most of the factors, as we have demonstrated. Thus, our next questions were whether formal Jewish education affects the strength of Jewish identity as we have measured it, whether its impact was different for men and for women, and whether it narrows or widens the gender gap in Jewish identity.

We can see clearly from Figure 6.8 that both gender and formal Jewish education have an impact on strength of Jewish identity. Among men, those who have received formal Jewish education have a stronger Jewish identity than those who have not, with respect to every aspect that we have measured; a similar impact can be seen for Jewish women. At the same time, among those with or without formal Jewish education, women have a stronger Jewish identity than men with respect to almost every aspect measured. There are two exceptions to this pattern. First, with respect to the observance of personal rituals, men are more observant than women among those with no formal Jewish education; and among those with formal Jewish education, there is no gender difference. Second, men have a stronger

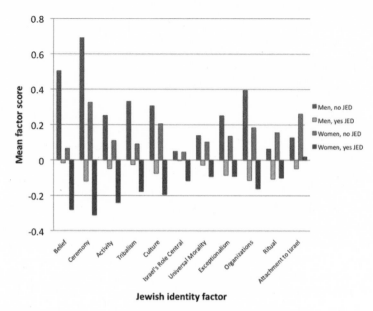

Figure 6.8. Mean scores on Jewish identity factors, by Jewish education (JED) and gender.

personal attachment to Israel—the main reason being, as already mentioned, that men are more familiar with the political and social situation in Israel than women are, and this gap remains even when men and women have received Jewish education (current familiarity with the Israeli situation is influenced very little by formal Jewish education).

Finally, we added years of Jewish education to the multivariate analysis of variance of each Jewish identity factor (presented in Table 6.3), controlling for denomination (with dummy variables of Orthodox, Conservative, and Reform/Reconstructionist), education, age, and gender (Table 6.5). The results show that gender differences remain statistically significant even when we control for years of Jewish education, denomination, education, and age. The three exceptions are Ritual (which we saw earlier), Attachment to Israel, and Organizations (which we saw earlier as well). This multivariate analysis of variance gives us adjusted means for each identity factor for men and women, once denomination, education, age, and years of Jewish education have been controlled for. The resulting means are presented in Figure 6.9. If we compare the results in Figure 6.9 with those in Figure 6.5, we see that the main effect of taking into account Jewish education is that men's scores on the identity factors are somewhat strengthened; however, the basic differences between the genders change very little.

Table 6.5 Multivariate Analysis of Variance of Jewish Identity Factors, by Denomination, Gender, Education, Jewish Education, and Age

Jewish Identity Factor	Type of identity factor[a]	Gender	Orthodox	Conservative	Reform/Reconstructionist	Education	Age	Years of Jewish education	R^2
Activity	Priv (mixed)	0.190*	-1.428*	-0.883*	-0.470*	0.031*	0.000	-0.023*	.267
Ritual	Priv religious	0.001	-1.786*	-0.479*	0.130*	0.045*	0.002*	-0.023*	.391
Belief	Priv religious	0.248*	-1.368*	-0.934*	-0.528*	0.078*	0.000	-0.027*	.268
Tribalism	Priv ethnic	0.176*	-1.485*	-0.897*	-0.466*	-0.015	-0.010*	-0.028*	.283
Culture	Priv ethnic	0.186*	-1.266*	-0.648*	-0.23*	-0.116*	-0.005*	-0.049*	.245
Attachment to Israel	Priv ethnic	-0.022	-0.961*	-0.232*	0.130*	-0.148*	-0.008*	-0.042*	.190
Universal	Pub (mixed)	0.092*	0.151*	-0.133*	-0.158*	-0.058*	-0.004*	-0.010*	.026
Ceremony	Pub religious	0.187*	-0.835*	-1.015*	-0.8598	-0.053*	-0.004*	-0.046*	.263
Exceptionalism	Pub ethnic	0.069*	0.003	-0.112*	-0.098*	-0.156*	0.010*	-0.018*	.085
Organizations	Pub ethnic	0.035	-0.487*	-0.474*	-0.247*	-0.049*	-0.010*	-0.029*	.164
Israel's Role Central	Pub ethnic	0.081*	-0.814*	-0.672*	-0.413*	0.052*	0.000	-0.002	.099
(Unweighted n)									(2406)

*Significant at $p < 0.05$;

[a] *Pub* denotes public; *Priv*, private.

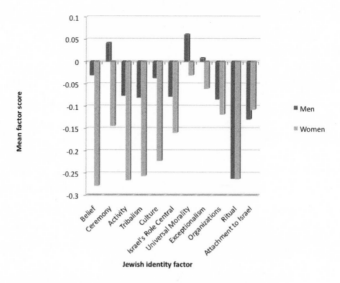

Figure 6.9. Mean scores on Jewish identity factors, by gender (controlling through analysis of variance for age, education, denomination, and amount of Jewish education).

SUMMARY AND CONCLUSIONS

We began this chapter by presenting a number of reasons to expect little gender difference in Jewish identity. The greatest gender differences in religiosity have been found in relation to belief and spirituality, which are only one part of Jewish identity. American Jewish men and women both have invested highly in secular achievements, given their high educational level and occupational standings, so that the "structural location" thesis of gender differences in religiosity was expected to be muted in this population. Furthermore, women's involvement in the labor force in the past was associated with weaker Jewish identity, even as men's involvement in the labor force was associated with stronger Jewish identity; and as women's labor force participation has continued to increase (men's more or less remaining stable), this might weaken women's gender identity relative to men's. Another reason for women's stronger religious and ethnic identity in the past has been the reliance on family during immigrant transitions and diasporas, which preclude institutional establishments; with many American Jews being third- and even fourth-generation Americans, this impetus for women's stronger identity was expected to be dampened. The growth of gender equality in public religious roles among the larger Jewish denominations in the United States (Reform and Conservative) might also be expected to spill over into greater gender equality in both private and public expressions of individual Jewish identity.

On the other hand, gender differences in spirituality have been found even when education is controlled for. Moreover, the persisting centrality of the home and voluntary institutions in transmitting Jewish identity suggests the continuation of women's greater involvement in Jewish identity compared with men. Finally, the increased accessibility of formal Jewish education to women, as well as men, with the concomitant strengthening of Jewish identity, could be expected to result in the persistence of gender differences found in the past, albeit at stronger levels of identity.

So it was with considerable interest that we demonstrated persisting gender differences in expressions of Jewish identity of all types—religious, ethnic, public, and private. Although gender differences were most apparent in religious belief and public rituals (the Ceremony factor), gender differences were significant with respect to indicators of both public and private ethnic identity as well. Furthermore, these gender differences persist even when age (which controls for life cycle and birth cohort), denomination, secular educational level, and exposure to Jewish education are controlled for. The denomination with the strictest gender division in terms of ritual practice and public religious roles is indeed characterized by gender difference in Jewish identity; however, the gender differences among the Orthodox are actually narrower than among the other denominational groups, and in many respects are greatest among the unaffiliated. Moreover, there is no significant gender difference in ritual observance among the Orthodox: women do not fall significantly below the level of ritual observance that men express, despite men's having more obligatory commandments to perform. Women do not appear to be daunted in their identification with Jewishness by any inequalities in public religious roles that persist in some of the denominations. Women continue to receive lower levels of formal Jewish education, especially unaffiliated and Reform women, but having less formal Jewish education does not appear to weaken their identity. In addition, gender differences persist when exposure to formal Jewish education is controlled for.

As we turn to the following chapters, we ask whether women's stronger Jewish identity is also reflected in a stronger relationship between their Jewish identity and their family behaviors and secular achievements than we find among men. In Chapter 8, we also explore further the thesis of "structural location," examining the relationship between Jewishness and labor force participation and occupational achievement.

CHAPTER 7

How Jewishness is Related to Family Patterns of American Jews

The relationship between Jewishness and family behavior is complex. Family serves as a metaphor for the entire Jewish people: "From the Bible forward the Jewish people is portrayed at its core as a large extended family descended from the patriarch Jacob" (Berger, 2005, p. 1). Institutionally, especially as Jews lived as minorities for most of their history, from the destruction of Solomon's Temple in 586 B.C.E. until the modern-day founding of Israel, the family was "in many cases, the primary vehicle for preserving distinctiveness from the majority culture" (Berger, 2005, p. 1), and still is, in many respects. Marriage and family are seen as part of the "sanctification of Israel" in the rabbinic tradition, and many rabbinic rules revolve around family ritual and behavior. "Among the most important of these [family-related] commandments are that: (1) men are to marry, (2) they are to procreate . . . and (3) they are obligated to teach their children about the religious traditions of Israel. (4) Women, as conceived by rabbinic Judaism, above all, are to attend to their children" (Wertheimer, 2005c, p. 245). In modern times Jews began to assimilate themselves into their surroundings: " 'Be a Frenchman outside and a Jew at home' became the formula for successful integration, granting the family . . . an even more central role in the preservation of Jewish identity" (Berger, 2005, p. 11).

Such an admonition may apply to either ethnic or religious identity, although the implication is that one should privatize religion while allowing ethnicity or nationality to be one's public face. The tendency to privatize religion was thought to accompany modernization (Berger, 1967; Luckmann, 1967), which relegated it to the private sphere dominated by the family: "The private sphere may seem to be, in a macro sense, peripheral in the modern world, but it nevertheless is where a bedrock of mutually reinforcing relations between family and religion is found" (Pankhurst and Houseknecht, 2000, p. 24). The persistent and even resurgent presence of religion in public life, even in an ostensibly secular country like the United States, challenges the notion of religious privatization, and the public functions of the family have been noted as well (Cherlin, 2005; Pankhurst and Houseknecht, 2000). So the mutually reinforcing relationship between religion and family, whether in the private or public sphere, is well established.

Edgell (2006) and Christiano (2000), among others, discuss the persisting association between religiosity and traditional familism, albeit one that is challenged by contemporary economic pressures and practices both in the broader society and in individual families. At the same time, however, Christiano (2000) notes the opposite tendencies among Jews (e.g., delayed marriage, low fertility), which are not explained by demographic and educational factors alone. Family texts routinely point to ethnic patterns of variation in familistic behavior (e.g., Benokraitis, 2002; Eshleman and Bulcroft, 2006; although Jews are rarely considered a relevant ethnic group and are not described in either of these sources). Little research is able to juxtapose religious and ethnic identity within the same group in the same way that is possible among Jews, however. By using ethnic and religious, private and public indices of Jewish identity, we seek in this chapter to sort out the relationships between family behavior and various types of Jewish identity.

In addition to the influence of Jewish religious and ethnic culture on family behavior, the norms of the broader society also have an influence on American Jewish life. The tendencies in contemporary U.S. society toward delayed marriage, high divorce rates, and small families are all evident among American Jews as well (Berger, 2005). Furthermore, the stress on individualism in the United States may well take its toll on the American Jewish family, as it has in the broader society (Bellah et. al., 1985/1996). As Cohen and Eisen (2000) found, contemporary American Jews are first and foremost motivated by a "profound individualism," a "sovereign self," yet their choices are often framed in the context of their family situations, which remain extremely important settings for practicing and actualizing their Jewishness.

The issues that we address in this chapter are the extent to which family behavior patterns are related to the denominational and Jewish identity patterns shown in the preceding chapter, and whether the distinctiveness of American Jewish family behavior that we saw in comparison with the broader American population is related to stronger or weaker expressions of Jewish identity and tradition. Because family patterns involve gender relations in the intimate setting, and are strongly related to both men's and women's secular educational and economic achievement, we see this as an important step in understanding patterns of gender equality and inequality among American Jews. We look first at denominational variation in the family behavior of men and women, then explore the relationship between Jewish identity and family roles, and finally look at how Jewish identity interacts with denominational variation in family behavior and whether this interaction is similar for men and women in each denomination.

DENOMINATION AND FAMILY BEHAVIOR

We look first at denominational variation in family behavior (Table 7.1). A clear result is that Orthodox family behavior is different from that of the non-Orthodox. The Orthodox are more likely to marry, to marry younger, to be married (at the time of the survey), and to have had only one marriage and are less likely to ever divorce, to have children when they are younger, and to have more children than those in other denominations. Among the Orthodox, more than 80% of men and nearly 90% of women have ever married, compared with 70–75% of non-Orthodox men and 70–85% of non-Orthodox women. Less than 13% of Orthodox men and less than 10% of Orthodox women have ever divorced, compared with 15–25% of non-Orthodox men and 15–20% of non-Orthodox women. On average, Orthodox men marry about a year earlier than non-Orthodox men, and Orthodox women marry about 2 years earlier than non-Orthodox women.

Less than 20% of Orthodox women are childless, compared with 26–44% of non-Orthodox women. Confining this observation to women aged 45 and over, we find that only 5% of Orthodox women have not given birth, compared with 14.7, 17.3, and 22.9% of Conservative, Reform/Reconstructionist, and unaffiliated women, respectively. Further confining our observation to women over 45 who have been married at least once, the differences are smaller but in the same direction: 4% of Orthodox women, 8.5% of Conservative women, 12.1% of Reform/Reconstructionist women, and 17.3% of unaffiliated women.

Orthodox women start having children on average 1–2 years earlier than non-Orthodox women and have an average of one or two more children than non-Orthodox women. More than a quarter of Orthodox women have four or more children, compared with less than 10% of Conservative women and less than 4% of Reform/Reconstructionist or unaffiliated women.

Another observation with regard to denomination is that the unaffiliated are less likely to be married or to have ever married, are more likely to have divorced and to be divorced (at least among men), and are more likely to have fewer children than the affiliated. It is especially striking that 25% of unaffiliated men have divorced, compared with 12–19% of the affiliated, and 11.8% of them were divorced at the time of the survey, compared with less than 7% of affiliated men. (It is interesting that unaffiliated women are similar to Reform/Reconstructionist women with regard

Table 7.1 Family Behavior of American Jews, by Denomination and Gender

Family indicator	Orthodox	Conservative	Reform/ Reconstructionist	Unaffiliated
Men				
Married (%)	71.7	62.2	64.2	53.7
Ever married (%)	81.5	75.1	76.4	71.8
Median age at first marriage	25.8	26.4	26.7	26.7
Mean number of marriages	1.2	1.2	1.3	1.3
Divorced (%)	5.4	6.7	6.2	11.8
Ever divorced (%)	12.7	15.1	18.9	25.1
(n)[a]	(109)	(278)	(347)	(295)
Women				
Married (%)	62.2	62.7	55.6	50.5
Ever married (%)	89.0	84.7	79.4	71.6
Median age at first marriage	22.4	24.2	24.3	24.2
Mean number of marriages	1.1	1.1	1.2	1.2
Divorced (%)	3.9	8.6	11.1	10.4
Ever divorced (%)	9.0	15.4	20.8	20.2
Childless (%)	19.0	26.2	31.2	44.0
Mean age at birth of first child	24.0	26.1	26.4	25.4
Mean number of children	2.7	1.8	1.4	1.1
4+ children (%)	26.8	9.2	3.6	3.9
(n)[a]	(92)	(420)	(522)	(346)

[a]Unweighted n in parentheses; calculations performed using person-weights provided with dataset.

to proportion divorced.) Forty-four percent of unaffiliated women are childless, compared with 19–31% of the affiliated. This may well be a clue to their lack of affiliation with the main denominations (or, conversely, may reflect the greater tendency of those with children to be affiliated with a denomination).

In order to better understand the denominational variation in family behavior, we used a multivariate regression analysis to predict age at marriage—the first step in formally creating a family of one's own.[1] As mentioned earlier, Wertheimer (2005b) asks what it is about the Orthodox that accounts for their higher fertility: is the reason primarily demographic, that is, a function of their marrying at younger ages, or do other factors explain their propensity to have more children? We start with age at marriage—attempting to explain the denominational variation in age at first marriage by conventional characteristics such as education and age cohort. Although we recognize that education may continue after marriage, for most people education takes place before marriage or signifies the respondent's orientation to education by the time of marriage (i.e., while a newly married man or woman may be in graduate school, the intention to complete a graduate degree is usually in place at the time of marriage, especially among those marrying later),[2] so we use it as a dependent variable influencing age at the time of marriage (Table 7.2). We look at respondents 45 and over, most of whom have already had a first marriage, and we look at men and women separately, because the prediction of their age at marriage may differ.

Denomination is not related to men's age at marriage, explaining less than 1% of the variance in age at marriage (model 1, $R^2 = 0.002$). The only variable we control for in this analysis that *is* related to men's age at marriage is their education, as can be seen in model 2. For women, however, being Orthodox (as opposed to belonging any of the other denominational groups) does explain an earlier age at marriage, even when we control for age cohort and educational level in model 2. Education is a more

Table 7.2 Multiple Regression of Age at First Marriage of American Jews (Ages 45 and Over), by Gender[a]

Independent variable	Men				Women			
	Model 1		Model 2		Model 1		Model 2	
Orthodox[b]	0.743	(.038)	0.878	(.045)	−1.476	(−.071)	−1.321	(−.063)*
Conservative[b]	0.498	(.035)	0.576	(.041)	−0.294	(−.024)	−0.093	(−.008)
Reform[b]	0.969	(.072)	0.960	(.071)	−0.319	(−.027)	−0.317	(−.027)
Unaffiliated[b]	0.890	(.064)	0.979	(.071)	0.534	(.295)	0.567	(.043)
Age			−0.005	(−.010)			−0.027	(−.058)*
Education			0.351	(.073)*			0.532	(.114)*
R	.040		.084		.088		.232	
R^2	.002		.007		.008		.054	
(Unweighted n)		(870)						(1,196)

[a]Data are unstandardized coefficients and (in parentheses) standardized coefficients, ß.
[b]Using dummy variables, 0 represents "does not identify with denomination"; 1 represents "identifies with denomination." The category "Reconstructionist" was omitted.
* $p < 0.05$.

Table 7.3 Multiple Regression of Age at Birth of First Child and Number of Children for American Jewish Women (Ages 45 and Over)[a]

Independent variable	Age at birth of first child				Number of children			
	Model 1		Model 2		Model 1		Model 2	
Orthodox[b]	−1.655	(−.092)*	−0.653	(−.036)	0.672	(.157)*	0.581	(.136)*
Conservative[b]	0.029	(.003)	0.408	(.039)	−0.091	(−.033)	−0.127	−(.046)
Reform[b]	0.111	(.011)	0.260	(.025)	−0.217	(−.081)**	−0.213	−(.080)*
Unaffiliated[b]	0.242	(.022)	0.021	(.002)	−0.527	(−.185)*	−0.498	(−174)*
Age			−0.014	(−.034)			0.011	(.108)*
Education			0.506	(.593)*			−0.037	(−.037)
Age at marriage			0.786	(.196)*			−0.032	(−.155)*
Age at birth of first child							−.049	(−.190)*
R	.095		.659		.240		.429	
R²	.009		.435		.058		.184	
(n)	(1,027)		(1,024)		(919)		(919)	

*$p < 0.05$; ** $p < 0.10$.

[a]Data are unstandardized coefficients and (in parentheses) standardized coefficients, ß.

[b]Using dummy variables, 0 represents "does not identify with denomination"; 1 represents "identifies with denomination." The category "Reconstructionist" was omitted.

effective predictor of age at marriage (more educated women get married at an older age), as is age cohort (younger women marry at an older age). Generally, we can explain more of the variance in age at marriage for women with these variables than we can for men, but still these variables account for only 5% of the variance.

The same set of variables explains more of the variance in age at first birth and number of children (for women only) (Table 7.3). We limit our analysis to women aged 45 and over, most of whom have completed their childbearing.[3] When we predict age at birth of first child, there is a significant relationship between being Orthodox and (earlier) age at birth of first child, but its significance is eliminated when we control for age at marriage, education, and age. In other words, denomination is likely to affect age at birth of first child by influencing age at marriage (as we saw earlier). Education is the strongest predictor of age at birth of first child, but age at first marriage has an effect independent of education.

When we use the same variables to predict the number of children born, and add age at birth of first child as an independent variable (right half of

Table 7.3), we find the difference in the number of children between the Orthodox and non-Orthodox groups (which we saw earlier) expressed in the significant regression coefficient for being Orthodox, a more potent explanation of number of children than being Reform, which is significantly related to lower fertility. Being Reform and especially having no denominational preference are significantly associated with having fewer children, as noted earlier; being unaffiliated has the strongest correlation with number of children of all the denominational groups. Being Conservative does not have an independent relationship with how many children a woman gave birth to.

When we add to the regression analysis the woman's age cohort, age at first marriage, age at birth of first child, and level of education, the effect of denominational preference remains significant for being Orthodox, Reform, and unaffiliated. In fact, the unstandardized regression coefficients for denominational preference change relatively little from model 1 to model 2 (about 12.5% for the Orthodox, less than 2% for the Reform, and less than 7% for the unaffiliated), indicating that the correlation between denomination and fertility is not related to demographic factors such as

Table 7.3 Multiple Regression of Age at Birth of First Child and Number of Children for American Jewish Women (Ages 45 and Over)[a]

Independent variable	Age at birth of first child				Number of children			
	Model 1		Model 2		Model 1		Model 2	
Orthodox[b]	−1.655	(−.092)*	−0.653	(−.036)	0.672	(.157)*	0.581	(.136)*
Conservative[b]	0.029	(.003)	0.408	(.039)	−0.091	(−.033)	−0.127	−(.046)
Reform[b]	0.111	(.011)	0.260	(.025)	−0.217	(−.081)**	−0.213	−(.080)*
Unaffiliated[b]	0.242	(.022)	0.021	(.002)	−0.527	(−.185)*	−0.498	(−174)*
Age			−0.014	(−.034)			0.011	(.108)*
Education			0.506	(.593)*			−0.037	(−.037)
Age at marriage			0.786	(.196)*			−0.032	(−.155)*
Age at birth of first child							−.049	(−.190)*
R	.095		.659		.240		.429	
R[2]	.009		.435		.058		.184	
(n)	(1,027)		(1,024)		(919)		(919)	

*p < 0.05; ** p < 0.10.

[a]Data are unstandardized coefficients and (in parentheses) standardized coefficients, ß.

[b]Using dummy variables, 0 represents "does not identify with denomination"; 1 represents "identifies with denomination." The category "Reconstructionist" was omitted.

age, age at marriage, age at birth of first child, or educational level. In contrast to age at marriage and age at birth of first child, denomination has a strong independent relationship to the number of children a woman gives birth to, for the Orthodox, the Reform, and the unaffiliated (in opposite directions); the effects of these denominational preferences are comparable to those of age at marriage and age at birth of first child.

Age, age at marriage, and age at birth of first child are each associated inversely with number of children (i.e., the older the woman, the younger her age at marriage, and the younger her age at the birth of her first child, the more children she has). Education, however, does not have a significant independent effect on number of children once age, age at marriage, and age at birth of first child are controlled for.

Finally, we look at the influence of denomination on number of times married, when we control for age, education, and age at first marriage, for men and women separately (Table 7.4). When we look at the relationship between denomination and number of marriages, without controlling for any other variables (model 1), we see that for men denomination explains little variation ($R^2 = 0.005$, indicating that 0.5% of the variance is explained). For women, a little more variation is explained, and several of the denominational groups have statistically significant relationships with number of times married: Orthodox Jews have significantly fewer marriages, whereas Reform Jews and the unaffiliated are more likely to have multiple marriages. We doubt that the denomination actually increases the likelihood of multiple marriages; rather it seems likely that divorced or remarried people feel more comfortable among the Reform than the other denominations, which tend to be more traditionally familial in their activities and emphasis; it is even more likely that people who have divorced or remarried are less comfortable in any of the denominations and therefore probably do not express a denominational preference. Because remarriage is more likely to involve non-Jewish spouses, which may increase the lack of affiliation or preference for the denomination most tolerant of intermarriage (Reform), we control for whether or not the respondent is currently married to a Jewish spouse (in model 3) and find that the significant correlation between being Reform or unaffiliated and number of marriages disappears, as does the correlation with being Orthodox. The significant influences on marrying more than once, for both men and women, are age (older cohorts have more stable first marriages) and earlier age at marriage.

In summary, denominational preference, especially being Orthodox, has an independent influence on the family behavior of women, even after demographic factors have been controlled for, but is not related to the family

Table 7.4 Multiple Regression of Number of Marriages for American Jewish Men and Women[a]

Independent variable	Men			Women		
	Model 1	Model 2	Model 3	Model 1	Model 2	Model 3
Orthodox[b]	−0.038 (−.024)	−0.033 (−.020)	0.005 (.003)	−0.104 (−.066)*	−0.123 (−.078)*	−0.067 (−.042)
Conservative[b]	0.026 (−.022)	0.027 (.022)	0.023 (.019)	0.010 (.009)	−0.002 (−.002)	0.007 (.007)
Reform[b]	0.009 (.008)	0.022 (.019)	−0.026 (−.023)	0.078 (.075)*	0.076 (.026)*	0.053 (.051)
Unaffiliated[b]	0.081 (.069)	0.093 (.080)**	0.018 (.015)	0.087 (.079)*	0.094 (.086)*	0.041 (.037)
Age		0.004 (.136)*	0.005 (.180)*		0.002 (.067)*	0.003 (.106)*
Age at marriage		−0.010 (−.114)*	−0.013 (−.143)*		−0.016 (−.185)*	−0.018 (−.207)*
Education		−0.003 (−.007)	−0.002 (−.006)		0.004 (.010)	0.005 (.011)
Current spouse Jewish[c]			−0.235 (−.204)*			−0.222 (−.195)*
R	.071	.189	.264	.114	.232	.292
R²	.005	.036	.070	.013	.054	.085
(Unweighted n)	(851)			(993)		

*$p < 0.05$; **$p < 0.10$.

[a]Data are unstandardized coefficients and (in parentheses) standardized coefficients, ß.

[b]Using dummy variable, 0 represents "does not identify with denomination"; 1 represents "identifies with denomination." The category "Reconstructionist" was omitted.

[c]Using dummy variable: 0 represents "current spouse is not Jewish"; 1 represents "current spouse is Jewish."

behavior of men. This finding may be related to the stronger expressions of Jewish identity among women that we saw in the preceding chapter; their stronger identity may have a greater impact on their family (and other) behavior. Or women may be more greatly influenced by the norms associated with their denominational reference group or environment. In the following section, we explore this further by looking at the ways family behavior is related to expressions of Jewish identity.

JEWISH IDENTITY AND FAMILY BEHAVIOR

When looking at the relationship between Jewish identity indices and family behavior, we expected stronger relationships between family behavior and private expressions of Jewish identity than between family behavior and public expressions of Jewish identity (since family behavior is private). We expected some relationship between familistic tendencies and commitment to Jewish religion or ritual, because Jewish commandments include those concerning marriage and having children. We also expected that stronger ethnic identity might lead to stronger family behavior as a commitment to perpetuate the Jewish people.

To relate the factors to family behavior, we correlated the scores on each factor (which range from strong Jewish identity [low] to weak Jewish identity [high]) with seven indicators of family behavior: ever married (0, no; 1, yes); age at first or only marriage; number of times married; ever divorced (0, no; 1, yes); ever gave birth (0, no; 1, yes); age at birth of first or only child; and number of children. The correlations in Table 7.5 show the direction of the relationships and whether or not they are statistically significant at $p < 0.05$.

Nearly 70% of the correlations between family behavior and expressions of private Jewish identity (i.e., attitudes or behaviors centered on personal or family situations) are statistically significant: believing that being Jewish is about activity in contemporary Jewish life, personal tribalistic attachment to the Jewish people, and commitment to Jewish culture (private ethnic expressions of Jewish identity) are significantly related to getting married at least once, earlier age at first marriage, marrying fewer times, less likelihood of being divorced, less likelihood of being childless, and having more children. Personal attachment to Israel is significantly related to getting married, not divorcing, and having more children. Stronger religious beliefs are related to almost all of the familistic behaviors, and commitment to personal ritual behavior is related to less divorce and more children. In contrast, less than half of the expressions of public Jewish ethnic identity are significantly related to family behavior. Commitment to collective rituals is related to almost all of the familistic behaviors; belonging to Jewish organizations is related to several of the behaviors. But believing that being Jewish is about

Table 7.5 Pearson Correlations Between Jewish Identity Factors and Family Behavior for American Jews (Ages 45 and Over)[a]

Type of identity factor[b]	Jewish identity factor[c]	Ever married (0, no; 1, yes)	Age at first marriage	Age at birth of first child	Number of times married	Ever divorced (0, no; 1, yes)	Childless (0, has children; 1, no children)	Number of children ever born
Priv (mixed)	Activity	-.051* (2,246)	.057* (1,914)	.033 (1,024)	.087* (2,030)	.117* (2,230)	.091* (1,285)	-.160* (1,262)
Priv R	Ritual	-.014 (2,135)	.026 (1,837)	.038 (972)	.056* (1,936)	.109* (2,123)	.055 (1,211)	-.173* (,1191)
Priv R	Belief	-.027 (2,271)	.123* (1,949)	.076* (1,046)	.066* (2,061)	.102* (2,258)	.120* (1,299)	-.176* (1,285)
Priv E	Tribalism	-.089* (2,016)	.087* (1,717)	-.022 (889)	.148* (1,817)	.173* (2,004)	.201* (1,118)	-.206* (1,107)
Priv E	Culture	-.094* (2,179)	.055* (1,861)	-.011 (985)	.084* (1,967)	.090* (2,167)	.115* (1,229)	-.169* (1217)
Priv E	Attachment to Israel	-.048* (2,284)	-.024 (1,953)	-.017 (1,048)	.040 (2,067)	.078* (2,269)	.041 (1,308)	-.067* (1,291)

Pub (mixed) Universal	.018 (2,246)	.014 (1,914)	-.052 (1,024)	-.012 (2,030)	-.003 (2,230)	.004 (1,285)	.001 (1,262)
Pub R Ceremony	-.104* (2,135)	.069* (1,837)	-.052 (1,026)	.107* (1,936)	.127* (2,123)	.182* (1,211)	-.182* (1199)
Pub E Exceptionalism	-.013 (2,016)	-.060* (1,818)	-.074* (889)	.001 (1,817)	-.047* (2,004)	-.020 (1,118)	.084* (1,964)
Pub E Organizations	-.048* (2,308)	.037 (1,970)	-.036 (1,056)	.031 (2,087)	.083* (2,293)	.077* (1,322)	-.168* (2,156)
Pub E Israel's role	-.013 (2,284)	.031 (1,953)	.031 (1,048)	.042 (2,067)	.047* (2,269)	.048 (1,308)	-.079* (1,299)

[a] Unweighted (n) in parentheses.

[b] Pub, public; Priv, private; R, religious; E, ethnic.

[c] Questions with high loading on each factor presented in Appendix, Table A-4.

*$p < .05$ (two-tailed) (in bold). Nonsignificant correlations italicized.

commitment to a universal moral heritage (as opposed to a particularistic identity) is not related significantly to any of the family behavior indicators. It is interesting that believing that American Jews are characterized by exceptionalism is related to non-familistic behavior more than to familistic behavior.

Looking at the correlations from the standpoint of the family behaviors themselves, we can see that some of the behaviors seem to be more closely related to expressions of Jewish identity than are others. Remaining in a stable marriage (not divorcing) and having more children are more strongly related to Jewish identity than are the other behaviors; age at birth of first child has the weakest relationship to the Jewish identity factors.

JEWISH IDENTITY, DENOMINATION, AND FAMILY BEHAVIOR
We wanted to know whether the denominations differed in family behavior even when we controlled for Jewish identity, and vice versa. That is, are denomination and Jewish identity two separate factors, or do they overlap so much that they cannot be distinguished? Note that we cannot entangle which comes first—types of Jewish identity, denominational preference, or family behavior—with the data we use.

To study the first direction of inquiry, we selected those Jewish identity factors that were significantly correlated with family behavior: from private expressions of Jewish identity—Activity (mixed religious and ethnic expressions of identity), Belief (religious), Tribalism (ethnic), and Culture (ethnic)—and from public expressions of Jewish identity—Ceremony (religious). We studied their relationship with age at marriage (for men and women separately) (Table 7.6), number of children (for women only) (Table 7.7),[4] and number of times married (for men and women separately) (Table 7.8). For each, family behavior was the dependent variable in a multiple regression, in which the identity factors, denomination (dummy variables for Orthodox, Conservative, Reform, and unaffiliated denominational groups, the excluded group being Reconstructionist), age, education, and the preceding family variables (e.g., age at marriage and age at first birth) were included as independent variables predicting number of children. It should be cautioned that while age cohort and completed education usually can be understood as preceding age at first marriage (as explained earlier), denominational affiliation and Jewish identity factors may themselves be influenced by family behavior, so that we cannot draw conclusions about the direction of causality. The regression analysis provides us with an understanding of the strength and independence of relationships, but not necessarily a prediction of family behavior. We confine our analysis to American Jews aged 45 and older, by which time most first marriages have already occurred.

Looking at the multiple regression analysis of age of marriage (Table 7.6), we present two models, one in which only the selected identity factors are entered, and another in which the identity factors, denominational variables, and demographic variables are entered. We see in model 1 that the ethnic factor of personal tribalistic attachment is related to the age of marriage of men, and religious belief or spirituality is related to the age of marriage of women. This is not surprising, given that women's religious identity is stronger than men's. When we control for denominational affiliation, age, and education, we see that for men, personal tribalistic attachment to the Jewish people continues to be significantly related to age at marriage, as is education—the Jewish identity factor being somewhat more important than education in its relationship to age at marriage (seen by comparing the standardized regression coefficients: 0.107 for Tribalism and 0.080 for education). Note that the two are related in opposite directions: the stronger the tribalistic attachment to Jews, the earlier the age at marriage; the higher the level of education, the later the age at marriage. Among women, religious belief has the strongest relationship to age at marriage (the stronger the religious belief, the earlier the age at marriage); education also has a statistically significant relationship with age at marriage (the higher the level of education, the later the age at marriage). Age cohort is also related, reflecting the fact that the older cohorts of women married at a younger age. For women, being Orthodox has a weakly significant relationship ($p = 0.064$) with age at marriage, independent of identity and demographic factors.

Thus, we see that expressions of private Jewish identity are related to age at marriage, independently of denominational factors or demographic factors. However, denomination is only weakly related to age at marriage once the identity factors have been controlled for, and then only for women. We also see that, for men, personal ethnic identity is related to age at marriage, whereas for women, it is their personal religious identity that is related to age at marriage.

We next consider to what extent Jewish identity and denomination explained the variation in a woman's age at the birth of her first child (Table 7.7). When we analyzed age at birth of first child earlier, using only denominational preferences as independent variables (Table 7.3), we were not able to explain much of the variation. The Jewish identity factors explain somewhat more, though still only a fraction of the variation. The two religious factors Belief and Ceremony appear to have the strongest correlation with age at marriage. When, however, we control for denomination, age, age at first marriage, and level of education (model 2, Table 7.7), the picture changes. The relationship between Belief and age at first marriage virtually disappears, while the ethnic factors of personal attachment to the Jewish people (Tribalism) and attachment to Jewish culture (Culture) have stronger

Table 7.6 Multiple Regression of Age at First Marriage for Jewish American Men and Women (Ages 45 and Over)[a]

Independent variable	Men				Women			
	Model 1		Model 2		Model 1		Model 2	
Jewish identity factor:								
Activity	−0.420	(−.068)	−0.273	(−.076)	−0.354	(−.061)	−0.345	(−.063)
Tribalism	0.487	(.077)	0.566	(.089)**	−0.015	(−.002)	−0.362	(−.057)
Belief	0.278	(.038)	0.239	(.040)	1.093	(.178)*	0.868	(.141)*
Ceremony	−0.010	(−.002)	0.084	(.014)	0.103	(.017)	0.281	(.046)
Culture	0.488	(.078)**	0.595	(.095)*	−0.315	(−.054)	−0.091	(−.016)
Denominational Preference:								
Orthodox[b]			1.441	(.080)**			−1.233	(−.059)**
Conservative[b]			0.726	(.052)			−0.057	(−.005)
Reform[b]			0.615	(.046)			−0.177	(−.015)
Unaffiliated[b]			0.193	(.014)			0.268	(.021)
Age			0.010	(.019)			−0.039	(−.083)
Education			0.431	(.090)*			0.433	(.093)*
R			.121	.162			.144	.206
R²	.015		.026		.021		.042	
(Unweighted *n*)				(774)				(994)

*p < 0.05; ** p < 0.10.

[a]Data are unstandardized coefficients and (in parentheses) standardized coefficients, ß.

[b]Using dummy variables, 0 represents "does not identify with denomination"; 1 represents "identifies with denomination." The category "Reconstructionist" was omitted.

relationships; the religious factor Ceremony retains a weak relationship (significant at *p* < 0.10) with age at birth of first child. Being Orthodox continues to have an independent weak relationship with age at birth of first child, and apparently it subsumes the effect of personal religiosity. The most important relationships with age at birth of first child are education (standardized coefficient of 0.602) and age at first marriage (standardized coefficient of 0.212). Thus, being Orthodox and personal religious belief have an indirect effect on age at birth of first chld, through their relationship to age at first marriage (which we saw in Table 7.6), but ethnic identity factors become important in determining age at birth of first child as well.

We next considered number of children born (right side of Table 7.7). In the first model, only the Jewish identity factors are included as dependent variables. In model 2, we add to the regression model denominational preferences, age, education, age at first marriage, and age at birth of first child. In the first regression model, three of the Jewish identity factors are related significantly to number of children born: personal tribalistic attachment to the Jewish people (Tribalism), the personal religious factor (Belief), and the public religious factor of collective ritual (Ceremony). The stronger each type of Jewish identity, the more children the woman has. This suggests that the relationship between fertility and Jewish identity is based on both religious and ethnic, private and public considerations. Controlling for denominational preference in model 2 eliminates many of the independent relationships between fertility and Jewish identity; only the religious factor Ceremony retains a significant relationship. Each of

Table 7.7 Multiple Regression of Age at Birth of First Child and Number of Live Births for American Jewish Women (Ages 45 and Over)[a]

Independent variable	Age at birth of first child				Number of live births			
	Model 1		Model 2		Model 1		Model 2	
Jewish identity factor								
Activity	0.072	(.015)	0.245	(.049)	0.001	(.000)	0.016	(.012)
Tribalism	−0.286	(−.053)	−0.612	(−.113)*	−0.143	(−.102)*	−0.067	(−.048)
Belief	0.777	(.147)*	−0.147	(−.028)	−0.130	(−.095)*	−0.011	(−.048)
Ceremony	−0.513	(−.097)*	−0.301	(−.057)**	−0.092	(−.068)**	−0.182	(−.134)*
Culture	−0.092	(−.018)	0.419	(.083)**	−0.047	(−.037)	−0.074	(−.054)
Denominational preference								
Orthodox[b]			−0.850	(−.047)**			0.531	(.125)*
Conservative[b]			0.237	(.022)			−0.231	(−.084)*
Reform[b]			0.043	(.004)			−0.236	(−.089)*
Unaffiliated[b]			0.224	(.020)			−0.297	(−.102)*
Age			−0.019	(−.046)**			0.012	(.111)*
Age at Marriage			0.854	(.212)*			−0.027	(−.122)*
Education			0.519	(.602)*			−0.051	(−.049)
Age at birth of first child							−0.057	(−.222)*
R	.147		.679		.236		.460	
R²	.021		.453		.056		.201	
(Unweighted *n*)		(919)				(919)		

*$p < 0.05$; ** $p < 0.10$.
[a]Data are unstandardized coefficients and (in parentheses) standardized coefficients, ß.
[b]Using dummy variables, o represents "does not identify with denomination"; 1 represents "identifies with denomination." The category "Reconstructionist" was omitted.

the denominational groups has independent relationships with fertility (Orthodox women having more children than Conservative, Reform, and unaffiliated women). The strongest effect on fertility is the age at which the woman began having children. Age at first marriage also has a significant relationship to fertility, as does age cohort (older cohorts having more children). Note that the independent relationship between education and number of children is apparently eliminated when age at first marriage and age at birth of first child are controlled for.

We can conclude that women's family behavior is certainly related to the norms of their preferred denominational groups, while the identity factors are also related to age at first marriage and age at birth of first child.

Table 7.8 Multiple Regression of Number of Times Married for American Jewish Men and Women (Ages 45 and Over)[a]

Independent variable	Men		Women	
	Model 1	Model 2	Model 1	Model 2
Jewish identity factor				
Activity	0.025 (.043)	0.019 (.034)	0.013 (.033)	0.000 (.001)
Tribalism	0.065 (.111)*	0.079 (.135)*	0.085 (.143)*	0.070 (.118)*
Belief	−0.024 (−.038)	−0.010 (−.018)	−0.016 (−.028)	−0.004 (−.007)
Ceremony	0.036 (.065)	0.039 (.071)	0.015 (.026)	0.024 (.042)
Culture	−0.021 (−.036)	−0.057 (−.012)	0.006 (.010)	−0.005 (−.004)
Denominational preference				
Orthodox[b]		0.029 (.016)		0.100 (.051)
Conservative[b]		0.018 (.014)		0.006 (.005)
Reform[b]		−0.060 (−.049)		0.064 (.057)
Unaffiliated[b]		−0.074 (−.058)		0.070 (.057)
Age		0.000 (.006)		−0.002 (−.038)
Education		0.015 (.035)		−0.002 (−.004)
Age at first marriage		−0.012 (−.128)*		−0.018 (−.191)*
R	.148	.205	.166	.259
R^2	.022	.042	.028	.067
(Unweighted *n*)	(774)		(994)	

*$p < 0.05$.

[a]Data are unstandardized coefficients and (in parentheses) standardized coefficients, ß.

[b]Using dummy variables, 0 represents "does not identify with denomination"; 1 represents "identifies with denomination." The category "Reconstructionist" was omitted.

Our inability to determine causality is even more apparent when we look at the multiple regression analysis of number of times married (Table 7.8). For both men and women, early age at marriage is a strong predictor of multiple times married. This is no surprise, as early age at marriage is associated with the likelihood of divorce. None of the denominational groups have significant relationships with number of times married. Having a strong tribalistic attachment to the Jewish people is, however, associated with fewer times married. But this may reflect weaker integration into the Jewish community of those who have remarried, particularly if the remarriage is an intermarriage. Indeed, when we enter an additional independent variable, of whether or not the current spouse is Jewish, the significant relationship with any Jewish identity factor disappears for both men and women. Therefore, number of times married does not appear to be directly related to the strength of Jewish identity or denominational grouping.

SUMMARY AND CONCLUSIONS

We began the chapter by asking how denomination and Jewish identity are related to family behavior among American Jewish men and women. Concentrating first on denominational differences in family behavior, we confirmed previous research and anecdotal evidence that Orthodox Jews are more familistic in their behavior (are more likely to marry, to marry at a younger age, to have children at younger ages, to have more children, and to remain in their first marriages) than are men and women in the other denominational groups and that the unaffiliated group demonstrates the least familistic behavior. In fact, this is quite a paradox. In Chapter 3, we showed three main ways in which the family behavior of American Jews is distinct from that of the broader white population, even when education is controlled for: they marry later, they are less likely to divorce, and they have fewer children. Yet these very characteristics that distinguish American Jewish family behavior from that of the broader white population in the United States are the opposite of the characteristics that distinguish those who are strongly identified with being Jewish from those who are not; similarly, those most traditional in terms of denominational affiliation do not share all of the characteristics that distinguish American Jews from the broader white U.S. population.

Being less likely to divorce does characterize Orthodox Jews compared with non-Orthodox Jews and those more strongly identified with both Jewish ritual behavior and Jewish ethnic identification. However, the Orthodox and those more strongly identified with being Jewish are more likely to marry younger and to have more children. In fact, Orthodox women are much more like women in the broader U.S. white population than are women of other denominational groups in terms of age at marriage, average number of children, and proportion having four or more children.

Because the Orthodox are a minority among American Jews, their more familistic behavior does not define the distinctiveness of American Jews compared with the broader U.S. population. However, the familistic tendencies associated with strong Jewish identity explain some of the anomalies found in our comparison with the broader population. Although American Jews marry later and have smaller families, commensurate with their higher educational level, they have more stable marriages and are less likely to remain childless even when they are highly educated. Hence, the centrality of the family among American Jews persists.

A second issue that we addressed in this chapter is whether contemporary family behavior, to the extent that it is related to Jewish identity, is more closely related to ethnic or to religious expressions of Jewish identity. By using ethnic and religious, private and public indices of Jewish identity, we sought to disentangle the relationships between family behavior and various types of Jewish identity. First, we found that expressions of private Jewish identity are more closely related to family behavior than are expressions of public Jewish identity. This finding reinforces the close association persisting between family and religion in the private sphere that we mentioned earlier. An exception was the relationship between family behavior and public religious Jewish identity, much of which involves families participating in communal settings.

Second, we found that religious identity was more closely related to some family behavior of women, whereas ethnic identity was more closely related to some family behavior of men. Thus, age at first marriage was related to men's ethnic identity and women's religious identity; for women, age at birth of first child and number of children were related to both religious and ethnic identity; and number of times married was related to ethnic identity for both men and women. Fertility is also related to denominational preference (independent of expressions of Jewish identity), which we suggest is related to the norms of family size in a the woman's surrounding (Jewish) community.

We also found that some family behavior appears to influence religious identity more than the other way around. Thus, the relationship between ethnic feelings of attachment to the Jewish people appears to be weakened by multiple marriages, particularly when the spouse in the second or subsequent marriages is not Jewish. This reciprocal relationship between Jewish identity and family behavior, and between denominational preference and family behavior as well, calls for a more complex research design that can disentangle the reciprocal effects more systematically. Cohen and

Eisen's (2000) qualitative research is a step in this direction, though it was not designed specifically to disentangle the various types of religious and ethnic identity and their respective relationships to family behavior.

Just as Jewish identity and denominational preference are related to familistic behavior, age cohort and education retain similar relationships with family behavior, as they do in the broader population. So religious and ethnic influences on family behavior appear to coexist—or even compete—with other social influences, sometimes being more important, sometimes as important, and sometimes less important. Also, patterns of familistic behavior have a significant effect on subsequent familistic behavior. Thus, early marriage, which is related to Jewish identity and, for women, being Orthodox, has a strong effect on age at birth of first child, and age at birth of first child has the strongest effect on a woman's fertility. Thus, the effects of Jewish identity on family behavior are not only direct, but also indirect, through its past influences on family behavior, augmenting its importance.

An important conclusion from this analysis is the persisting influence of American Jewish religious and ethnic identity, which often overlaps with denominational preference and norms, on the family behavior of both men and women.

CHAPTER 8

How Jewishness is Related to Gendered Patterns of Secular Achievement

We saw in the preceding chapter that Jewishness is related to variation in family behavior, and we were able to isolate some particular elements of Jewishness that are related to such variation. The most striking variation is that the family behavior of Orthodox Jews is very different from that of the other denominational groups, and we could trace some of the reasons for this difference. The difference could be explained partly by demographic features (such as age and age at marriage) and partly by strength of religious Jewish identity, expressed by the Orthodox in their commitment to halachic ritual and religious belief. Family situation also seemed to be closely related to affiliation or lack thereof.

In this chapter we turn to secular achievement—education, labor force participation, occupational achievement, and occupational rewards (occupational prestige, annual earnings)—and again ask whether any of the patterns of secular achievement are related to different expressions of "Jewishness." In Chapters 3 to 5, we considered whether Jewish secular achievement patterns were distinct from those of the broader U.S. population. Here we ask whether Jewish secular achievement varies in ways that are consonant with different expressions of Jewishness, as presented in Chapter 6. By focusing on this relationship, we address the question of whether investment in Jewish "cultural capital," "religious capital," "ethnic capital," or "social capital" might be related to patterns of secular achievement. The literature that has linked the high educational and occupational achievement of Jews to "cultural particularity" and Jewish social networking (summarized in Burstein, 2007) suggests that there is a link between at least certain aspects of Jewish identity and educational and economic achievement. Hurst and Mott (2006) suggest that men and women who have "moderate" Jewish religious connections and behaviors (as opposed to connections that are extremely particularistic or observant, on the one hand, or extremely secular, on the other) have higher secular achievement. In this chapter we hope to shed further light on this relationship and the patterns of gender (in)equality in educational and labor force achievement. We build on our earlier research based on the 1990 National Jewish Population Survey (Hartman and Hartman, 1996a, 1996b). In this work, we found that Jewishness was related to higher education among both men and women, but that the relationship between labor force activity and Jewishness differed for men and women. Married Jewish men tended to work longer hours, as providers; married Jewish women curtailed their labor force participation and consequently had lower occupational achievement:

> Apparently Jewish involvement, because of the Jewish familial orientation, increases the gender differentiation in the family, which in turn affects the relationship between gender and labor force participation. This gender differentiation in turn affects occupational achievement. Jewishness, however, is not directly related to labor force participation or to occupational achievement; that is, there seem to be no proscriptions of women's secular achievement, only a positive value attached to family life, which has its own effect on secular achievement. (Hartman and Hartman, 1996a, pp. 247–48)

Inquiry into the relationship between secular behavior and Jewishness is important not only from a Jewish standpoint, but in terms of understanding the role that religion and ethnicity play more generally in contemporary society. Although the classical "secularization thesis," which posited a decline of religion in the contemporary world, has largely been debunked, the interpretation of secularization as a disjunction between religion and secular behavior, especially in the public arena, has to a greater extent been validated (see discussions in Christiano, Swatos, and Kivisto, 2002, ch. 3, and Furseth and Repstad, 2006, ch. 5). Yet it too has been plagued by contradictions, such as the impact of religion on politics, and religion's impact on gender roles in the economy. Although with our data set we cannot uncover the mechanisms of influence, we can determine the extent to which the secular and religious or ethnic arenas are related for American Jews. Furthermore, we can determine whether it is the "private" or "public" expressions of Jewish identity that are more strongly related to public economic behavior.

Because we have separate measures of ethnic and religious identity, we can also address the question of whether religious or ethnic Jewish identity has a stronger relation to secular achievement. Because of secularization, it may be that religious identity has less to do with secular achievement than does ethnic identity, which involves both cultural and social ethnic capital, conceivably more helpful in terms of educational achievement and the labor market.

We are limited in that we cannot tell which came first—Jewish identity or secular behavior (or whether they are mutually reinforcing), and actually we have little knowledge in general of how Jewish identity changes over the life course (Horowitz, 2000, has shown us the importance of such a longitudinal perspective). So we are looking at the relationship between secular achievement and Jewish identity rather than the impact of one on the other. It could well be, for example, that secular education changes Jewish identity or vice versa, that certain occupations are accompanied by lifestyles that reinforce or undermine religious or ethnic contacts and identity, and that certain types of Jewish identity facilitate certain kinds of occupations or occupational lifestyles. This analysis also lets us reexamine the "structural location" hypothesis regarding gender differences in religious identity, that is, whether women who have secular positions similar to those of men have similar Jewish identity or continue to have stronger Jewish identity. But again, we cannot test the causal effect, only the relationship.

We begin by looking at variations in achievement by denominational identification, and then we examine how secular achievement is related to various expressions of Jewish identity. We consider gender equality in achievement within the various subgroups of American Jews in this chapter, and within married couples in Chapter 9.

One way in which denominations differ that is relevant to this inquiry is the extent to which integration into the broader society is promoted (both structurally and ideologically). Ideologically, the denominations promote greater or lesser integration with the broader non-Jewish community, with the most particularistic being the Orthodox and the least being the Reform groups, which have aspired to diminish the differences between Jews and the broader community; however, Conservative denominations also promote integration into the broader community while also preserving a strong particularistic Jewish identity. There is also a sizable minority of Jews who do not identify with any of the main American Jewish denominations, who have been categorized in our analysis as "unaffiliated." They are expected to be the least separate from the broader population and, in this analysis, to have the least dissimilarity in occupational distribution. The degree of particularism or separation from the broader society may influence which reference group provides the most salient norms of secular achievement and gender equality in such achievement, both within families and in the general patterns of American Jews.

Denomination, as we have already suggested, also reflects how traditional the orientation to Jewishness is, the extent to which it accommodates secularity or modernity, and how demanding it is in terms of particularistic obligation or commitment. Jewishness is by no means monolithic—that is, there is much variation within denominations, and much overlap as well, especially since denominational affiliation may be quite fluid (see, e.g, Hartman and Hartman, 1999, based on 1991 New York data). Nevertheless, denominational categories are often used to denote variation between American Jews and therefore are useful to examine. They are important to look at from a practical standpoint also; that is, by describing differences between denominational groups, we may help denominational leaders to understand their affiliates (or, in this case, at least those who identify with their denomination).

But as we have seen, denomination does not capture the "messy nuances" of variation in Jewish identity (Mayer, 2001), and our multiple measures of Jewish identity are a step in that direction. By considering later in the chapter whether ethnic or religious, public or private expressions of Jewish identity are most related to secular behaviors, and how they interact with denominational preferences, we come closer to understanding the persistent ties of religion to contemporary secular behavior, and the roles of Jewish and ethnic identity in promoting or mitigating gender equality in secular achievement.

DENOMINATIONAL DIFFERENCES IN THE EDUCATION OF AMERICAN JEWS

We confine our analysis to men and women aged 25–64, so that on the young end of our sample spectrum we will not be confounding the results with students still completing their education, and on the older end we will not be confounding the results with the different patterns of educational attainment we saw earlier for those 65 and over (especially women). We see in Table 8.1 that there are differences in educational attainment between the denominations: the Orthodox have the lowest proportion with college degrees, slightly more than half, followed by the unaffiliated, with slightly more than 60%, whereas more than 70% of Conservatives and Reform/Reconstructionists have college degrees. This pattern of difference is similar for men and women, although in each denomination men have a higher education than women. The denominational difference is not just a result of the age composition of the denominational groups, or of the tendency among Orthodox Jews to marry at a younger age than Jews in other groups: in a multiple regression of educational achievement (not shown here), educational variation is significantly related (negatively) to being Orthodox or unaffiliated (for men), even when age and age at first marriage are controlled for, and is positively related to age (the older having higher

Table 8.1 Educational Attainment, Educational Dissimilarity between Genders, and Educational Dissimilarity from Broader Population (Ages 25–64)

Denomination	B.A. or higher (%)			Dissimilarity between men and women's educational attainment	Dissimilarity between denominational group and non-Hispanic white U.S. population	
	Total	Men	Women		Men	Women
Orthodox	55.1 (196)[a]	58.7 (104)	50.8 (92)	9.5	32.3	29.9
Conservative	70.0 (695)	74.1 (277)	66.9 (418)	15.5	47.7	44.8
Reform/ Reconstructionist	74.5 (867)	79.6 (346)	69.9 (521)	13.1	53.2	49.1
Unaffiliated	62.9 (633)	64.8 (294)	60.8 (339)	4.7	38.4	39.9

Data sources: NJPS, 2000–01; U.S. Census, 2000.

[a]Unweighted *n* in parentheses; calculations performed using person-weights provided with dataset.

educational achievement) and age at first marriage (the older one is at the time of one's first marriage, the higher the educational achievement). Among women, being Orthodox is significantly related to lower educational achievement, even when age and age at first marriage are controlled for; being younger and marrying at an older age are related to higher educational achievement.

The denominational variation in education results in the unaffiliated and the Orthodox being the least dissimilar from the broader white U.S. population; the Conservative and the Reform/Reconstructionist groups show the greatest dissimilarity.[1] The low degree of dissimilarity between the unaffiliated and the broader population is actually the only finding that is consonant with our expectations: if the unaffiliated can be considered more marginal to the Jewish community, we would expect them to be least differentiated from the broader population. That a higher proportion of unaffiliated are intermarried reinforces this expectation (see also Chapter 10). That they are joined in this low degree of dissimilarity by the Orthodox, however, does not conform to the explanation of Jewish distinctiveness as marginality or as integration into the broader society.

In terms of gender difference, we expected that the more egalitarian the denomination in terms of religious roles, the greater the similarity would be between men and women in terms of their educational attainment. However, this was not what we found. First of all, there is not much dissimilarity between men and women in any denomination: dissimilarity coefficients between men and women's educational distribution within any denomination do not exceed 15.5% who would have to change their education in order for men's and women's distributions to be similar. The highest coefficients of dissimilarity between men and women within a denomination are found among the Conservatives and the Reform/Reconstructionists, presumably because more of the men go on to get doctoral and professional degrees than do women. The lowest degree of dissimilarity is found between men and women among the unaffiliated and the Orthodox. The latter is similar to a finding of 1990—greater gender equality regarding education and occupation among the Orthodox than among other denominational groups (Hartman and Hartman, 1996a)—and recalls the historical roots of gender equality in Jewish secular achievement that we discussed earlier.

DENOMINATIONAL DIFFERENCES IN LABOR FORCE PARTICIPATION

Overall, there are few differences in labor force participation rates between the denominations, with the overall labor force participation rate for those aged 25–64 hovering around 80%. The same is true when we compare men in different denominational groups, the labor force participation rate hovering around 87% (Figure 8.1). However, when we compare women, we see that the Orthodox women have the lowest labor force participation rate. As a result, the ratio of female to male participation in the labor force is lower for the Orthodox (71%) than for the other denominational groups (82–89%).

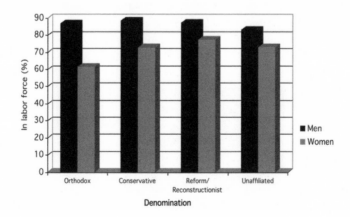

Figure 8.1. Percentage in labor force (ages 25–64), by gender and denomination.

Even more striking are the denominational differences in full-time employment of women (Figure 8.2). Slightly more than half of Orthodox women are employed full time, compared with around 70% of Conservative and Reform/Reconstructionist women and nearly 80% of the unaffiliated.

Is the reason Orthodox women are less likely to be employed full time that they have more and younger children at home or that they are less likely to have a college degree? The multiple regression analysis presented in Table 8.2 addresses this question. Hours of employment is the predicted variable; the independent variables are education (highest degree achieved), age at first marriage, and age at birth of first child (to indicate how early family roles were entered), current marital status, age of youngest child under 18 in the household, and number of children under 18 in the household (to indicate current childcare and marital obligations); age is controlled for to adjust for any cohort or life-cycle variation above and beyond education and family characteristics.

When we control for education (model 1), being Orthodox or Conservative does not have an independent effect on hours of work; being Reform or unaffiliated is significantly associated with more hours of work, even when education is controlled for. However, once we control for family characteristics (model 2), none of the denominational groups have independent relationships with hours of work. Comparing the unstandardized regression coefficients of model 1 and model 2 shows that the relationship between each of the denominational groups and hours of employment decreases considerably when family characteristics are controlled for. The only significant relationships are between hours of employment and current marital status (married women are employed fewer hours) and number of children under 18 in the household (the more young children, the fewer the hours the mother is employed)—both practical influences (non-married women need to support themselves; young children are more likely to need a caregiver in the home,

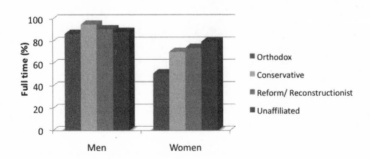

Figure 8.2. Percentage employed full time (ages 25–64), by gender and denomination.

Table 8.2 Multiple Regression Analysis of Hours of Employment for American Jewish Women (Ages 25–64)[a]

Independent variable	Model 1		Model 2	
Orthodox[b]	−0.094	(−.062)	−0.029	(−.019)
Conservative[b]	0.084	(.062)	0.040	(.037)
Reform[b]	0.127	(.130)**	0.064	(.066)
Unaffiliated[b]	0.150	(.131)*	0.074	(.065)
Education	0.000	(.001)	0.001	(.002)
Age at first marriage			0.005	(.047)
Age at birth of first child			0.002	(.021)
Current marital status			−0.168	(−.148)*
Age of youngest child under 18 in household			0.005	(.106)
Number of children under 18 in household			−0.070	(−.172)*
R	.152		.305	
R^2	.023		.093	
(Unweighted n)	(586)			

* $p < 0.05$; ** $p < 0.10$.
[a]Data are unstandardized coefficients and (in parentheses) standardized coefficients, ß.
[b]Using dummy variables, 0 represents "does not identify with denomination"; 1 represents "identifies with denomination." The category "Reconstructionist" was omitted.

which often makes it economically impractical for one of the parents to work full time). Thus, education, marital status, and number of children under 18 in the household appear to explain the denominational differences in the number of hours women are employed. These are more important than familistic indications such as age at first marriage, age at birth of first child, or age of youngest child, which are also included in the model.

DENOMINATION AND OCCUPATION

Next we turn to denominational differences in the occupations of men and women. Given the slight differences in educational attainment between the denominations, we might expect somewhat different occupational distributions. We might also expect greater similarity between the occupations of men and women in the more egalitarian denominations (Reform/Reconstructionist) and the least similarity among the Orthodox (although our findings in 1990 suggested greater occupational similarity between Orthodox men and women than in other denominations).

Although there are commonalities in the occupational distributions across denominational groups, there are also differences within each gender

(Table 8.3). Among the men, the most common types of occupation are professional; sales and management executive are the next most common; technical and service occupations are the least common in all denominational groups of men. While there is a higher proportion of managers/executives among Conservative and Reform/Reconstructionist men than among the Orthodox or unaffiliated, dissimilarity coefficients between men in different denominations do not exceed 13.5, which indicates strong similarity across all denominational groups (less than 14% of men in each denomination would have to change their occupations for all of the denominations to have identical occupational distributions).

There is a similar pattern of consistency among women: professional occupations are the most common, followed by management/executive, sales, and occupational support. Among the Orthodox, however, more than half of employed women have professional occupations, in contrast to about 40% of women in the other groups. As a result, the highest degree of dissimilarity is between Orthodox and Conservative women, at 17.3; the dissimilarity coefficients between women in other denominational groups do not exceed 11.9 (indicating that less than 12% of women in one denominational group would have to change occupations to have an occupational distribution identical to that of women in another group, using the broad occupational categories).

Comparing the occupations of men and women in each denomination, we find the greatest degree of dissimilarity among the Orthodox (17.1) and the Reform/Reconstructionists (16.5). In these two groups there is a disproportionate percentage of women in the professions, compared with men. In the Conservative and unaffiliated groups, the distributions of men's and women's occupations are more similar.

Looking at more detailed occupations, we can compare the top 10 (detailed) occupations (with the highest proportion employed in each denomination) in each denominational group. We see that there is quite a bit of overlap between the denominations (Table 8.4). Among men, 6 of the top 10 occupations are shared by all denominational groups; 9 of 10 occupations in the non-Orthodox groups are shared by at least one other group. It is the Orthodox who differ the most from the other denominations, with 3 of their top 10 occupations not appearing in the other groups: sales representatives, wholesale and manufacturing (although retail salespersons appears in all denominations); directors of religious activities and education; and butchers, meat, poultry, fish (presumably at kosher facilities).

There is a similarly consistent pattern among women: half of the top 10 occupations are common to all denominational groups (teachers, retail

Table 8.3 Occupational Distribution for American Jews (Ages 25–64) by Denomination and Gender[a]

	Orthodox	Conservative	Reform/ Reconstructionist	Unaffiliated
Men				
Management/executive	10.3	15.2	13.7	9.0
Business/finance	7.5	12.1	8.1	4.9
Professional	38.0	37.4	39.2	42.2
Technical	1.7	3.8	2.5	3.8
Service	2.5	2.2	3.1	5.4
Sales	12.5	14.1	17.6	19.1
Office/ administrative support	6.7	3.7	3.1	3.4
Blue collar	8.8	4.7	5.7	5.0
Other	12.0	6.7	7.1	7.1
Total	100.0	100.0	100.0	100.0
Women				
Management/executive	9.3	15.3	12.2	10.2
Business/finance	4.6	8.1	5.6	5.1
Professional	53.4	36.2	43.1	41.0
Technical	2.4	3.3	5.0	4.8
Service	1.9	0.8	5.2	5.6
Sales	12.8	11.6	11.2	13.7
Office/ administrative support	11.8	13.6	12.6	13.4
Blue collar	0.6	3.5	1.1	2.0
Other	3.1	7.5	4.1	4.2
Total	100.0	100.0	100.0	100.0
Dissimilarity coefficient between men and women's occupations	17.1	10.4	16.5	11.1

[a]Data are percentages.

salespersons, managers, and secretaries), and another 4 occupations occur in three denominational groups (lodging managers, registered nurses, lawyers, and office clerks). Again, it is the Orthodox who are the most highly differentiated from the other denominational groups, with 5 occupations that do not appear in the top 10 of the other groups: secondary school teachers, preschool and kindergarten teachers (although other teachers are in all groups), bookkeepers (although accountants appear in other groups), computer scientists, and occupational therapists.

Table 8.4 Top Ten Occupations of American Jewish Men and Women by Denominational Preference[a]

	Orthodox	Conservative	Reform/Reconstructionist	Unaffiliated
Men	Retail salespersons (6.3)	Physicians and surgeons (6.7)	Retail salespersons (10.8)	Retail salespersons (12.3)
	Other teachers and instructors (5.7)	Retail salespersons (6.6)	Lawyers (7.3)	Computer programmers (4.9)
	Accountants/auditors (5.1)	Accountants/auditors (6.5)	Chief executives (4.1)	Other teachers and instructors (4.2)
	Computer programmers (5.0)	Managers, all other (6.1)	Other teachers and instructors (4.0)	Chief executives (3.9)
	Engineers, all other (4.3)	Lawyers (5.8)	Physicians and surgeons (3.9)	Engineers, all other (3.2)
	Sales Representatives, wholesale and manufacturing (3.1)	Management analysts (4.8)	Managers, all other (3.3)	Postsecondary teachers (3.0)
	Lawyers (3.0)	Engineers, all other (3.2)	Management analysts (3.0)	Accountants/auditors (2.0)
	Directors, religious activities and education (2.9)	Real estate brokers/sales agents (3.0)	Engineers, all other (3.0)	Physicians and surgeons (2.8)
	Managers, all other (2.4)	Chief executives (3.0)	Real estate brokers/sales agents (2.5)	Managers, all other (2.6)
	Butchers, meat, poultry, fish procesing workers (2.3)	Driver/sales workers and truck drivers (2.7)	Post-secondary teachers (2.4)	Medical assistants/health support (2.4)

Women			
Elementary and middle school teachers (16.8)	Retail salespersons (7.8)	Retail salespersons (5.7)	Retail salespersons (7.6)
Retail salespersons (9.5)	Elementary and middle school teachers (5.9)	Other teachers and instructors (4.9)	Secretaries, administrative assistants (5.8)
Other teachers and instructors (7.5)	Lodging managers (4.9)	Elementary and middle school teachers (4.2)	Other teachers and instructors (5.7)
Managers, all other (5.1)	Accountants/auditors (4.2)	Managers, all other (3.5)	Managers, all other (5.6)
Secondary school teachers (5.1)	Other teachers and instructors (4.2)	Office clerks, general (3.3)	Elementary and middle school teachers (4.8)
Preschool and kindergarten teachers (5.0)	Office clerks, general (4.1)	Registered nurses (3.1)	Social workers (3.7)
Bookkeeping, accounting, auditing clerks (3.3)	Managers, all other (3.8)	Lodging managers (3.0)	Office clerks, general (2.8)
Secretaries, administrative assistants (3.1)	Registered nurses (3.3)	Lawyers (3.0)	Registered nurses (2.7)
Computer scientists, systems analysts (3.0)	Secretaries, administrative assistants (3.2)	Social workers (3.0)	Sales and related workers, all other (2.6)
Occupational therapists (2.9)	Lawyers (3.1)	Secondary school teachers	Lawyers (2.2)

▮ Occupation occurs in two columns only.   ▮ Occupation occurs in one column only.

[a] Percentage of total occupational distribution in that gender and denomination in parentheses.

Between the men and women in each denominational group, there is an overlap of only 3 or 4 occupations. Physicians and surgeons, which are in the top 10 occupations of three of the men's denominational groups, do not appear in the top 10 occupations of any of the women's groups, nor do chief executives, real estate brokers/sales agents, post-secondary teachers, or engineers. In the women's groups but not the men's are lodging managers; registered nurses; secretaries; office clerks; secondary school, elementary/middle school, and preschool/kindergarten teachers; and social workers. It seems that gender differences in specific occupations persist across all denominations

The denominational groups show much more similarity to each other than to the broader population, among both men and women. Overall, the denominations show little variation in their dissimilarity from the broader white population (Table 8.5). In all of the denominational groups and the unaffiliated, slightly more than a third would need to change occupations to have occupations similar to those of the broader white population. Among men, only the Orthodox show a slightly greater degree of similarity (dissimilarity coefficient, 37.7) to the broader population than the Conservative, Reform, or unaffiliated groups (dissimilarity coefficients, 43.3, 42.1, and 43.2, respectively). The younger age and somewhat lower educational level of the Orthodox in the NJPS sample, compared with the Conservative, Reform, and unaffiliated, may account for this difference. Among the women, the Orthodox are somewhat less similar (dissimilarity coefficient, 39.0) to the broader female population than are the Conservative, Reform, or unaffiliated (33.1, 31.1, 29.2, respectively). This is because, as we have seen, there is an especially high proportion of Orthodox women in professional occupations (55%), compared with women in the other denominations and in the broader population of white women.

Because of the great disparity in education between Jews and the broader white population, we also looked at differences in occupational distribution, among those with college degrees only, between each denomination and the broader population (based on the occupational distributions in Table A-5 of the Appendix). Here there is somewhat more variation. Among the men, it is the unaffiliated who stand out, with a dissimilarity coefficient of 26.0, compared with dissimilarity coefficients of 15.0, 16.8, and 14.0 among the Orthodox, Conservative, and Reform, respectively. In comparison with their affiliated counterparts with college degrees, relatively fewer unaffiliated men are employed in management or business and finance, and relatively more unaffiliated men are in sales. As men with college degrees in the broader white population are more likely to be in management and somewhat less likely to be in sales than are Jewish men with college degrees, this increases the difference

Table 8.5 Occupational Dissimilarity Coefficients between American Jews and Non-Hispanic Whites (Ages 25 andOver) by Gender, Education, and Denominational Preference

Denomination	Total		B.A.+	
	Men	Women	Men	Women
Orthodox	37.7	39.0	15.0	28.6
Conservative	43.3	33.1	16.8	11.7
Reform/Reconstructionist	42.1	31.1	14.0	9.0
Unaffiliated	43.2	29.2	26.0	13.5

Data sources: U.S. Census, 2000; NJPS, 2000–01.

in occupational distribution for the unaffiliated. Among women with college degrees, the Orthodox are particularly different from their counterparts in the broader population, resulting from a high proportion of college-educated Orthodox women (more than 78%) with professional occupations, compared with only 58% of their counterparts in the broader population. There is a lower percentage of college-educated Orthodox women than of college-educated women from other groups in sales occupations.

DENOMINATION AND OCCUPATIONAL REWARDS

The occupational differences just described result in significant income differences between the various denominations among men but not women (Table 8.6). Among men, the highest earnings are found among Conservatives and Reform/Reconstructionists; the unaffiliated and Orthodox have lower incomes. When we consider only those who are employed full time, the unaffiliated achieve considerably lower earnings than the Orthodox. There is much less variation in women's earnings; among women who are employed full time, Orthodox women achieve higher earnings than non-Orthodox women (but because they are a relatively small group, this difference does not result in a statistically significant analysis of variance).

The higher the men's income, the lower is the ratio of women's to men's income. Among the Orthodox, the ratio changes considerably when we compare the total with those employed full time, indicating that much of the gender difference in income in this group results from the greater tendency for Orthodox women to work part time. Among full-time employees, women make nearly 85% of what men make, quite high even compared with the broader U.S. population. In the other groups, controlling for full-time employment does not alter the comparison of men's with women's income: for Conservatives and Reform/Reconstructionists, women make about half of men's earnings; unaffiliated women make about two-thirds.

The denominational differences in income disappear when education, marital status, and number of children at home are controlled for. In the multiple regression of annual earnings presented in Table 8.7, dummy variables for each of the main denominations are entered (the omitted category is Reconstructionist), whereas age, education, current marital status, and number of children under 18 in the household are controlled for. We can see that denominational differences in income are not statistically significant. The main explanatory variables for income differences are education, age, and, for men, number of children in the household: the higher the education, the higher the earnings; the older the respondent (and hence the more seniority), the higher the earnings; and for men, the greater the number of children in the household, the higher the earnings. Note also that women's income is not well explained by these variables. Education explains about half of the variation in women's income as it does in men's (comparing the unstandardized regression coefficients), and generally less than 8% of the variation in women's income is explained by these variables.

To sum up the denominational differences in secular achievement, there are denominational differences in education and extent of labor force participation, especially among women. However, denominational differences in labor force participation can be explained by educational differences and

Table 8.6 Occupational Rewards for American Jews (Ages 25–64), by Denomination and Gender[a]

| Denomination | Mean annual earnings ($) | | | | Mean occupational prestige | | | |
	Men[b]		Women		Ratio M/W	Men		Women	
Orthodox	80,785	(71)	52,077	(42)	64.5	54.04	(89)	53.54	(71)
Conservative	119,190	(146)	55,869	(154)	46.9	55.95	(223)	52.66	(230)
Reform/									
Reconstructionist	94,358	(237)	50,025	(269)	53.0	53.58	(333)	53.51	(407)
Unaffiliated	78,520	(210)	50,056	(186)	63.7	52.30	(263)	50.94	(257)
Full time only									
Orthodox	90,493	(61)	76,477	(23)	84.5	56.17	(79)	53.10	(38)
Conservative	122,370	(132)	56,332	(106)	46.0	56.00	(204)	52.27	(172)
Reform/									
Reconstructionist	97,440	(216)	53,367	(205)	54.8	53.89	(300)	54.69	(307)
Unaffiliated	81,955	(189)	53,408	(145)	65.2	52.38	(229)	51.73	(205)

[a]Unweighted n in parentheses; calculations performed using person-weights provided with dataset.
[b]Anova of denomination significant at $p < 0.05$ (for both total and full time).

Table 8.7 Multiple Regression Analysis of Annual Earnings of American Jewish Men and Women (Ages 25–64), Employed Full Time

Independent variable	Men		Women	
Orthodox[a]	–1.469	(–.066)	1.654	(.079)
Conservative[a]	0.974	(.060)	0.587	(.047)
Reform[a]	–0.008	(.000)	0.320	(.650)
Unaffiliated[a]	–0.568	(–.036)	0.780	(.285)
Education	2.022	(.329)*	1.222	(.245)*
Marital status[b]	0.463	(.032)	0.320	(.029)
Number of children under 18 in household	0.533	(.085)*	0.096	(.015)
Age	0.070	(.100)*	0.050	(.097)*
R^2	.390		.274	
R	.152		.075	
(Unweighted n)		(600)		(483)

* $p < 0.05$.

[a]Using dummy variables, 0 represents "does not identify with denomination"; 1 represents "identifies with denomination." The category "Reconstructionist" was omitted.

[b]0, not married; 1, married.

family situation. The main occupational differences are between the Orthodox and non-Orthodox denominations, and they do not result in income or prestige differences that cannot be explained by education, age, or family characteristics. Thus, denominational differences in occupational rewards do not appear to be a result of denomination per se, and are related only indirectly to denomination through educational differences.

As we have already mentioned, denomination is a very imprecise indicator of Jewish identity and does not get at the nuances of different types of Jewish identity. Should we, then, expect that expressions of Jewish identity will be more closely related to secular achievement? In the following section we explore the relationship between expressions of Jewish identity and secular achievement, and observe whether the relationships that we find are similar in the various denominations.

JEWISH IDENTITY AND SECULAR ACHIEVEMENT

In this section, we analyze the extent to which various ways of expressing Jewish identity are related to patterns of secular achievement. This relationship is critical for understanding why American Jews are such high achievers: if it is because of the Jewish religion or culture, we would expect strong expressions of religious or ethnic identity to be related to higher secular achievement. Because we have both religious and ethnic identity indicators, we can distinguish between what in the Jewish heritage is most closely related to higher secular achievement. If it is the religious tradition of education that is spilling over to secular achievement, we will find religious expressions of Jewish identity more strongly related to secular achievement; if it is the identification with the Jewish people and accompanying norms of behavior, the ethnic expressions of Jewish identity are likely to be more strongly related to secular achievement. We can also distinguish between personal, familistic expressions of Jewish identity and more public, collective expressions of that identity. More public, collective identity is likely to reflect social norms associated with American Jews, whereas personal expressions of Jewish identity may reflect more ideological orientations. On the other hand, involvement in a job may take time away from involvement in Jewish activities, such as volunteer work at Jewish organizations. Employment may also indicate greater involvement in the secular world and may thus be associated with less particularistic Jewish identification. We consider these relationships separately for men and women, as participation in the labor force and the accompanying occupational achievement follow different patterns for men and women.

To begin with, we divided each of the Jewish identity factors into "strong Jewish identity" and "weak Jewish identity" (two sample groups of approximately equal size) and compared (with t-tests) secular achievement between the two groups for men and women separately. As measures of secular achievement, we looked at the percentage of those who were college educated, the percentage of those participating in the labor force, the percentage of those working full time in the labor force (Table 8.8), the percentage of those engaged in managerial/business/professional occupations, the mean annual earnings, and the mean occupational prestige (Table 8.9).

Striking differences are found in the proportion of both college-educated men and women with stronger and weaker Jewish identity. For the private expressions of religious identity, stronger Jewish identity is associated with a lower level of education; for the private expressions of ethnic identity, stronger Jewish identity is associated with a higher education. For the public religious and ethnic expressions of Jewish identity, stronger identity is associated with a higher education (with one exception: those who have a stronger identity with Israel's central role have a lower level of education than those who have weaker identity in this respect). Also striking is the difference in percentage of women employed full time in the labor force: for every Jewish identity factor, those with stronger Jewish identity are much less likely to be employed full time than are those with weaker Jewish identity (Figure 8.3).

Table 8.8 Educational Attainment, Labor Force Participation, and Full-time Employment of American Jews (Ages 25–64), by Jewish Identity Factor and Gender[a]

Jewish identity factor	B.A.+ (%)		Employed in labor force (%)		Employed full time (35+ hours per week) (%)	
	Strong Identity	Weak Identity	Strong Identity	Weak Identity	Strong Identity	Weak Identity
Men						
Activity (private mixed)	72.9 (509)	73.9 (628)	86.4 (508)	87.0 (622)	92.5 (439)	88.2* (541)
Universal Morality (public mixed)	74.5 (591)	72.3 (546)	86.0 (587)	87.5 (543)	89.7 (505)	90.5 (475)
Ritual (private religious)	68.4 (373)	76.6* (735)	87.7 (373)	87.0 (732)	88.7 (327)	90.4 (637)
Belief (private religious)	70.3 (569)	75.1** (590)	86.6 (569)	86.8 (585)	89.5 (492)	90.4 (508)
Ceremony (public religious)	79.7 (596)	67.5* (532)	91.1 (574)	83.1* (531)	91.2 (523)	88.2 (441)
Tribalism (private ethnic)	77.3 (463)	70.6* (657)	88.0 (465)	86.0 (652)	89.7 (409)	90.7 (561)
Culture (private ethnic)	77.0 (478)	69.3* (671)	88.7 (476)	85.8 (668)	89.1 (422)	90.1 (573)
Attachment to Israel (private ethnic)	80.2 (408)	69.8* (721)	88.0 (409)	85.2 (915)	87.5 (360)	91.5** (609)
Exceptionalism (public ethnic)	76.7 (639)	69.0* (481)	88.4 (635)	84.9** (482)	89.3 (561)	91.7 (409)
Organizations (public ethnic)	79.7 (394)	69.6* (750)	88.9 (396)	85.3** (742)	88.9 (352)	90.1 (633)
Israel's Role Central (public ethnic)	71.2 (614)	76.3* (515)	85.8 (613)	86.7 (511)	89.7 (526)	90.3 (443)

Table 8.8 (continued)

Jewish identity factor	B.A.+ (%)		Employed in labor force (%)		Employed full time (35+ hours per week) (%)	
	Strong Identity	Weak Identity	Strong Identity	Weak Identity	Strong Identity	Weak Identity
Women						
Activity	62.5 (712)	68.9* (684)	72.8 (713)	75.7 (680)	69.9 (519)	80.2* (515)
Universal Morality	68.6 (821)	61.4* (575)	74.2 (819)	74.2 (574)	74.3 (608)	76.1 (426)
Ritual	58.5 (424)	69.8* (886)	67.8 (425)	77.7* (883)	68.4 (228)	78.1* (686)
Belief	60.7 (837)	72.1* (556)	71.0 (835)	77.7* (556)	72.8 (593)	77.6** (432)
Ceremony	68.2 (761)	63.2** (549)	74.6 (761)	74.2 (547)	71.3 (568)	80.8* (406)
Tribalism	66.2 (616)	66.9 (706)	71.4 (616)	77.8* (704)	70.5 (440)	79.4* (548)
Culture	69.1 (647)	63.3* (711)	73.0 (648)	75.6 (705)	70.8 (473)	78.8* (533)
Attachment to Israel	71.2 (497)	63.4* (890)	74.0 (499)	74.7 (886)	70.5 (369)	78.0* (662)
Exceptionalism	73.3 (765)	57.3* (559)	76.3 (764)	72.8 (556)	74.6 (583)	76.5 (405)
Organizations	69.6 (517)	63.1* (839)	72.7 (516)	74.3 (638)	69.6 (375)	79.6* (623)
Israel's Role Central	63.2 (828)	70.7* (559)	73.6 (825)	75.7 (560)	72.5 (607)	79.3* (424)

t-Test significant at p < .05; ** significant at *p* < 0.1.

[a]Unweighted *n* in parentheses; calculations performed using person-weights provided with dataset.

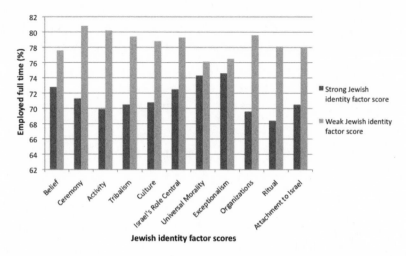

Figure 8.3. Percentage of women (ages 25–64) employed full time, by strength of Jewish identity.

Occupational achievement is also related to Jewish identity: both men and women with strong Jewish identity, especially ethnic identity, are more likely to have a managerial, business, or professional occupation (Table 8.9). Men with stronger Jewish identity are more likely to have higher annual earnings than men with weaker Jewish identity; and occupational prestige is higher among those with stronger Jewish identity. The relationships are particularly strong and consistent for ethnic identity.

Thus, relationships between Jewish identity and secular achievement seem to be fairly consistent, with higher secular achievement among those with stronger Jewish identity. Women are the exception: they are less likely to be employed full time when they have strong Jewish identity. This fits with the pattern we saw earlier among dual earners, where compared with wives in the broader U.S. population Jewish wives were more likely to be "secondary earners," that is, employed part time when family roles beckoned.

JEWISH IDENTITY, DENOMINATIONAL PREFERENCE, AND SECULAR ACHIEVEMENT

Many of the denominational differences we observed in secular achievement disappeared once we held family and demographic characteristics constant. We also want to see whether any denominational differences remain once we control for Jewish identity, demographic variables, and family characteristics. As we mentioned earlier, in 1990 we found that Jewishness influenced family characteristics more than it influenced labor force participation and subsequent occupational achievement and rewards

Table 8.9 Occupational Attainment and Rewards of American Jews (Ages 25-64), by Jewish Identity and Gender[a]

Jewish identity factor	In managerial/ business/ professional occupations (%)		Mean annual earnings ($)		Mean occupational prestige score	
	Strong Identity	Weak Identity	Strong Identity	Weak Identity	Strong Identity	Weak Identity
Men						
Activity	62.7	57.4*	105,810	94,874	54.0	53.4
	(474)	(594)	(283)	(358)	(426)	(529)
Universal Morality	61.9	57.5	96,055	103,340	53.9	53.4
	(551)	(517)	(360)	(321)	(494)	(461)
Ritual	60.6	58.4	115,260	94,319*	54.7	52.8**
	(358)	(694)	(217)	(411)	(324)	(612)
Belief	59.8	57.6	108,010	91,797*	54.0	52.7
	(535)	(559)	(313)	(345)	(476)	(502)
Ceremony	63.8	53.9*	112,600	90,509*	54.8	52.0*
	(551)	(501)	(314)	(314)	(497)	(439)
Tribalism	65.3	55.1*	112,440	90,231*	55.4	52.0*
	(435)	(624)	(255)	(390)	(255)	(390)
Culture	64.1	54.7*	108,620	90,892*	54.2	52.7
	(451)	(634)	(269)	(381)	(407)	(562)
Attachment to Israel	61.7	57.0	112,930	91,143*	54.8	52.5*
	(389)	(672)	(231)	(409)	(347)	(597)
Exceptionalism	61.0	57.0	108,200	86,655*	54.2	52.3*
	(613)	(446)	(370)	(275)	(553)	(394)
Organizations	66.1	54.2*	114,050	91,268*	55.2	52.3*
	(378)	(699)	(219)	(424)	(339)	(621)
Israel's Role Central	59.6	57.7	101,930	95,631	53.6	53.1
	(576)	(485)	(343)	(297)	(518)	(426)
Women						
Activity	60.8	59.6	53,445	57,394	53.1	52.2
	(607)	(591)	(312)	(329)	(560)	(547)
Universal Morality	62.3	57.2**	56,182	54,389	53.4	51.6*
	(700)	(498)	(387)	(254)	(646)	(461)
Ritual	57.6	60.9	54,026	56,459	51.7	52.9
	(347)	(779)	(172)	(430)	(323)	(722)

Belief	60.4	59.9	55,172	57,598	52.5	52.8
	(702)	(489)	(364)	(280)	(647)	(456)
Ceremony	61.9	57.0	55,754	55,776	53.6	51.2
	(656)	(470)	(338)	(470)	(605)	(440)
Tribalism	61.6	60.0	57,548	55,978	53.9	52.1*
	(516)	(627)	(259)	(363)	(465)	(591)
Culture	65.0	56.1*	56,364	56,076	54.4	51.1*
	(554)	(611)	(286)	(344)	(510)	(569)
Attachment to Israel	63.4	58.1**	56,030	56,281	54.1	52.0*
	(426)	(768)	(233)	(408)	(393)	(710)
Exceptionalism	64.5	55.3*	58,804	53,566	53.9	51.4*
	(676)	(467)	(364)	(258)	(625)	(431)
Organizations	64.1	56.6*	60,205	52,865**	54.0	51.5*
	(434)	(734)	(220)	(397)	(400)	(670)
Israel's Role Central	60.5	59.2	54,340	58,779	52.8	52.8
	(704)	(490)	(379)	(262)	(657)	(446)

*t-test significant at $p < 0.05$; ** significant at $p < 0.10$.

[a]Unweighted n in parentheses; calculations performed using person-weights provided with dataset.

(Hartman and Hartman, 1996a; 1996b). According to our findings, Jewish identity is stronger for women than for men; we wanted to see whether Jewish identity has a greater effect on the secular achievement of women than of men, once we control for denominational preference, demographic variables, and family characteristics. We also found somewhat different relationships between Jewishness and secular achievement for older and younger respondents in 1990, so we wanted to control for age cohort as well.

We continue our analysis by presenting the results of a series of regression analyses, which have as dependent variables various indicators of secular achievement (education, extent of labor force participation, occupation, earnings, and occupational prestige); the independent variables are denominational preference (dummy variables for Orthodox, Conservative, Reform, and unaffiliated, with Reconstructionist the omitted category), selected Jewish identity factors (those factors that in the t-test analyses had the strongest relationships to secular achievement), demographic variables (age cohort), and family characteristics (age at first marriage, number of children under 18 in the household, and current marital status).[2] We analyze the relative strength of each of these independent variables in explaining the secular achievement of Jewish men and women, respectively.

We summarize our findings in Table 8.10 (results of the detailed regression analyses are available from the authors upon request). Only independent variables that had regression coefficients with a statistical significance of $p < 0.10$ or $p < 0.05$ are presented. The results with respect to labor force participation of men are omitted, as less than 10% of the men aged 25–64 were not participating in the labor force and the results of the analysis were inconclusive. Otherwise, there is a regression analysis for men and women, respectively, for each of the dependent variables. The dependent variables of labor force participation and occupation are dichotomies (participation in the labor force or not; managerial/professional/business occupation or not) and therefore were analyzed by means of binary logistic regression. The other analyses were multiple regression analyses. The effects of each of the independent variables are those that remain after the other independent variables are held constant.

We see that of the denominational variables, being Orthodox has a weak negative relationship with three of the secular achievement indicators for men (education, occupation, and mean annual earnings) and a weak positive relationship with annual earnings for women (possibly because Orthodox women are so much more likely to be in professional occupations, as we saw earlier). Controlling for denomination does not eliminate many of the relationships between secular achievement and the measures of Jewish identity. So even after controlling for denomination, demography, and family characteristics, stronger ethnic identity is related to higher educational achievement, occupation, and occupational prestige; but stronger religious identity (Ritual, Ceremony) is associated with a lower educational level for both men and women and a lower-status occupation for men. However, stronger religious identity is associated with higher occupational prestige and earnings for men. For men, it is possible that the strong ethnic identification is a result of secular achievement rather than a force toward secular achievement. (As we cautioned before, we cannot determine the causal direction with these data, and both secular achievement and Jewish identity may influence each other.) For women, personal ethnic attachment to the Jewish people (Tribalism) is negatively associated with labor force participation and occupational achievement. However, women who have higher occupational prestige are more likely to be active in Jewish organizations.

Occupation and occupational rewards are strongly and positively related to education for both men and women (as is labor force participation for women).

Few family characteristics figure in the secular achievement of men. However, for women, the number of children at home curtails labor force participation and full-time employment (as we have already seen). Currently married women are employed fewer hours than non-married women, and they are more likely to be in managerial, business, or (even more likely) professional occupations.

Thus, we have refined the findings from the 1990 NJPS that "Jewishness" affects labor force participation, occupation, and ensuing rewards only through its influence on education or family characteristics. We see that there is a relationship between ethnic Jewish identity and higher occupational achievement that does not disappear when denomination, education, age, and family characteristics are controlled for. We also see that there is a relationship between secular achievement and stronger religious identity, although it tends to be weak, as well as a relationship between occupational prestige and earnings and weaker religious identity. Relationships between Jewishness and secular achievement tend to be similar for men and women, with one exception: strong ethnic identity for women (Tribalism) is associated with lower labor force participation and (weakly) with lower occupational attainment.

We do not see evidence that Jewishness affects women's secular behavior to a greater extent than it affects men's; rather, there are more aspects of Jewish identity that retain independent relationships with occupational achievement among men than women. So it seems that some of the correlation between secular achievement and Jewishness for women results from the influence of Jewishness on family behavior (as we saw in the preceding chapter); for men, however, secular achievement is less closely related to family characteristics than to education and Jewish identity. It is possible that occupational achievement enables men to become better integrated into the Jewish communal scene, which reinforces their Jewish identity.

We suspected that Jewish identity might carry more weight for the Orthodox, for whom Jewish identity seems to be central to many aspects of life, than for the other denominational groups, especially the Reform/Reconstructionist and the unaffiliated, who tend to be more secular in orientation. To study this, we repeated the earlier regression analyses for separate denominational groups to see whether the same expressions of Jewish identity were related to secular achievement in each denomination and gender (the regression models are the same as used earlier, minus the dummy variables for denomination). We summarize the results of our analyses in Table 8.11 (detailed results of the regression analyses are available from the authors upon request).

With regard to educational attainment, it is clear that ethnic Jewish identity is related in a similar positive way in each of the denominational groups and for each gender. The identity factor Activity (believing that being Jewish encompasses being active in the contemporary American Jewish community

Table 8.10 Relationships among Secular Achievement, Denomination, Jewish Identity Factor Scores, Demographic Variables, and Family Characteristics of American Jews (Ages 25–64) by Gender[a]

Independent variable	Education	Labor force participation[b]	Weekly hours of employment	Managerial/ business/ professional occupation[b]	Occupational prestige score	Mean annual earnings (for full-time-employed)
Men						
Denomination	−Orthodox**		—	−Orthodox**	—	−Orthodox*
Jewish identity factor	−Activity* −Ritual** +Culture* +Exceptionalism*		+Activity*	Ceremony** +Tribalism**	+Ritual* +Tribalism*	+Ritual
Demographic variables				+Education*	+Education*	+Education*
Family characteristics	+AgeMarr*		+Marital*		—	—

Women

Denomination	+Orthodox**	—	—	—	—
Jewish identity factor	—	−Tribalism** +Organizations**	—	+Ceremony* −Tribalism*	−Activity* −Ritual* +Culture* +Exceptionalism*
Demographic variables	+Education*	+Education*	+Age*	+Education*	−Age*
Family characteristics	—	+Marital*	+Marital* −Chh*	−Chh*	+AgeMarr* −Chh*

aDenominational preference: Orthodox, Conservative, Reform, unaffiliated (0, no; 1, = yes). Jewish identity factor scores: Activity, Ritual, Ceremony, Tribalism, Exceptionalism, Culture, Organizations (weak—>strong). Demographic variables: Age, education. Family characteristics age at first marriage (AgeMarr), number of children under 18 in household (Chh), current marital status (Marital) (0, not married; 1, married). Independent variables with statistically significant regression coefficients, based on multiple regressions unless otherwise indicated (−, negative relationship; +, positive relationship).
b 0, no; 1, yes. Based on logistic regression.

Table 8.11 Relationships among Secular Achievement, Jewish Identity Factor Scores, Demographic, and Family Characteristics of American Jews (Ages 25–64), by Gender and Denominational Preference[a]

Denominational preference	Education	Labor force participation[b]	Weekly hours of employment	Managerial professional occupation[b]	Occupational prestige score	Mean annual earnings (for full-time-employed)
Men						
Orthodox	+Exceptionalism** +Culture* +Age* +AgeMarr*		—	+Organizations* −AgeMarr*	+Tribalism* +Education* −AgeMarr*	+Exceptionalism* +Organizations* +Education*
Conservative	+ Exceptionalism* +Culture*		—	+Organizations** +Education*	+Education*	+Ritual* +Education**
Reform/ Reconstructionist	−Activity* −Ritual** +Exceptionalism** +Culture** +Agemarr* +Marital*		+Marital*	+Education*	+Ritual* +Education*	+Education**
Unaffiliated	−Activity* + Exceptionalism* +Culture* + Organizations**		—	+Tribalism* +Education*	+Tribalism** +Education*	+Education*

Women						
Orthodox	−Activity* +Ritual* +Culture* +AgeMarri −Chh**	+Education* +Marital*	−Tribalism*	+Ritual* +Education*	−Tribalism** +Education* +Chh*	−Culture** +Organizations* +Chh*
Conservative	−Activity* +Tribalism** +Exceptionalism* −Age* +AgeMarri*	+Ritual* +Ceremony* +Tribalism* −Age* +AgeMarri*	+AgeMarri* −Chh* −Marital*	−Activity** +Ritual* +Education*	+Education* +Marital**	—
Reform/ Reconstructionist	+Exceptionalism* +Culture* −Age* +AgeMarri*	+Activity* +Ceremony* −Tribalism** +Education* −Age*	−AgeMarri* −Chh* −Marital*	−Tribalism** +Education* +Marital*	+Education*	+Education**
Unaffiliated	−Tribalism* +Exceptionalism* +Culture** +Organizations*	−Activity* +Tribalism** +Education*	+Ceremony* +Agemarri* −Chh* −Marital*	+Education*	+Education* +Age*	−Culture** +Education*

[a]Jewish identity factor scores: Activity, Ritual, Ceremony, Tribalism, Exceptionalism, Culture, Organizations (weak → strong); age at first marriage (AgeMarri), number of children under 18 in household (Chh), current marital status (Marital, 0, not married; 1, married). Independent variables with statistically significant regression coefficients, based on multiple regressions, except where indicated (−, negative relation; +, positive).
[b]0, no; 1, yes. Based on logistic regression.

and practice) is related negatively to educational attainment, as is personal religious identity (Ritual) in Reform/Reconstructionist and unaffiliated groups of men, and among Orthodox and Conservative women. So here we see that, for Orthodox and Conservative men, ritual observance is not an obstacle to higher education, but it is for women in these groups; and it is for men in the less observant denominational groups.

Among Orthodox, Conservative, and unaffiliated women, activity in the Jewish community is related negatively to secular achievement, but among Reform/Reconstructionist women, it is related positively to secular achievement. It is possible that the different denominational reference groups place different value on women's integration into the labor force and certain occupations.

Whereas, for Orthodox and unaffiliated men, personal ethnic identity (Tribalism) has a positive relationship to secular achievement, for women, it has different relationships to secular achievement. It has a positive relationship to education and labor force participation among Conservative women, a positive relationship to education but a negative relationship to labor force participation among the unaffiliated, a negative relationship to labor force participation and occupational attainment among the Reform/Reconstructionist, and a negative relationship to occupational prestige among the Orthodox. Again, it is possible that the different denominational groups have different communal norms for women's labor force achievements, so that sometimes Jewishness competes with women's secular involvement, and sometimes it reinforces or supports it. For Orthodox women, the more hours they are employed, the weaker their ethnic identity, but this relationship is not found in the other denominational groups, among whom the most important variables affecting hours of employment are the number of children at home and whether or not a woman is currently married. Consistent across all denominations and both genders is the importance of education for occupational achievement and rewards (hence indirectly affected by Jewishness).

SUMMARY AND CONCLUSIONS

This chapter has answered some of the questions we started out with and raised other issues for further research. Denominational groups tend to differ with respect to labor force participation and occupational achievement, particularly among women, and particularly comparing the Orthodox with the non-Orthodox. Much of this difference among women can be explained when we control for family characteristics. Some of the difference among men can be explained by the somewhat lower educational attainment of Orthodox men. The denominational groups appear to exert two kinds of influence on secular achievement: they reflect norms about familism, which are related to age at marriage, age of childbearing, and number of children, which in turn are related to the labor force involvement of women and their subsequent occupational achievement. They also provide reinforcement for high secular achievement, particularly among men.

But many of the denominational differences can be explained by strength of Jewish identity in its various forms. Therefore, when we control for expressions of Jewish identity and denomination, it is expressions of Jewish identity more than denominational preference that are related to secular achievement. Some aspects of Jewish identity are related to secular achievement in all denominational groups. We cannot say that Jewish identity has a relationship to secular achievement only among the Orthodox; and we do not find that religious identity (as opposed to ethnic identity) has a greater influence among the Orthodox than the other denominational groups. However, among women in particular, ethnic Jewish identity has a different relationship to secular achievement when we compare denominational groups. Thus, among the Orthodox, personal ethnic identity is lower among women who are more involved in the labor force, but among Conservatives, personal ethnic identity is higher among women active in the labor force. Among Reform and Reconstructionist women, there is also a negative relationship between personal ethnic identity and labor force involvement.

What we can conclude is that some types of Jewish identity retain an independent relationship with secular achievement in each of the denominational groups and for each gender; that this relationship is different for men and women in the denomination; and that this relationship differs between denominations. But the fact that there is an independent relationship to secular achievement, for the most part positive, suggests that the American Jewish community is not completely secularized; its particularistic investments in Jewish social and cultural capital are often related to higher secular achievement, especially for men.

We recall from our discussion about gender and Jewish identity in Chapter 6 that one of the explanations for women's greater religiosity (found not only among Jews) is that women have a less structural stake in secular status (e.g., less occupational achievement). However, Orthodox and Conservative women who are more personally religious (on the identity factor Ritual) are more likely to have higher-status occupations (managerial, business, or professional), Conservative and Reform/Reconstructionist women who are more personally religious are more likely to be in the labor force, and the unaffiliated who are more personally religious are likely to be employed more hours per week. This certainly undermines this structural hypothesis. Orthodox and unaffiliated women who achieve higher annual earnings are less involved in Jewish culture, but Orthodox women with high earnings are more involved in Jewish organizations.

To better understand the influences of the different denominational milieus on women's labor force involvement, or the influence of women's labor force involvement on integration into a denomination's ethnic milieu, we suggest more qualitative research to uncover the mechanisms of the interrelationships.

CHAPTER 9

How Jewishness is Related to American Jews' Dual-Earning Patterns

In the preceding two chapters, we considered whether an individual's Jewishness was related to his or her behavior with respect to family formation, childbearing, labor force participation, and occupational achievement and rewards. In this chapter, we look at the family as a unit to get some insight into how Jewishness is related to the division of economic roles in the family. We want to know how Jewishness is related to both spouses being engaged in economic roles outside the home and whether the effect of having young children at home on the parents' economic behavior is modified by their Jewishness. If Jewishness is related to family decisions about economic behavior, what aspect of Jewishness is responsible: the religious and/or the ethnic? Do religious identity and ethnic identity have similar effects on couples' economic behavior in all denominations of American Jews? Note that we have information only on how the respondent expresses Jewishness, that is, the respondent's denominational preference and expressions of Jewish identity. We do know whether or not the spouse is identified as Jewish, and we will explore the relationship of secular achievement to this aspect of Jewishness in the next chapter. Here we focus on the relationship between the couple's economic roles and the respondents' denominational preferences and expressions of Jewish identity.

We see this as a further inquiry into the ways in which religious identity and ethnic identity penetrate family decisions and secular behavior. If we find that Jewish denomination and expressions of Jewish identity are *not* related to a couple's allocation of economic roles and the spouses' relative contributions to the family economy, we will have an indication of secularization; that is, Jewishness will be separate from such decisions and behavior. If we find a relationship between Jewishness and a couple's economic roles and rewards, we will have insight into one mechanism by which religious identity and ethnic identity on the individual level are translated into everyday behavior for Jewish men and women. In turn this may be a model for how other religious and ethnic identities influence the day-to-day activities and orientations of individuals and families expressing other contemporary identities.

We begin by looking at denominational differences in dual-earning patterns; we follow this with a consideration of scores on the Jewish identity factors.

DENOMINATION AND DUAL EARNING

The purpose of this section is to examine whether the denominations differ in terms of the economic roles of married couples. As we have already mentioned, intimate relations often mirror the broader social and cultural context, and certainly are influenced by patterns in the surrounding society. Denominational groups may form reference groups for norms affecting marital patterns, and therefore couples within a particular denomination may differ from those in another. We measure here, however, only the denomination of the respondent, not the denominational preference of the spouse.

One hypothesis regarding dual earning and denominational preference is that the more traditional the denomination, the more "Jewish" is the dual-earning pattern, following the distinctiveness of the Jewish dual-earning pattern shown in Chapter 5. That is, we would expect more traditional Jews to have a higher proportion of dual earners than their counterparts in other denominational groups; we would also expect a great degree of homogeneity between spouses in terms of education and occupation and large contributions by wives to joint earnings, though at the same time we would anticipate that wives act as secondary earners in the face of family need, such as the presence of many children at home or a husband's low salary/husband's income lower than the wife's. A somewhat contradictory hypothesis is that the more egalitarian the denomination, the closer to equality are the spouses in terms of economic roles (extent of labor force participation, contribution to earnings, homogeneity in terms of occupational prestige and earnings). A final hypothesis is that denomination is not related to the pattern of dual earning: that the variation among Jews in terms of dual earning is primarily a result of educational differences between the spouses and childrearing responsibilities. Our earlier findings, that denominational differences in labor force participation and occupational achievement appear to result from educational differences and family roles of women, suggest that the last might be the strongest hypothesis.

We see that among married Jewish couples in each denomination, the majority are dual earners, as was found in 1990 (Fishman, 1993). Along

Table 9.1 Percentage of Married American Jews in Dual-Earner Couples, by Denomination and Age of Respondent[a]

Denomination	Age of respondent					
	25–44[b]		44–64		65+[c]	
Orthodox	48.0	(106)	58.0	(92)	11.1	(44)
Conservative	63.0	(145)	54.2	(237)	6.6	(174)
Reform/Reconstructionist	66.7	(263)	62.3	(348)	9.5	(162)
Unaffiliated	66.1	(147)	58.2	(222)	2.8	(131)

[a]Unweighted n in parentheses; calculations performed using person-weights provided with dataset.

[b]Anova of denomination significant at $p < 0.05$.

[c]Anova of denomination significant at $p < 0.10$.

with this, we find a lower proportion of dual earners among the Orthodox than among Conservative, Reform, and unaffiliated Jews. We can see that these denominational differences are concentrated in the main age group (25–44) of people involved in childbearing and childrearing, among whom the Orthodox have a significantly lower proportion of dual-earner couples than do the other denominational groups (Table 9.1). In the oldest age group, in contrast, the Orthodox do not have fewer dual-earner couples than the other groups (although the unaffiliated group does).

It is reasonable to expect that the denominational differences are strongly related to childbearing and childrearing, as we found in 1990 (Hartman and Hartman, 1996a, ch. 6) and above for the whole sample. As we have seen, the Orthodox have more children than the other denominational groups: they are also more likely to have four or more children under 18 at home, and fewer of them have no young children at home.

If we control for number of children and denomination, we see that number of children does not, however, explain all of the denominational differences in dual earning (Figure 9.1). Denominational differences persist, but the proportion of dual earners does not vary linearly by number of children at home for any denominational group. Families with three or more children may have higher proportions of dual earners than families with fewer children, perhaps because of the need for more income in large families. For some groups, there are more dual earners when there are no children under 18 at home; among the Orthodox, there is a lower proportion of dual earners in this category.

To get a better understanding of this variation, and because the extent of the wife's labor force participation contributes the most variation in the

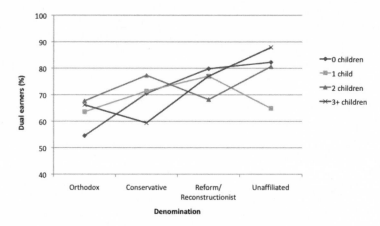

Figure 9.1. Percentage of dual-earner households, by denomination and number of children under age 18.

likelihood and pattern of dual earning, we analyzed the wife's labor force participation by a logistic regression for each denominational group separately (Table 9.2). The dependent variable was the wife's labor force participation (0, not employed; 1, employed). The independent variables were the husband's and wife's age, the husband's and wife's education (and hence earning potential), and the number of children under 18 at home.

In each denominational group, the wife's education was the most important factor related to her labor force participation, which indicates her career orientation and earnings potential (and opportunity costs if she does not participate in the labor force). The number of children under 18 at home was significantly related to the extent of the wife's labor force participation among Conservatives and Reform/Reconstructionists, but it does not have as strong a relationship as does the wife's education to her labor force participation. It is interesting that the number of children had the smallest effect among the Orthodox (seen by comparing the unstandardized regression coefficients for number of children across denominational groups). Perhaps the variation among Orthodox Jews, most of whom have at least one young child at home, is not great enough to explain differences in the wife's labor force participation.

Even more strongly affected by number of children under 18 at home are the wife's hours of employment (Table 9.3). Among dual-earner families with more children under 18 at home, wives are less likely to be employed full time than those in families with fewer children. Among the Orthodox, fewer wives are employed full time, especially among those with two or more children at home; among those with three or more children at home, only 27.5% are employed full time. Among Conservatives, those with two children at home are employed considerably fewer hours than those with one child or no children at home; and among those with three or more children at home, only 27.8% are employed full time. Among Reform/Reconstructionists with three or more children at home, only 13.8% are employed full time. There are also denominational differences that persist when number of children at home is controlled for: Orthodox women are least likely to have full-time employment, except among those with three or more children; unaffiliated and Reform/Reconstructionist women are most likely to be employed full time when they have no children or two children at home; among women with one child at home, Conservative women are most likely to be employed full time. Certainly educational differences affect these work hours, but apparently there are denominational norms, which also have an influence.

Table 9.2 Logistic Regression Analysis of Labor Force Participation by American Jewish Wives (Ages 25–64), by Spousal and Family Characteristics and Denomination[a]

	Denomination			
Independent variable	Orthodox	Conservative	Reform/ Reconstructionist	Unaffiliated
Wife's age	0.025	0.026	0.020	0.027
	(1.026)	(1.027)	(1.020)	(1.028)
Husband's age	0.007	−0.005	−0.004	−0.026
	(1.007)	(0.995)	(0.996)	(0.975)
Wife's education	0.365	0.261	0.431	0.346
	(1.440)**	(1.298)	(1.539)*	(1.413)*
Husband's education	0.051	−0.077	−0.108	−0.213
	(0.950)	(0.926)	(0.898)	(0.808)
Number of children under 18 at home	−0.027	−0.236	−0.332	−0.178
	(0.973)	(0.790)**	(0.717)*	(0.837)
Predicted correctly (%)	68.7	81.2	80.7	83.5
Nagelkerke R^2	.083	.050	.081	.046
(Unweighted n)	(134)	(271)	(455)	(249)

*Significant at $p < 0.05$.; ** significant at $p < 0.10$.

[a]Data are unstandardized coefficients; exponential coefficients are in parentheses.

Table 9.3 Percentage of Wives Employed Full Time among Dual-Earner Families, by Number of Children and Denomination[a]

Denomination	Mean number of children under 18 at home			
	0	1	2	3+
Orthodox	72.3 (40)	64.7 (27)	48.2 (13)	27.5 (33)
Conservative	78.8 (125)	80.8 (47)	50.6 (54)	27.8 (21)
Reform/Reconstructionist	82.3 (204)	64.2 (89)	65.8 (84)	13.8 (22)
Unaffiliated	85.5 (119)	66.0 (45)	70.8 (51)	—[b]

[a]Unweighted n in parentheses; calculations performed using person-weights provided with dataset.

[b]Less than 10 (unweighted) cases.

Probably because of the difference in the number of children under 18 at home, there are significant differences between the denominations in terms of how work hours compare between the spouses (χ^2 significant at $p < 0.05$). Orthodox couples are the most conventional, with 68.2% of husbands employed more hours per week than wives. Conservative couples are the next most conventional, with 63.2% of husbands employed more hours than wives. In Reform/Reconstructionist couples, slightly more than half of husbands are employed more hours than wives. Finally, among the unaffiliated, the couples in which the wife is employed as much as or more than the husband outnumber conventional couples, in which the husband is employed more hours than the wife (Figure 9.2).

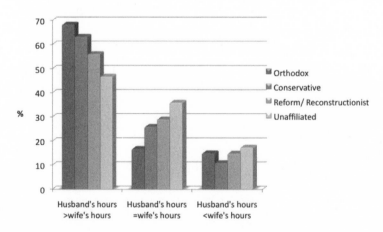

Figure 9.2. Comparison of husband's and wife's hours of employment, by denomination.

To study the effect of children and the husband's hours of employment on wives' hours of employment in dual-earner couples, we entered wife's mean hours of employment per week as the dependent variable in a multiple regression analysis, with the independent variables being wife's and husband's ages, wife's and husband's levels of education, number of children at home, and husband's mean hours of work per week (Table 9.4). The wife's and husband's ages were entered as control variables, with the expectation that the older the age (of either), the lower would be the hours of employment. Their ages might also reflect the ages of the children at home, however, with younger wives expected to have younger children and therefore to have fewer hours of paid employment. Education of the wife was expected to have a positive relationship with hours of paid work, as higher education is associated with higher-level careers and career commitment. Higher education is also related to a higher income, which would make it more worthwhile to work longer hours in the labor force.[1] The husband's education, having a similar relationship to his occupation and income, might be inversely related to the wife's hours of paid work, as the lower his education level, the lower his income might be and hence the greater the need for the wife's income. We expected number of children to be inversely related to the wife's hours of paid work, as the more children at home, the greater the demands on her time outside the labor force (her unpaid labor). Finally, we expected the husband's hours of employment to be inversely related to the wife's hours of employment—the fewer hours he is employed, the greater the need for her labor hours and income (and vice versa). Because of the greater number of children among the Orthodox, it was expected that their work hours would be most responsive to the number of children at home, whereas in the other denominations, the wife's hours of employment might be related more to the wife's characteristics (e.g., education) and less hindered by the number of children at home, since there would be fewer of them.

Our expectations were not borne out. In all of the denominational groups, the number of children under 18 in the household is the dominant influence on the wife's hours of employment—the more children at home, the fewer are the hours the wife works. Comparing the relationship of number of children at home with hours of employment across the denominations (using unstandardized regression coefficients), we can see that number of children has a smaller effect on the hours of employment of Orthodox wives than on those of non-Orthodox wives. On the other hand, the effect of the husband's education is stronger (at least double the unstandardized coefficient) among the Orthodox than the other

Table 9.4 Multiple Regression Analysis of Weekly Hours of Employment of American Jewish Wives (Ages 25–64), by Spousal and Family Characteristics and Denomination[a]

Independent variable	Orthodox	Conservative	Reform/ Reconstructionist	Unaffiliated
Wife's age	−0.066	0.076	0.106	−0.157
	(−.049)	(.054)	(.072)	(−.114)
Husband's age	0.280	−0.350	−0.113	0.120
	(.203)	(−.267)**	(−.082)	(.092)
Wife's education	2.142	0.010	1.568	1.714
	(.187)	(.001)	(.124)*	(.151)*
Husband's education	−2.853	−1.169	−1.096	−1.580
	(−.240)**	(−.117)	(−.093)**	(−0.150)*
Number of children under 18 at home	−1.687	−4.971	−4.306	−5.057
	(−.223)*	(−0.403)*	(−.306)*	(−.370)*
Husband's weekly hours of employment	0.091	−0.045	0.007	0.260
	(.081)	(−.049)	(.005)	(.237)*
Multiple R	0.357	0.440	0.328	0.444
R^2	0.127	0.194	0.108	0.092
(Unweighted n)	(84)	(208)	(354)	(195)

* Significant at $p < 0.05$; ** significant at $p < 0.10$.

[a]Data are unstandardized coefficients and (in parentheses) standardized coefficients.

groups, indicating that when the husband's education level (and hence his earning potential) is lower, Orthodox wives are more likely to compensate by working more hours in the labor force. Rather than children being the only consideration in terms of weekly hours of employment, Orthodox wives also respond to the larger family situation, especially the husband's income. This is true in the other denominational groups as well. The wife's own education is also related to more hours of employment, except among Conservatives. The Conservatives are the only group in which the husband's age is a significant factor in how many hours the wife works (the older the husband, the less likely the wife is to work long hours).

One clue about this variation in wife's hours of work is related to self-employment. Orthodox women are more likely to be self-employed than are women in the other denominational groups (Figure 9.3), and Orthodox women who are self-employed are more likely to work full time than women in other denominations (Figure 9.4); however, Orthodox women employed by others are much less likely to work full time.

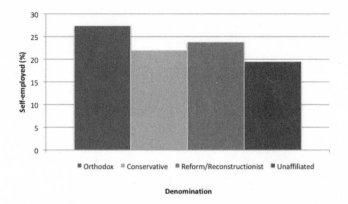

Figure 9.3. Percentage of women (ages 25–64) self-employed, by denomination.

Although we do not have information on the self-employment of both spouses (only on that of the respondent), we do have information on the occupations of both spouses (as presented in Chapter 5). Using broad occupational groupings, we see that about a third of all wives are employed in the same occupation as their husbands, across all denominations. There is some variation as to what kinds of occupational combinations we find. Classifying the occupations as managerial/business/professional or not, we observe that the highest proportion of couples in all denominational groups are those in which both husband and wife are in managerial/business/professional occupations (as we see for couples in

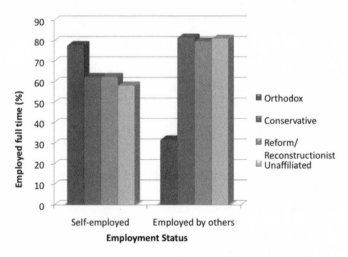

Figure 9.4. Percentage of women (ages 25–64) employed full time, by employment status and denomination.

Table 9.5 Occupational Combinations of American Jewish Spouses (Ages 25–64), Employed Full Time, by Denomination[a]

Husband's occupation	Wife's occupation	Orthodox	Conservative	Reform/ Reconstructionist	Unaffiliated
MBP	MBP	51.4	46.8	47.6	38.7
MBP	Not MBP	7.7	15.3	14.9	19.5
Not MBP	MBP	24.8	20.6	20.7	21.6
Not MBP	Not MBP	16.1	17.3	16.8	20.2
(n)[b]		(40)	(122)	(24)	(120)

[a]Data are percentages. MBP denotes "managerial/business/professional."

[b]Unweighted n in parentheses; calculations performed using person-weights provided with dataset.

which both spouses are employed full time; Table 9.5). When spouses have different occupations, it is more likely that the wife's occupation is professional, as we have already seen, so the next most common combination is one in which the wife is in a managerial/business/professional occupation and the husband is not. There are slight variations in this pattern by denomination: the Orthodox are the most likely to have both spouses in managerial/business/professional occupations, and the unaffiliated are the least likely; among the unaffiliated, more than the other denominational groups, neither spouse is likely to be in these occupations. This makes the unaffiliated most like the broader white U.S. population (as shown in Chapter 5).

These occupational patterns are reflected in the comparison of occupational rewards between spouses across denominations, as we see in the next section.

DENOMINATION, OCCUPATIONAL REWARDS, AND DUAL EARNERS

Income differs somewhat for husbands and wives in the different denominational groups (Table 9.6): Orthodox men have relatively lower incomes than non-Orthodox men, which may be related to educational and age differences between the denominations; unaffiliated men have the next lowest incomes, followed by Reform/Reconstructionist. The highest earnings are found among Conservatives (Anova of income variation by denomination significant at $p < 0.05$). The variation among women in the different denominations is smaller, with Conservative women earning more than the others, perhaps related to their somewhat older age, and Orthodox women earning the least of the groups, perhaps related to their fewer hours of employment per week. Looking only at husbands and wives employed full time (the bottom half of the table), we find that the denominational differences are smaller and not statistically significant. Orthodox women's lower income disappears, relative to the other denominations.

Among couples in which both husband and wife are employed full time, both Orthodox and Conservative couples reach near parity in spouses' incomes, with wives contributing almost half of the family's earnings. The unaffiliated have the lowest ratio of wife's to husband's earnings, with wives earning on average only 58% of what husbands earn. When hours of employment are not controlled for (top half of the table), unaffiliated husbands earn almost double their wives' income, whereas Conservative women make three-quarters of what their husbands earn. Thus, hours of employment explain much of the disparity in earnings among the Orthodox and Conservative groups, but less so among the Reform/Reconstructionist and unaffiliated groups.

In terms of further comparisons between husbands and wives, in each denomination the dominant pattern is that of conventional education, income, and occupational prestige differences; that is, in comparison with their wives, most husbands have the same or higher education, the same or higher income, and the same or higher occupational prestige. Although there are some minor denominational variations in terms of the incidence

Table 9.6 Median Annual Earnings of American Jewish Couples (Ages 25–64) by Denomination

Denomination	Median annual earnings of husbands ($)	Median annual earnings of wives ($)	Wives' earnings/ husbands' earnings	(n)[a]
Total				
Orthodox	52,000	37,500	67.6	(92)
Conservative	82,500	52,500	76.5	(155)
Reform/ Reconstructionist	72,500	42,500	61.1	(269)
Unaffiliated	62,500	42,500	53.9	(173)
Both husband and wife employed full time				
Orthodox	72,500	52,500	88.2	(25)
Conservative	62,500	62,500	89.2	(69)
Reform/ Reconstructionist	72,500	42,500	73.3	(136)
Unaffiliated	67,500	47,500	58.0	(85)

[a]Unweighted *n* in parentheses; calculations performed using person-weights provided with dataset.

of unconventional spousal differences (Table 9.7), they are balanced by slightly higher percentages of spouses whose education, incomes, or occupational prestige are equal. (For example, although in Orthodox couples the proportion of couples in which the wife has completed more education than her husband is slightly lower than in the other denominations, there is a higher percentage of Orthodox wives having the same education as their husbands.) The denominational variation is not statistically significant for any of the comparisons. Thus, traditional patterns of male dominance do not seem to vary by denomination.

In summary, in this section we explored whether a preference for a more traditional Jewish denomination would lead to the dual-earner patterns that distinguish Jews from the broader population. The results were mixed. The Orthodox (the most traditional denomination) do not have a higher proportion of dual earners than the other denominations, partly because they have more children. However, the extent of Orthodox wives' labor force participation is affected by their husband's earning power and their own earning power even more than it is by the number of children at home. One of the reasons might be the need for greater income when there are more children at home. Another might be a more pervasive familism that indicates commitment to the family's needs, which can result in greater labor force participation on the part of the wife. With regard to the equality of the spouses in terms of education, income, and occupational prestige, we found no significant differences between the denominations, which does not support the idea that the more traditionally Jewish a couple is, the more the "Jewish" pattern of dual earners is followed.

Table 9.7 Unconventional Spousal Differences for American Jewish Couples (Ages 25–64), by Denomination

Husband–wife comparisons	Orthodox	Conservative	Reform/ Reconstructionist	Unaffiliated
Wife has more education than husband (%)	25.3	27.0	25.0	24.8
Wife has higher occupational prestige than husband (%)	41.8	48.7	48.5	46.8
Wife has higher annual earnings than husband (%)	17.0	22.3	14.5	20.2
$(n)^a$	(178)	(348)	(543)	(319)

[a]Unweighted n in parentheses; calculations performed using person-weights provided with dataset.

In this section we analyze the extent to which various ways of expressing Jewish identity are related to patterns of dual earning. We expected that there would be a number of ways in which the dual-earning pattern might intersect with Jewish identity: if Jewish identity is expressed in a more traditional way, it may reflect strong familistic values, which in turn may restrict women's labor force participation to the extent that it conflicts with family roles. Therefore, more traditional Jewish identity may be associated with a lower incidence of dual-earner couples, especially if there are children at home. Furthermore, some ritual behavior may take time away from career commitment, which might limit the dual-earning pattern. Strong ethnic and public expressions of Jewish identity may reflect exposure to social norms that influence the respondent's behavior, suggesting that the relationship between Jewishness and secular behavior and achievement may be a result of social networks.

On the other hand, involvement in a job may take time away from participation in Jewish activities, such as volunteering for Jewish organizations. Employment may also indicate greater involvement in the secular world, and thus be associated with less particularistic identification as a Jew.

Most of the indicators of Jewish identity reflect the respondent's personal attitudes about what being Jewish means or what the Jewish community is about. Some are related to the respondent's behavior (e.g., attachment to Jewish culture or involvement in formal Jewish organizations), and a few are related to rituals observed by anyone in the household (e.g., commitment to *halacha*, which may involve someone in the household lighting Sabbath candles, keeping kosher at home, as well as practicing personal rituals). Therefore, we are looking primarily at the relationship between married respondents' expressions of Jewish identity and the dual-earning patterns of their family.

We divided each of the Jewish identity factors into "strong Jewish identity" and "weak Jewish identity" (approximately two groups of equal size). We then compared the proportion of dual earners in each group (Table 9.8). Generally there were only small differences between the two groups of strong versus weak Jewish identity on any of the factors, and the differences were statistically significant for only three factors. Furthermore, the direction of the differences was not the same for all factors. Thus, for the factor of Jewish identity called Activity—indicating that being Jewish means being active in the contemporary Jewish community—there was a higher percentage of dual earners among those with a stronger identity than among those with a weaker identity. For the private ethnic expression of involvement in Jewish culture (Culture) and the public ethnic expression

Table 9.8 Percentage of Dual Earners for American Jewish Couples by Strength of Jewish Identity[a]

Jewish identity factor	Type of factor	Strong identity (%)		Weak identity (%)	
Activity	Private (mixed)	57.1	(790)	49.5*	(710)
Universal Morality	Public (mixed)	61.4	(825)	58.6	(675)
Ritual	Private religious	57.3	(513)	61.9	(914)
Belief	Private religious	58.9	(882)	61.3	(629)
Ceremony	Public Religious	60.3	(924)	60.8	(503)
Tribalism	Private ethnic	63.6	(722)	58.1	(710)
Culture	Private ethnic	57.2	(742)	62.7**	(736)
Attachment to Israel	Private ethnic	58.3	(561)	62.0	(923)
Exceptionalism	Public ethnic	58.5	(816)	63.1*	(616)
Organizations	Public ethnic	61.7	(599)	58.5	(865)
Israel's Role Central	Public ethnic	61.4	(881)	60.3	(603)

[a]n in parentheses; mean for weighted sample; significance tests on unweighted n.

*t-test significant at $p < 0.05$.

**t-test significant at $p < 0.10$.

of American Jewish exceptionalism (Exceptionalism), there was a higher percentage of dual earners among those with stronger identity than among those with weaker identity. Because the differences are small and in different directions, it does not seem that Jewish identity has a strong relationship with proportion of dual earners. We will revisit this at the end of the chapter when we predict the proportion of dual earners by denomination, Jewish identity, family characteristics, and demographic factors.

Looking at the weekly hours of employment by strength of Jewish identity revealed more differences. The couple's combined hours of employment are somewhat lower for dual-earner couples in which the respondent has a strong Jewish identity on most of the factors, and some of these differences are statistically significant (Table 9.9). Respondents with a stronger Jewish identity in terms of personal commitment to halachic ritual, participation in public religious ceremonies, and personal attachment to Jewry (Tribalism) and to Israel have fewer combined work hours than those more weakly identified (most at the level of significance of $p < 0.05$). Most of the other differences are in the same direction, even if not statistically significant. The reason appears to be the fewer hours of employment of the wife among dual-earner couples in which the respondent has a stronger Jewish identity for almost all of the factors (eight of which are statistically significant). Thus, stronger Jewish identity is associated with fewer hours of paid employment for the wife, which usually results in a smaller number of combined couple hours of employment per week.

In terms of comparisons between husbands and wives, the occurrence of unconventional differences (i.e., when the wife is employed more hours than the husband, has a higher education than the husband, has higher annual earnings than the husband, and has higher occupational prestige than the husband) does not appear to be related to the strength of Jewish identity. We looked at correlations between the Jewish identity factors and the variables comparing husband's and wife's education, weekly hours of

Table 9.9 Mean Weekly Hours of Employment in Dual-Earner Couples (Ages 25–64), by Strength of Jewish Identity

Jewish identity factor	Mean combined hours of employment		Mean hours of employment of husband		Mean hours of employment of wife	
	Strong identity	Weak identity	Strong identity	Weak identity	Strong identity	Weak identity
Activity	81.2	82.0	46.3	45.5	34.5	37.0*
	(421)	(400)	(577)	(525)	(488)	(464)
Universal Morality	83.6	82.5	46.7	46.4	36.6	36.9
	(455)	(366)	(595)	(507)	(535)	(417)
Ritual	79.3	82.3*	45.8	45.7	33.3	36.9*
	(260)	(529)	(368)	(696)	(308)	(607)
Belief	80.9	82.4	45.7	46.2	35.1	36.6**
	(486)	(342)	(652)	(464)	(557)	(404)
Ceremony	80.5	83.0**	45.9	45.4	34.5	37.8*
	(522)	(267)	(711)	(353)	(596)	(319)
Tribalism	80.8	83.0**	46.1	46.0	34.7	37.2*
	(393)	(414)	(542)	(536)	(443)	(481)
Culture	80.6	82.5	46.3	45.6	34.5	37.0*
	(393)	(421)	(543)	(549)	(459)	(483)
Attachment to Israel	78.6	83.3*	45.3	46.3	33.4	37.2*
	(294)	(531)	(412)	(688)	(349)	(602)
Exceptionalism	82.6	80.9	46.5	45.5	36.2	35.7
	(482)	(325)	(630)	(448)	(548)	(376)
Organizations	80.6	82.4	46.3	45.4	34.3	37.1*
	(335)	(464)	(446)	(624)	(382)	(545)
Israel's Role Central	80.9	82.4	45.5	46.5	35.3	36.3
	(491)	(334)	(646)	(454)	(563)	(388)

*Anova significant at $p < 0.05$; ** significant at $p < 0.1$.

[a]Unweighted n in parentheses; mean for weighted n; significance tests on unweighted n.

employment, annual earnings, and occupational prestige; there was only one statistically significant correlation. We also looked at comparisons of respondents expressing strong and weak identity on each of the Jewish identity factors in terms of the proportion of couples with "unconventional" spousal differences (the wife employed more hours than the husband, the wife having a higher education than the husband, the wife earning more than the husband, and the wife having higher occupational prestige than the husband); there were very few statistically significant differences (measured by χ^2 analysis). We concluded that Jewish identity does not seem to be related to the occurrence of unconventional spousal differences in economic behavior or rewards.

However, looking at the proportion of "equally dependent spouses," that is, the proportion of couples in which the wife earns 40–59% of the joint earnings, we do find a consistent pattern (Figure 9.5). The proportion of "equally dependent spouses" is lower among those with stronger Jewish identity. Among those couples with a stronger Jewish identity, husbands are more likely to earn more than their wives (probably because the wives are employed fewer hours). Thus, the wives among those with stronger Jewish identity are clearly in the pattern of "secondary earners," with weaker career commitments than their husbands.

Whether this is because of family roles or Jewish identity itself will be explored in the next section, when we analyze the relative importance of

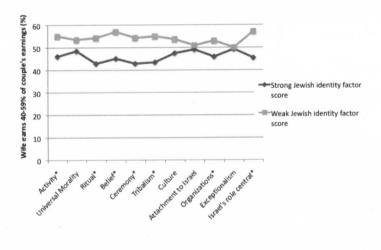

Figure 9.5. Percentage of "equally dependent spouses," by strength of Jewish identity factor. (*Asterisk indicates *t*-test significant at $p < 0.05$.)

Table 9.10 Scores on Jewish Identity Factors for Respondents in Single-Earner and Dual-Earner Couples

Jewish identity factor	Single-earner couples	Dual-earner couples
Activity	−.423	−.327
Universal Morality	.090	−.075*
Ritual	−.453	−.284*
Belief	−.352	−.284
Ceremony	−.492	−.541
Tribalism	−.590	−.500
Culture	−.456	−.386
Attachment to Israel	−.190	−.187
Organizations	−.278	−.324
Exceptionalism	.009	−.206*
Israel's Role Central	−.341	−.197
$(n)^a$	(1183)	(991)

*t-test between respondents in single-earner and dual-earner couples significant at $p < 0.05$.
[a]Unweighted n in parentheses; mean score of weighted n; significance calculated on unweighted n.

denomination, Jewish identity, family characteristics, and demographic factors in explaining the occurrence of equally dependent spouses.

Finally, following the research that suggests that greater involvement in the secular labor force might affect how religiosity is expressed, we looked at the difference in Jewish identity scores between respondents in dual-earner and single-earner families to see whether the dual-earning pattern might be related to how Jewish identity is expressed (Table 9.10). Perhaps the first thing to be noted is that the differences in scores between respondents in single-earner and dual-earner couples are statistically significant only for three of the Jewish identity factors. On two of these factors, respondents in dual-earner couples express stronger Jewish identity than those in single-earner couples; on one of these, respondents in single-earner couples express stronger Jewish identity than those in dual-earner couples.

Dual-earner couples are more likely to see being Jewish as being part of a universal moral community and heritage. This viewpoint minimizes the particularistic, tribal aspects of being Jewish, and emphasizes Jews' aspiration to make the world "a better place." It fits in well with other "universalistic" worldviews offered by other mainstream religions in the United States (Heilman, 2003–4). It also minimizes the conflict between being Jewish and fitting into the broader U.S. context. At the same time, dual-earner couples are more likely to understand being Jewish as being part of a cultural, ethnic, religious group of a worldwide people (Exceptionalism). This too fits with the mainstream U.S. orientation toward coexistent denominations and does not raise any conflicts between being Jewish and fitting into the broader U.S. context. Dual-earner couples are less likely, however, to express personal commitment to halachic rituals, such as keeping kosher, keeping the Yom Kippur fast, and keeping the Sabbath, which often do conflict with involvement in the broader U.S. society. Therefore, dual-earner couples are more likely to minimize the difference being Jewish presents in the broader U.S. context and to emphasize the universal aspects of being Jewish.

In the same direction, but not statistically significant, are the findings that dual-earner couples are less likely than single-earner couples to understand being Jewish as being active in the Jewish community and in Jewish practice; to personally be attached to the Jewish people, to Israel, and to the Jewish culture; and to have strong beliefs about religion (e.g., the belief that religion is important in one's life, the belief that one can pray in one's own words, the belief in God).

Being in a dual-earner couple apparently does not take time away from involvement in formal Jewish organizations, as can be seen by the lack of statistical significance in the comparison of the factor scores of dual-earner and single-earner couples.

SUMMARY ANALYSES OF DENOMINATION, JEWISH IDENTITY, AND DUAL-EARNING PATTERNS

Both denomination and Jewish identity appear to have weak relationships with dual-earning patterns. In the final section of this chapter, we look at whether any of the "Jewishness" indicators have independent relationships with dual-earning patterns once we take into account the educational background of both spouses, ages of spouses, and indicators of family roles (number of children at home). We use regression analyses that include dummy variables of denomination (Orthodox, Conservative, Reform, and unaffiliated, with Reconstructionist being omitted), selected Jewish identity factor scores (representing private religious, public religious, private ethnic, and public ethnic expressions of Jewish identity), demographic characteristics (age, education), and family variables (number of children under 18 in the household) to explain the likelihood of being in a dual-earner couple, the hours of work of the dual-earner couple, and the wife's contribution to the couple's annual earnings.

In the logistic regression of the likelihood of being in a dual-earner couple (Table 9.11), we see that being Orthodox is significantly associated with a lower likelihood of dual earning, as is the public religious expression of Jewish identity (Ceremony), even with the other variables controlled for. In fact, being Orthodox has the strongest relationship (negative) with the likelihood of being a dual earner, and this is after the number of children and the wife's level of education have been controlled for. As expected, being a dual-earner couple is more likely the higher the wife's education, the smaller the number of children under 18 in the household, the older the wife, and the younger the husband. Together these variables explain about 10% of the variance, predicting correctly just slightly more than two-thirds of the cases (67.3%). Thus, we see that Jewish identity and denominational norms do have an effect on the couple's economic behavior, beyond the demographic and familistic indicators associated with Jewishness.

The extent to which the couple is involved in the labor force (their joint weekly hours of employment) is related mainly to the number of children under 18 in the household (Table 9.12), which affects primarily the wife's hours of work, as we have seen in Chapter 5. None of the denominational

Table 9.11 Logistic Regression Analysis of Dual Earning, by Denomination, Jewish Identity, Spousal Characteristics and Number of Children

Independent variable	Unstandardized regression coefficient	Exponential coefficient
Denominational preference		
Orthodox	−0.578	0.561*
Conservative	−0.424	0.654**
Reform	−0.300	0.741
Unaffiliated	0.015	1.016
Jewish Identity Factor		
Ritual (private religious)	−0.099	0.906
Ceremony (public religious)	−0.185	0.831*
Culture (private ethnic)	0.136	1.145
Exceptionalism (public ethnic)	−0.067	0.936
Husband's education	−0.008	0.992
Wife's education	0.332	1.393*
Husband's age	−0.051	0.951*
Wife's age	0.037	1.038*
Number of children		
under 18 in household	−0.169	0.845*
Nagelkerke R^2	.097	
(Unweighted *n*)	(1,124)	

* $p < 0.05$; ** $p < 0.10$.

Table 9.12 Multiple Regression Analysis of Weekly Hours of Employment for American Jewish Couples (Ages 25–64), by Denomination, Jewish Identity, Spousal and Family Characteristics

Independent variable	Unstandardized coefficient	Standardized coefficient (ß)
Denominational preference		
Orthodox	−1.012	−.017
Conservative	.841	.020
Reform	−0.491	−.013
Unaffiliated	-2.021	−.050
Jewish identity factor		
Ritual (private religious)	0.180	.009
Ceremony (public religious)	0.017	.001
Culture (private ethnic)	0.583	.032
Exceptionalism (public ethnic)	−0.328	−.016
Husband's education	0.133	.009
Wife's education	1.067	.067
Husband's age	0.005	.006
Wife's age	0.025	.027
Number of children		
under 18 in household	−3.576	−.220*
R	0.251	
R^2	0.063	
(Unweighted n)	(788)	

* $p < 0.05$; **$p < 0.10$.

groups have independent relationships with the couple's hours of employment that are statistically significant at $p < 0.05$, nor do any of the Jewish identity factor scores.

The likelihood of unconventional income differences—the wife earning more than the husband—is most strongly related to the spouse's education (the lower the husband's education and the higher the wife's education), as might be expected, as well as the number of children in the household (the more children, the less the wife is likely to work in the labor force and hence to earn more than the husband; Table 9.13). However, the public ethnic expression of Jewish exceptionalism (believing in the uniqueness of the Jewish people) is also related to unconventional differences in income, and being Orthodox is weakly related (negatively) as well (even after the number of children and the spouse's education are controlled for). Therefore, the Jewishness indicators are not the most important influences on the wife's contribution to the household income, but they are not completely unrelated either.

Finally, we analyzed whether the Jewish identity factors have the same relationship (or lack thereof) to the dual-earning patterns within denominational groups. We considered the percentage of dual-earner couples, the combined hours of employment of husband and wife, the ratio of wife's to husband's employment hours, and the contribution of the wife's earnings to the couple's earnings. We used regression analyses for each of these variables (a logistic regression analysis for the incidence of dual earners in the denominational group and multiple regression analyses for each of the other dependent variables), with the independent variables being representative of private religious expressions of Jewish identity (Ritual), public religious expressions (Ceremony), private ethnic expressions (Culture), and

Table 9.13 Multiple Regression Analysis of Contribution to Household Earnings of American Jewish Wives (Ages 25–64), by Denomination, Jewish Identity, Spousal and Family Characteristics[a]

Independent variable	Unstandardized coefficient	Standardized Coefficient (ß)
Denominational preference		
Orthodox	0.195	.095**
Conservative	0.019	.013
Reform	−0.118	−.087
Unaffiliated	−0.046	−.032
Jewish identity factor		
Ritual (private religious)	0.043	.063
Ceremony (public religious)	−0.038	−.059
Culture (private ethnic)	0.060	.094
Exceptionalism (public ethnic)	−0.111	−.156*
Husband's education	−0.111	−.156*
Wife's education	0.105	.189*
Husband's age	0.002	.073
Wife's age	0.002	.050
Number of children		
under 18 in household	−0.081	−.142*
R	.336	
R²	.113	
(Unweighted *n*)	(460)	

* $p < 0.05$; ** $p < 0.10$.

[a]Data represent the ratio of the wife's income to that of the husband.

public ethnic expressions (Exceptionalism)—as in the analyses in the preceding section; we also controlled for husband's education, wife's education, husband's age, wife's age, and number of children under 18 in the household.

We have indicated with bold type those regression coefficients that are statistically significant to make the relationships across denominational groups clearer. As an explanation of the incidence of dual earning, the wife's education is a significant factor in each of the denominational groups (Table 9.14). The husband's age is significant for the non-Orthodox (the younger the husband, the more likely is the couple to be dual earner). For the Conservative and the Reform/Reconstructionist groups, dual earning is negatively related to the number of children under 18 in the household. For the Orthodox and the unaffiliated groups, public expressions of Jewish identity are significantly related to the incidence of dual earning, even when education, age, and number of children are controlled for. For the Orthodox a public ethnic factor, and for the unaffiliated a public religious factor, have significant relationships with dual earning (the stronger the identity, the greater is the incidence of dual earning). It is interesting that among the Conservative and the Reform/Reconstructionist denominations (the largest American Jewish denominations), none of the Jewish identity factors have an independent relationship with dual earning. We will return to this point in the final section.

With respect to the couple's combined hours of employment, among both Orthodox and Conservative groups, ethnic Jewishness is significantly related to how many hours the couple works, but this is not the case for other groups (Table 9.15; again, the regression coefficients that are statistically significant are in bold). Among the Conservative and Reform groups, the age of the husband and wife, and the number of children under 18 in the household, are also important in explaining how many hours the couple is employed. For the unaffiliated groups, only number of children under 18 significantly explains the variation in the couple's hours of employment.

In the analysis of the wife's contribution to the couple's joint earnings (Table 9.16), we can see that Jewish identity is related to the wife's contribution in both Orthodox and Conservative groups , but not in Reform/Reconstructionist or unaffiliated groups (again, see the regression coefficients in bold, which are statistically significant at $p < 0.05$ or $p < 0.10$). The stronger the public religious identity, the greater is the wife's contribution to the household economy. However, the stronger the ethnic factors (for Conservatives), the lower is the wife's contribution. The public and ethnic nature of these relationships suggests the influence of the norms of the surrounding denominational culture; it is interesting that the influences are not all in the same direction.

Table 9.14 Logistic Regression Analysis of Dual Earning in American Jewish Couples in Each Denominational Group (Ages 25–64), by Jewish Identity, Spousal and Family Characteristics[a]

Independent variable	Orthodox	Conservative	Reform/ Reconstructionist	Unaffiliated
Jewish identity factor				
Ritual (private religious)	−0.211	−0.285	−0.065	0.018
	(0.809)	(0.752)	(0.937)	(1.018)
Ceremony (public religious)	−0.110	−0.041	−0.143	**−0.454**
	(0.896)	(0.959)	(0.867)	**(0.635)***
Culture (private ethnic)	0.041	0.283	−0.026	0.297
	(1.042)	(1.327)	(0.856)	(1.345)
Exceptionalism				
(public ethnic)	**−0.631**	−0.014	−0.047	0.050
	(.532)*	(.986)	(0.708)	(1.051)
Husband's education	0.030	0.023	−0.050	−0.006
	(1.030)	(1.023)	(0.591)	(0.994)
Wife's education	**0.465**	**0.313**	**0.295**	**0.343**
	(1.592)*	**(1.368)***	**(1.342)***	**(1.409)***
Husband's age	0.006	**−0.047**	**−0.060**	**−0.064**
	(1.006)	**(0.954)***	**(0.942)***	**−(0.938)***
Wife's age	0.027	0.028	0.036	**0.047**
	(1.027)	(1.029)	(1.037)	**(1.048)****
Number of children				
under 18 in household	−0.075	**−0.237**	**−0.254**	−1.005
	(0.928)	**(0.789)***	**(0.775)***	(0.995)
Nagelkerke R^2	.254	.078	.079	.124
(Unweighted *n*)	(250)	(632)	(993)	(738)

* $p < .05$; ** $p < 0.10$.

[a]Data are unstandardized regression coefficients and (in parentheses) exponential coefficients.

Among Orthodox Jews, the wife's contribution is greater when the couple is younger and there are fewer children in the household. Among Conservatives, only the Jewish identity factors are significantly related to the wife's income contribution. Among Reform/Reconstructionist Jews, only the number of children in the household is related to the wife's contribution. For the unaffiliated, the fewer the number of children and the higher the wife's education, the greater is the wife's contribution to the joint income.

What we see in the last two analyses is that Jewish identity has an independent relationship with the dynamics of the dual-earning pattern among the Orthodox and Conservative, even when demographic and family variables

Table 9.15 Multiple Regression Analysis of Combined Hours of Employment of American Jewish Couples in Each Denominational Group (Ages 25–64), by Jewish Identity, Spousal and Family Characteristics[a]

Independent variable	Orthodox	Conservative	Reform/ Reconstructionist	Unaffiliated
Jewish Identity Factor				
Ritual (private religious)	6.198	–1.339	0.919	–0.593
	(.208)	(–.746)	(.035)	(–.021)
Ceremony (public religious)	–1.736	–2.807	1.606	0.881
	(–.040)	(–.114)	(.087)	(.045)
Culture (private ethnic)	4.004	3.800	–1.725	–0.319
	(.150)	(.181)*	(–.091)	(–.015)
Exceptionalism				
(public ethnic)	–.4257	–1.151	–0.059	0.345
	(–.203)**	–(–.054)	(–.003)	(.017)
Husband's education	–0.102	–1.151	–0.283	–1.014
	(–.007)	(–.054)	(–.332)	(–.066)
Wife's education	1.858	–0.494)	2.107	1.736
	(.125)	(–.029)	(.138)*	(.104)
Husband's age	0.084	–0.170	0.089	–0.036
	(.076)	(–.203)*	(.115)*	(–.041)
Wife's age	0.138	–0.132	0.095	–0.013
	(.130)	(–.147)*	(.110)*	(–.015)
Number of children				
under 18 in household	0.140	–4.624	–5.192	–4.083
	(.015)	(–.249)*	(–.266)*	(–.188)*
R	.414	.408	.321	.226
R²	.172	.167	.103	.051
(Unweighted *n*)	(76)	(190)	(320)	(182)

*p < 0.05; **p < 0.10.

[a]Data are unstandardized regression coefficients and (in parentheses) standardized coefficients, ß.

have been controlled for; this is not so for the Reform/Reconstructionist or unaffiliated groups. This suggests that their Jewish identity has less to do with their secular economic behavior than it does for the Orthodox and Conservative groups.

SUMMARY AND CONCLUSIONS

In this chapter, we have asked whether Jewishness is related to the economic behavior of Jewish couples (in which at least one spouse is Jewish), looking at denomination and expressions of Jewish identity as indicators of "Jewishness." An affirmative answer limits the notion of secularization, suggesting that religious and ethnic identity continue to be related to secular behavior. Relationships between primarily ethnic and public expressions of Jewish identity would suggest that they have more to do with social networks and norms than with religiosity per se. The fact that we found that it is identification with public and ethnic expressions of Jewish identity that are related to the dual-earning patterns of American Jews suggests that the structural forces binding Jews together as a community are reinforced by patterns of economic behavior within American Jewish families. These results thus reinforce the dynamic suggested by Goldscheider and Zuckerman's (1985) work

Table 9.16 Multiple Regression Analysis of Wife's Contribution to Combined Earnings of American Jewish Couples in Each Denominational Group (Ages 25–64), by Jewish Identity, Spousal and Family Characteristics[a]

Independent variable	Orthodox	Conservative	Reform/ Reconstructionist	Unaffiliated
Jewish identity factor				
Ritual(private religious)	0.081	−0.212	0.016	0.085
	(.129)	(−.083)	(.021)	(.055)
Ceremony (public religious)	−0.258	−0.393	0.048	0.086
	(−.283)*	(−.145)**	(.087)	(.078)
Culture (private ethnic)	0.049	0.365	0.005	0.038
	(.088)	(.158)**	(.008)	(.032)
Exceptionalism (public ethnic)	−0.040	0.352	0.019	−0.032
	(−.091)	(.149)*	(.032)	(−.028)
Husband's education	−0.024	−0.143	−0.026	−0.106
	(−.039)	(−.093)	(−.059)	(−.123)
Wife's education	−0.039	−0.023	0.046	0.169
	(−.123)	(−.012)	(.100)	(.180)*
Husband's age	0.005	−0.006	0.001	0.005
	(.214)*	(−.062)	(.051)	(.098)
Wife's age	0.005	−0.009	0.002	0.005
	(.204)**	(−.095)	(.074)	(.095)
Number of children under 18 in household	−0.049	−0.089	−0.085	−0.178
	−.249)*	(−.043)	(−.146)*	(−.147)*
R	.516	.272	.202	.249
R²	.266	.074	.041	.062
(n)	(47)	(102)	(176)	(120)

*p < 0.05; **p < 0.10.

[a]Data are unstandardized regression coefficients and (in parentheses) standardized coefficients, ß.

on the "transformation" of the nature of American Jewry and what binds the American Jewish population together; they suggested that many American Jews are "bound tightly by occupational, residential, and other structural ties to the community" (p. 241) and that these ties reinforce "Jewish" norms regardless of variations in religious ideology and belief.

Looking at denominational preference as an indicator of traditional or egalitarian Jewishness, we found few indications that denomination itself is related to labor force behavior or couples' achievement. Orthodoxy does not seem to foster or impede the dual-earning pattern or equal achievement between spouses, nor do the more egalitarian Reform/Reconstructionist denominations. Rather, the influence of Orthodoxy seems to work through the greater familistic orientation (more children at home, the wife's determination of her hours of employment on the basis of the husband's occupation and age, and the wife's choice of an occupation that may be more flexible during her childrearing years), whereas the distinctiveness of the Reform/Reconstructionists seems to be a reflection of their somewhat higher educational achievement. The various indicators of Jewish identity were most strongly related to variation in the wife's work hours than to any patterns of achievement or labor force participation.

When we combined denomination, Jewish identity, demographic characteristics, and family indicators to predict the likelihood of a couple being dual earner, we were testing whether the weak effects of Jewishness that we had seen on couple's economic behavior and achievements were the result of differential age, education, and family characteristics rather than direct relationships with Jewishness. We found that being Orthodox and the strength of public ethnic Jewish identity had independent relationships with being a dual-earner couple and the wife's contribution to the couple's earnings. Therefore, the relationship between Jewishness and the couple's economic patterns could not be explained entirely by the demographic and family indicators we controlled for.

Finally, we looked at the denominations separately to see whether the same Jewish identity factors correlated with couple's economic patterns in each denomination. We wondered whether the Orthodox were guided more by religiosity than the other groups, whether Conservative and Reform/Reconstructionists might be guided more by ethnic identity, and whether the unaffiliated might be guided to a lesser extent by Jewishness than those respondents who had expressed denominational preferences. We found that public involvement in Jewishness was related to the extent of the wife's labor force participation (hours and contribution to household earnings) among both the Orthodox and the Conservative denominations, but not among the Reform/Reconstructionist or unaffiliated groups.

Involvement in public religious expression of Jewish identity was related to the wife's greater contribution to the couple's earnings. For the Orthodox, public ethnic expression of Jewish identity was related to the couple being involved more hours in the labor force, but for the Conservative group, stronger ethnic identity was related to less involvement of the wife in the labor force. That it is public involvement in Jewish identity that is related to this behavior suggests that the denominational community involves norms of behavior that spill over into the couple's economic functioning; it is possible that the denominational community also provides an infrastructure of support for such behavior, such as childcare facilities. That the Reform/Reconstructionist and unaffiliated groups are not as highly influenced in their secular behavior by their Jewish identity suggests greater secularization on their part, in the sense that their religious community has less effect on their secular economic behavior. Our findings thus refine Goldscheider and Zuckerman's (1985) conclusions by suggesting that the ties that bind secular behavior and Jewish identity are not equally distributed throughout the American Jewish population.

CHAPTER 10

Intermarriage and Gendered Patterns of Secular Achievement

Perhaps the most direct test of the integration of American Jews into the broader population is intermarriage. It might be expected that Jews married to non-Jews would be less differentiated from the broader U.S. society in a number of ways, and there is no reason to expect that secular achievement and patterns of gender difference would be exceptional in this respect. Intermarried Jews are typically less invested in their Jewish ethnic or religious capital than are other Jews (cf. Phillips and Fishman, 2006), and their social capital clearly extends beyond Jewish social circles. Their pool for marriage partners extends beyond Jews to the larger pool of non-Jews,[1] and from the evidence we have in the National Jewish Population Survey, supported by qualitative studies, this often is a persistent pattern since childhood: intermarried Jews are more likely than intramarried Jews to have had a non-Jewish parent, to say that their closest high school friends included non-Jews, and to have had less positive interactions in Jewish-oriented social environments (Phillips and Fishman, 2006).

Seeking, or being willing to accept, a non-Jewish marriage partner might reflect putting economic considerations above cultural or religious considerations, especially if the Jewish spouse has an occupational status that differs from that of the majority of American Jews. Status harmonization has been found to be a motivation for switching to a different religious denomination (Sherkat and Wilson, 1995; Wilson, 1966) and also for endogamy or intermarriage (O'Leary and Finnas, 2002). As the boundaries between Jews and non-Jews become blurred (Alba, 2006), however, status differences between the intermarried and the intramarried may also narrow.

Kalmijn (1994) found that economic homogamy is a more important factor than cultural homogamy for individuals who are older when they marry, and as we will see later in this chapter, intermarriages occur more often when the man and/or woman is older (either as later first marriages or remarriages). This may be a variant of "trading up" in remarriage—that is, giving up cultural homogamy for higher economic status or economic homogamy.

Once one has intermarried, social contacts and knowing how to get along among non-Jews (to the extent that this differs from getting along with Jews) provide social capital that might prove fruitful for getting a job or promotion, resulting in different occupational patterns and even rewards. In this chapter we consider the differences in the secular achievement of Jewish men and women who are intermarried from those who are intramarried and consider whether patterns of gender equality differ as well.

EDUCATION AND INTERMARRIAGE

Jews who have married non-Jews do not differ significantly from Jews who have married Jews in terms of their education (Table 10.1). Similar proportions have college degrees, graduate degrees, and doctoral or professional degrees. The slightly higher percentages of women with doctoral or professional degrees among intermarried women may well be attributed to the older average age of intramarried women. It certainly is not the case that the intermarried are more similar to the broader U.S. population than are the intramarried in this respect.

FAMILY BEHAVIOR AND INTERMARRIAGE

In terms of family behavior, we see certain differences between intramarried and intermarried American Jews (Table 10.2). Men and women who are intermarried were married (first marriage) at an older age than were intramarried Jews. Fishman's interviews with intermarried couples suggests that, for some, marriage was postponed *because* of the religious differences

Table 10.1 Educational Attainment of Married American Jews (Ages 25–64), by Intermarriage and Gender

	Men		Women	
Education	Jewish spouse	Non-Jewish spouse	Jewish spouse	Non-Jewish spouse
B.A.+ (%)	69.0	69.2	59.5	60.6
Graduate degrees (%)	37.3	35.4	26.1	29.2
Ph.D., professional degree (%)	14.5	14.5	4.3	7.4
$(n)^a$	(582)	(283)	(731)	(263)

[a]Unweighted *n* in parentheses; calculations performed using person-weights provided with dataset.

Table 10.2 Family Characteristics of Intramarried and Intermarried American Jews and Non-Hispanic Whites (Ages 35–64), by Gender

Family characteristic	Men			Women		
	Intramarried	Intermarried	U.S. non-Hispanic whites	Intramarried	Intermarried	U.S. non-Hispanic whites
Age at first marriage (mean)	26.2	28.5	22.4	24.3	25.7	20.2
Married more than once (%)	20.0	34.0*	27.4	15.5	29.1*	28.4
Ever divorced (%)	18.7	31.4*	33.2	14.7	26.8*	36.2
Age at current marriage (if remarried) (mean)	44.3	40.3		44.0	40.5	
Childless (%)				9.7	20.3*	16.3
Age at birth of first child (mean)				27.3	27.2	24.5
Age at birth of last child (mean)				32.1	31.6	30.1
Number of children (mean)				2.2	1.6*	2.1
Four or more children (%)				9.5	8.9	13.9
(n, thousands)[a]	(375.6)	(166.8)	(45,167.5)	(402.6)	(139.1)	(46,592.5)

Data sources: NJPS, 2000–01; SIPP, 2001.

*t-test between intramarried and intermarried men or women is significant at $p < 0.05$.

[a]Data for Jews weighted by person-weights provided with dataset.

(Phillips and Fishman, 2006); therefore, it would be inaccurate to conclude that intermarriage is a "last resort" when intramarriage has not happened. A clearer difference is seen with regard to remarriage: 35% of remarriages are intermarriages, compared with 19.7% of first marriages. This is true for both men and women, although there are somewhat higher proportions of inter-marriage among remarried men than among remarried women. Therefore, we see in Table 10.2 that both men and women who are intermarried are more likely to have been divorced and to have been married more than once than are men and women with Jewish spouses. Remarriages, however, do occur on the average at about the same age for those marrying Jews or non-Jews.

A second major difference that we see is in patterns of childbirth. A higher proportion of intermarried women have no children, and intermar-ried women have fewer children than intramarried women. The timing of childbirth among those who have children is similar for both groups of Jewish women.

The family characteristics of the intermarried are not more similar to the broader population than are those of the intramarried. Their older age at first marriage and fewer children actually make intermarried Jews less like those in the broader population than are intramarried Jews. There are similarities only in the proportion of those who have married more than once and the proportion of those who have ever been divorced.

HOMOGAMY AND INTERMARRIAGE

One question that may be asked is whether the intermarried have traded cultural homogamy (being of the same religion or ethnicity) for other kinds of marital homogamy. We look at educational homogamy and age homog-amy (husband and wife within 5 years of each other)—two characteristics that may well affect choice of marriage partner—for men and women who are intramarried and intermarried, for first and subsequent marriages (Table 10.3).

We see some tendency for intermarriages to be more homogamous with respect to education, but not with respect to age. Age homogamy is quite high in first marriages whether they are intra- or intermarriages, for both men and women (around 80% of first marriages are between spouses within 5 years of each other). Remarriages are less homogamous with re-spect to age, probably reflecting a more restricted marriage market, which makes age homogamy less likely. Intermarriage seems to be an obstacle to age homogamy for men, but not for women (remarried, intermarried men are the most likely to be more than 5 years older than their wives).

Educational homogamy tends to be greater for intermarriages, espe-cially for women and especially for those who have remarried (there is

Table 10.3 Age and Educational Homogamy of First Marriages and Remarriages, by Intermarriage and Gender

	Men		Women	
	Intramarried	Intermarried	Intramarried	Intermarried
First marriage (n)[a]	(495)	(198)	(677)	(194)
Within five years of spouse's age (%)	85.1	80.8	78.9	81.5
Same educational attainment as spouse (%)	40.7	41.4	37.0	44.8
Remarriage (n)[a]	(113)	(90)	(108)	(78)
Within five years of spouse's age (%)	58.4	42.9	59.4	62.6
Same educational attainment as spouse (%)	25.4	33.0	26.9	37.7

[a]Unweighted n in parentheses; calculations performed using person-weights provided with dataset.

hardly any difference in educational homogamy between intramarried and intermarried men in their first marriage). As with age, there is less educational homogamy in remarriages than in first marriages, for both men and women. But intermarried couples are more likely to have the same educational attainment, for both men and women in remarriages and for women in first marriages. Recalling from Chapter 3 that educational homogamy is greater among American Jews than in the broader U.S. population, we see again that the intermarried are even more distinct than the intramarried from the broader population.

LABOR FORCE PARTICIPATION PATTERNS AND INTERMARRIAGE

Intermarriages are also characterized by higher percentages of dual earners, that is, both husband and wife participating in the labor force, than are intramarriages. To some extent this is because a higher proportion of intermarried women have no children, but they are also more active in the labor force when they have no children than are women with no children who have Jewish spouses (Figure 10.1). We see this as part of a more general pattern among intermarried couples.

Intermarried wives are more likely to share the economic role of labor force participation with their husbands, especially when they have no young children at home. Intermarried couples are also more likely to have wives who earn more than their husbands when they are employed and to have higher occupational prestige than their husbands, as we shall see later.

Both Jewish husbands and wives who are intermarried are less likely to be in managerial/executive, business/finance, or professional occupations (Table 10.4). As a result, while there is only a slight difference in terms of occupational homogamy between intermarried and intramarried couples, when intramarried spouses have similar occupations, both are more likely to be in managerial/executive, business/finance, or professional positions, whereas both spouses in occupationally homogamous intermarried couples are more likely to have other kinds of occupations.

As a result, intermarried Jewish men are more similar in their occupational distribution to the broader white population than are Jewish men with Jewish spouses (Figure 10.2). Although the comparison among women shows a similar tendency, the difference between the two groups of Jewish women is smaller.

Figure 10.1. Percentage of dual-earner households, by gender, inter- or intramarriage, and presence of children under age 18.

Table 10.4 Occupations of Intermarried and Intramarried Couples

	Jewish spouse	Non-Jewish spouse
Husband's occupation		
manager/business/professional (%)	64.4	54.9
Wife's occupation		
manager/business/professional (%)	63.3	55.9
Spouses with same occupation		
for Jewish husbands (%)	35.2	34.1
Spouses with same occupation		
for Jewish wives (%)	30.9	27.6
Both spouses' occupation		
managerial/business/professional (%)	45.0	35.7
Husband, but not wife,		
manager/business/professional (%)	19.4	19.2
Wife, but not husband,		
manager/business/professional (%)	18.3	20.2
Neither spouse		
manager/business/professional (%)	17.3	24.9
(Unweighted n)[a]	(770)	(421)

[a]Unweighted n in parentheses; calculations performed using person-weights provided with dataset.

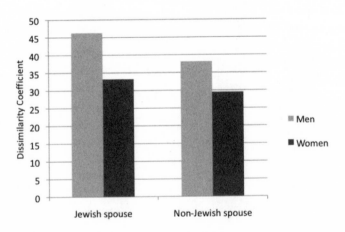

Figure 10.2. Occupational dissimilarity between American non-Hispanic whites and Jews, by gender and inter- or intramarriage, 2000–01. *Data sources:* NJPS, 2000–01; U.S. Census, 2000.

Given that there is little difference in education between respondents who have Jewish spouses and those who do not, the occupational differences may be a result of ties with the non-Jewish spouse and his or her family and friends, which provides social capital valued differently in the broader population.

INTERMARRIAGE, REMARRIAGE, AND SECULAR ACHIEVEMENT

Given that intermarriage is more common among the remarried and that remarriage is associated both with lower achievement of husbands and with women's high achievement relative to that of their husbands (Chapter 5), we wanted to see whether remarriage and intermarriage interact in terms of spouse's occupational achievement. That is, the findings about remarriage might be a result of the higher proportion of remarriages that are intermarriages; or the findings about intermarriage might be a result of the higher proportion of intermarriages that are remarriages. We therefore looked at respondents' occupational achievement by gender, controlling for whether the current marriage was a first marriage or a remarriage, as well as whether the respondent had a Jewish or a non-Jewish spouse (Table 10.5).

Looking first at respondents currently in their first marriage, women with Jewish husbands have somewhat lower educational achievement than intermarried wives, but are more likely to be in managerial/executive, business/finance, or professional occupations, have similar median annual incomes, and have higher occupational prestige. However, they are less likely to be in marriages where the wife has a higher education, higher annual earnings, or higher occupational prestige than the husband, suggesting that their Jewish husbands have an even higher occupational status than they do. Similarly, men with Jewish wives are more likely to be in managerial/executive, business/finance, or professional occupations, have a similar education but higher income, and have higher occupational prestige than intermarried husbands. Their wives are less likely than intermarried husbands to have a higher income or higher occupational prestige than they do.

Among second (or later) marriages, women with Jewish husbands are more likely to have higher education than their husbands, to be in a managerial/executive, business/finance, or professional occupation, to have greater occupational prestige than their husbands, and to have the same income as their husbands than are wives of non-Jewish husbands. However, intermarried wives are also somewhat more likely to be in marriages where they have a higher education, income, and occupational prestige than their husbands. Similarly, among the husbands, those with Jewish wives have a higher education and higher occupational prestige than those

Table 10.5 Education and Occupational Characteristics of Intermarried and Intramarried Men and Women[a]

	Spouse's religion			
	First marriage		Remarriage	
Characteristic	Jewish	Non-Jewish	Jewish	Non-Jewish
Women				
B.A. or higher (%)	57.5 (193)	63.9 (668)	59.4 (186)	50.9 (78)
Mgr/Exec/Bus/finance/ professional (%)	64.1 (424)	55.1 (159)	68.2 (106)	62.3 (67)
Mean occupational prestige	53.68 (398)	51.70 (154)	53.69 (77)	51.8 (64)
Median annual income ($)	37,500 (180)	37,500 (89)	42,500 (39)	42,500 (37)
Wife's education greater than husband's (%)	21.8 (653)	30.3 (191)	30.3 (182)	33.7 (76)
Wife's annual income greater than husband's (%)	18.1 (144)	19.0 (75)	17.2 (28)	21.8 (33)
Wife's occupational prestige greater than husband's (%)	50.3 (186)	57.8 (77)	62.4 (36)	67.2 (32)

Men

B.A. or higher (%)	68.0	(486)	71.2	(198)	70.2	(112)	62.4	(89)
Mgr/Exec/Bus/finance/ professional (%)	67.0	(354)	55.5	(181)	52.4	(77)	57.7	(67)
Mean occupational prestige	55.83	(329)	52.55	(165)	54.55	(67)	53.70	(61)
Median annual income ($)	72,500	(182)	67,500	(114)	72,500	(44)	72,500	(37)
Wife's education greater than husband's (%)	21.8	(653)	30.3	(191)	30.3	(182)	33.7	(76)
Wife's annual income greater than husband's (%)	18.1	(144)	19.0	(75)	17.2	(28)	21.8	(33)
Wife's occupational prestige greater than husband's (%)	50.3	(186)	57.8	(77)	62.4	(36)	67.2	(32)

[a] Unweighted *n* in parentheses; calculations performed using person-weights provided with dataset.

with non-Jewish wives, but income is the same for both sets of husbands, and intramarried men are slightly less likely to be in managerial/executive, business/finance, or professional occupations than their intermarried counterparts. Although remarried men who have Jewish wives are more likely to have wives with a higher education and income than they have, they are less likely to have wives with higher occupational prestige than they have.

Comparing the achievements of intramarried men and women who are in first versus second marriages, we find that the main difference between wives in their first marriage to Jewish men and those in their second or other marriage to Jewish men is that the latter are more likely to have a higher education, higher income, and greater occupational prestige than their husbands. This is also true for the husbands with respect to income and education, but not occupational prestige. Comparing the achievements of intermarried men and women who are in a first versus a second marriage, we find similarly that wives in second or other marriages are more likely to have a higher education, income, and occupational prestige than their husbands, even though they themselves are less likely to be college graduates. Comparing intermarried husbands in first marriages with those who are remarried, we see that the latter have lower educational achievement (are less likely to be college graduates), but have a slightly higher median annual income and occupational prestige; their wives are more likely to have a higher education and greater occupational prestige than intermarried husbands in first marriages, but they are less likely to be in marriages where the wife earns more than the husband.

In conclusion, intermarried men and women tend to have less occupational and educational achievement than their intramarried counterparts, in first marriages as well as in remarriages, but remarriage itself seems to have an effect, in that remarried husbands are more likely than husbands in first marriages to have wives with a higher occupational status than themselves. It seems that intermarriage offers intermarried men higher economic status through their wives, particularly men who have lower educational and occupational achievement than their intramarried male counterparts.

JEWISHNESS AND INTERMARRIAGE

It is not surprising that intermarried Jews tend to be less identified with Jewishness, in terms of both religion and ethnicity. On each of our Jewish identity factors, both men and women who are intermarried have weaker Jewish identity than their intramarried counterparts (Figure 10.3). From the NJPS data, we cannot determine whether this precedes intermarriage, though it is likely that weaker Jewish identity allows Jewish boundaries to

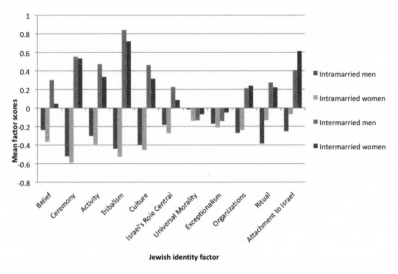

Figure 10.3. Jewish identity factor scores, by gender and inter- or intramarriage.

be permeated and then is not reinforced by the spouse's Jewish identity (unless the spouse converts and is committed to being Jewish; see also Fishman, 2004).

The biggest differences are found with respect to the understanding that being Jewish involves being active in contemporary Jewish life and practice (Activity), participating in collective rituals (Ceremony), and having personal attachment to the Jewish people (Tribalism). There are two factors on which the intermarried and the intramarried are very similar: that being Jewish expresses a universal morality and heritage (Universal Morality) and that American Jews are a distinctive group (Exceptionalism). These two factors are quite compatible with American pluralism from any perspective, religious or ethnic, Jewish or non-Jewish; they are also compatible with positive views of intermarriage that see it as an act transcending one's own narrow ethnic identity and opting for a more general "American" one, but not negating one's own roots (Fishman, 2004).

On almost every factor, women have stronger Jewish identity than men, and this is true for both intramarried and intermarried women. This may be one of the reasons that children of intermarried Jewish women are more likely to be raised in the Jewish tradition than are children of intermarried Jewish men (Fishman, 2004). However, the gender differences are somewhat smaller than we saw in Chapter 6 once we separate the intermarried and the intramarried. The gender differences are reversed for the intermarried on three factors: that being Jewish expresses a universal morality, American Jewish exceptionalism, and personal attachment to Israel. The gender differences are reversed for the intramarried on two factors as well: personal halachic ritual performance and personal attachment to Israel. As noted in Chapter 6, the critical variable in personal attachment to Israel on which there is this reversed gender difference is familiarity with the social and political situation in Israel. There is very little gender difference in organizational involvement for either group.

It is interesting that almost as high a proportion of the intermarried had some formal Jewish education (81.2% of men and 66.2% of women) as did the intramarried (83.5% of men and 72.2% of women), although the intermarried who had some Jewish education had fewer years on average (4.5 years for men and 3.5 years for women) than the intramarried (5.6 years for men and 4.8 years for women). Their exposure to formal Jewish education undermines the idea that there is something fundamentally different between those who marry Jews and those who do not; to some degree those who intermarry are probably exposed to similar "Jewish capital" as those who do not; but their fewer years of Jewish education suggest that not all of their Jewish experience was positive or continuous, and is one of the ways in which their upbringing provides less "Jewish capital" than does that of those who intramarried (Phillips and Fishman, 2006).

JEWISHNESS, SECULAR BEHAVIOR, AND INTERMARRIAGE

In this final section of the chapter, we consider how the different expressions of Jewish identity are related to the secular behavior patterns of intramarried and intermarried couples. We look first at a family characteristic that we have seen differs between intramarried and intermarried couples: fertility. We continue with the labor force participation of women and conclude with occupational prestige, a measure of occupational achievement (for both men and women).

We use a multiple regression analysis to predict the number of live children born to women 35 and older (for whom most childbearing has been completed) and perform separate analyses for intramarried and intermarried women (Table 10.6). Among the independent variables, as indicators of Jewish identity we chose one indicator of private religious behavior, Ritual; an indicator of public religious behavior, Ceremony; an indicator of private ethnic attachment, Tribalism; and an indicator of public ethnic behavior, Organizations. We included years of formal Jewish education as an independent variable, along with the common demographic variables related to variation in number of children born: age, as an indicator of age cohort; age at marriage; whether or not a woman has been married more than once; and her level of education.

Table 10.6 Multiple Regression Analysis of Number of Live Births for Intramarried and Intermarried Women (Ages 35 and Over), by Jewish Identity, Age, Family Characteristics, and Education[a]

Independent variable	Intramarried women		Intermarried women	
Jewish Identity Factor[b]				
Ritual	−0.449	(−.337)*	−0.087	(−.042)
Ceremony	−0.269	(−.138)*	−0.104	(−.090)
Tribalism	−0.025	(−.014)	0.104	(.061)
Organizations	0.083	(.072)**	−0.142	(−.083)
Formal Jewish				
education (years)	0.068	(.192)*	−0.027	(−.081)
Age	0.006	(.056)	0.001	(.009)
Age at first marriage	−0.070	(−.272)*	−0.099	(−.535)*
Number of marriages	−0.282	(−.076)*	−0.341	(−.131)**
Education	−0.148	(−.129)*	−0.061	(−.059)
R^2	0.301		0.297	
(Unweighted *n*)	(550)		(184)	

[a]Data are unstandardized coefficients and (in parentheses) standardized coefficients, ß.

[b]Stronger expressions of Jewish identity on these factors are lower; weaker expressions are higher.

*Statistically significant at $p < 0.05$; **significant at $p < 0.10$.

    Clearly, their Jewish identity has a greater impact on the fertility of intramarried than on that of intermarried women. Among the intramarried, both private and public religious expressions of Jewish identity are related positively to having more children, and involvement in public ethnic behavior (Organizations) is related negatively to having more children (actually, it may be the other direction of influence: women with fewer children may have more time to participate in volunteer organizations). In addition, the more years of formal Jewish education the woman has had, the more children she has. Comparing the standardized regression coefficients in parentheses, we can see that the private religious expressions of Jewish identity have the strongest influence on fertility, followed by the age at first marriage. None of these "Jewishness" factors have any relationship to the fertility of intermarried women.

    Intramarried women's fertility is most strongly related to their level of secular education (the more education, the fewer children). For both groups of women, an earlier age at marriage is related to having more children, and being married more than once is related to having fewer children. The former has a much stronger effect than the latter among both groups of women.

Jewish identity is also related to the extent of women's participation in the labor force for the intramarried, but not for the intermarried (Table 10.7), although the relationship is much weaker than that for fertility. In this multiple regression analysis, the dependent variable is the extent of labor force participation (0, none; 1, part time; 2, full time). The independent variables are, as in the preceding analysis, an indicator of private religious expression of Jewish identity (Ritual), public religious Jewish identity (Ceremony), private ethnic Jewish identity (Tribalism), and public ethnic Jewish identity (Organizations). Years of formal Jewish education are also independent variables. Secular education, age, age at marriage, number of marriages, and number of children under 18 in the household are also entered into the equation as independent variables. We limit the analysis to the main ages of labor force participation, 35–64. We are looking only at currently married women (so that we can divide them by the religion of their spouse).

Here we can see that for intramarried women, those who are more active in the civilian labor force are less active in Jewish volunteer organizations.

Table 10.7 Multiple Regression Analysis of Labor Force Participation of Intramarried and Intermarried Women (Ages 35–64), by Jewish Identity, Age, Family Characteristics, and Education[a]

Independent variable	Intramarried women		Intermarried women	
Jewish Identity Factor[b]				
Ritual	−0.015	(−.020)	−0.027	(−.020)
Ceremony	−0.066	(−.971)	−0.116	(−.153)
Tribalism	0.076	(.068)	0.026	(.107)
Organizations	0.091	(.117)*	0.026	(.019)
Formal Jewish education (years)	−0.004	(−.021)	0.005	(.025)
Age	−0.009	(−.117)*	−0.006	(−.067)
Age at first marriage	0.000	(.003)	0.017	(.016)
Number of marriages	0.325	(.133) *	0.161	(.141)
Number of children under 18 in household	−0.101	(−.174)*	−0.209	(−.280)*
Education	0.148	(.193)*	0.094	(.130)**
R^2	.111		.139	
(Unweighted *n*)	(443)		(211)	

[a]Data are unstandardized coefficients and (in parentheses) standardized coefficients, ß.
[b]Stronger expressions of Jewish identity on these factors are lower; weaker expressions are higher.
*Statistically significant at $p < 0.05$; **significant at $p < 0.10$.

This may be related to their allocation of time (the more one volunteers, the less time one has to work in the labor force full time and vice versa). For both groups of women, an important influence on the extent of labor force participation is having children under the age of 18 in the household. Education also has an important influence on how much women work in the labor force. So here we see, as we did earlier, that investment in Jewish identity does not hold women back from participating in the labor force, except to the extent that it introduces time constraints if they are involved in volunteer organizations.

Finally, we look at an indicator of occupational achievement, occupational prestige, for both men and women, intramarried and intermarried (Table 10.8). Our independent variables are again four expressions of Jewish identity—private religious (Ritual), public religious (Ceremony), private ethnic (Tribalism), and public ethnic (Organizations)—and years of formal Jewish education. Age, age at first marriage, number of marriages, number of children under 18 present in the household, and education are also entered as independent variables. We also introduce the variable of hours of work, which may influence occupational achievement.

Among all groups (men and women, intramarried or intermarried), of all the variables education has the strongest relationship by far with occupational prestige. For intermarried men and women, age is also related to occupational prestige (older men and women have higher occupational prestige). This suggests that perhaps the patterns of intermarriage are changing, with intermarriage occurring among Jews with less occupational achievement than used to be the case.

The various expressions of Jewish identity have no relationship to intramarried women's occupational prestige. For intramarried men, however, occupational prestige is higher among those with strong ethnic ties to other Jews, both in terms of personal attachment to the Jewish people (Tribalism) and involvement in Jewish organizations (Organizations). This suggests that men use their ethnic ties to further their occupational advancement. Among intermarried men and women, however, ties to fellow Jews appear to be negatively related to occupational prestige. Perhaps those who maintain strong ties to fellow Jews are not as well integrated into their non-Jewish circles or have investments in conflicting social capital, which hampers their achievement. This would seem to be an important avenue to explore in terms of understanding the impact of intermarriage on other aspects of secular and social life.

Finally, we wanted to see whether the likelihood of wives earning more than their husbands, which was more common among the intermarried than the intramarried, was at all related to Jewish identity factors. However,

Table 10.8 Multiple Regression Analysis of Occupational Prestige of Intramarried and Intermarried American Jews (Ages 35–64), by Jewish Identity, Age, Family Characteristics, and Education

Independent variable	Intramarried		Intermarried	
Women				
Jewish Identity Factor[b]				
Ritual	0.466	(.044)	−2.509	(−.120)
Ceremony	0.240	(.014)	−1.233	(−.103)
Tribalism	−1.364	(−.085)	3.757	(.215)*
Organizations	−1.024	(−.092)	−2.240	(−.104)
Formal Jewish education (years)	0.030	(.010)	−0.133	(−.034)
Age	0.023	(.020)	0.223	(.159)*
Number of marriages	−0.688	(−.020)	−2.322	(−.081)
Number of children under 18 in household	0.850	(.103)	−0.452	(−.039)
Education	4.235	(.384)*	5.625	(.494)*
R^2	0.166		0.297	
(Unweighted *n*)	(330)		(171)	
Men				
Jewish Identity Factor[b]				
Ritual	−0.578	(−.045)	−2.003	(−.095)
Ceremony	0.222	(.013)	−1.123	(−.094)
Tribalism	−2.897	(−.157)*	3.757	(.215)*
Organizations	−1.029	(−.092)**	−2.254	(−.105)
Formal Jewish education (years)	−0.213	(−.058)	−0.469	(−.114)
Age	−0.103	(−.073)	0.223	(.159)*
Number of marriages	0.958	(.026)	−2.322	(−.081)
Number of children under 18 in household	0.252	(.024)	−0.408	(−.035)
Education	4.875	(.402)*	4.887	(.390)*
R^2	0.177		0.157	
(Unweighted *n*)	(293)		(190)	

[a]Data are unstandardized coefficients and (in parentheses) standardized coefficients, ß.

[b]Stronger expressions of Jewish identity on these factors are lower; weaker expressions are higher.

*Statistically significant at $p < 0.05$; **significant at $p < 0.10$.

as Table 10.9 shows, Jewish identity factors have no significant relation-ships to the comparison of the husband's and wife's incomes. The only sig-nificant factors that we could identify are the husband's and wife's educa-tion (significantly related to the income comparison in most of the subgroups): the lower the husband's level of education, the higher is the wife's income relative to his; the higher the wife's level of education, the higher is her in-come relative to her husband's. The family situation (remarriage or first marriage, number of children under 18 at home), the Jewish identity fac-tors, age, and occupational homogamy are not related to the comparison of wife's to husband's income.

SUMMARY AND CONCLUSIONS

We have seen that intermarried American Jews differ from intramarried American Jews in that they marry later, have fewer children, are more likely to marry a spouse with similar education, are more likely to be dual earn-ers, and are more likely to be in marriages in which the wife earns more than her husband and has higher occupational prestige than her husband. Intermarried Jews are less likely to be in managerial/executive, business/ finance, or professional occupations than their intramarried counterparts. We suggested that among remarried men who are intermarried, cultural homogamy might be traded for the higher economic status their wives' contribute to the marriage. This is consonant with research that shows that economic motivations may outweigh cultural considerations when mar-riage is entered into by older men and women (Kalmijn, 1994), since inter-marriages are more likely to be remarriages, and remarriages take place when the couple is older than do first marriages. However, our results also refine earlier research, in that we show that there is a gender differentia-tion: men and women's intermarriage may be motivated by different fac-tors, or selection in the marriage market may work differently for men and women, at least among American Jews. The findings are consistent with the increasing importance of women's earning potential in determining their marriage prospects, here extended to the "remarriage market." Among men, the dynamic seems less straightforward: men's economic status seems to play an important role in the Jewish marriage market (just as women's economic status does), but men who do not measure up to the Jewish "standard" may feel more comfortable (or successful) seeking non-Jewish partners. Whether they themselves are opting out of the culturally homogamous marriage market or being pushed out remains to be demon-strated by other kinds of research.

It is not surprising that intermarried Jews express weaker Jewish iden-tity in almost every aspect. Furthermore, their Jewish identity has less to do

Table 10.9 Multiple Regression Analysis of Ratio of Wife's to Husband's Income in Intramarried and Intermarried American Jewish Couples (Ages 35 and Over), by Jewish Identity, Age, Family Characteristics, and Education

Independent variable	Intramarried		Intermarried	
Women				
Jewish identity factor[b]				
Ritual	−0.022	(−.036)	−0.118	(−.116)
Ceremony	0.024	(.027)	0.013	(.021)
Tribalism	0.012	(.014)	−0.079	(−.087)
Organizations	0.079	(.154)	−0.266	(−.255)
Formal Jewish education (years)	0.022	(.138)	0.011	(.066)
Age	0.002	(.039)	−0.005	(−.077)
Number of marriages	0.081	(.045)	−0.007	(−.005)
Number of children under 18 in household	−0.088	(−.174)	−0.110	(−.187)
Husband's education	−0.136	(−.287)*	−0.092	(−.188)
Wife's education	0.051	(.089)	0.108	(.190)
Occupational homogamy	0.010	(.007)	−0.060	(−.042)
R^2	0.126		0.162	
(Unweighted *n*)	(117)		(70)	
Men				
Jewish Identity Factor[b]				
Ritual	0.129	(.070)	−0.238	(.203)
Ceremony	−0.051	(−.061)	−0.100	(−.166)
Tribalism	−0.130	(−.175)	0.019	(.020)
Organizations	0.095	(.175)	0.006	(.008)
Formal Jewish education (years)	−0.001	(−.007)	−0.012	(−.066)
Age	−0.007	(−.168)	0.003	(.005)
Number of marriages	−0.002	(−.001)	−0.147	(−.107)
Number of children under 18 in household	−0.045	(−.092)	−0.129	(−.190)
Husband's education	−0.178	(−.386)*	−0.144	(−.270)*
Wife's education	0.122	(.254)*	0.144	(.272)*
Occupational homogamy	−0.039	(−.030)	0.249	(.179)
R^2	0.212		0.189	
(Unweighted *n*)	(103)		(76)	

[a]Data are unstandardized coefficients and (in parentheses) standardized coefficients, ß.

[b]Stronger expressions of Jewish identity on these factors are lower; weaker expressions are higher.

*Statistically significant at $p < 0.05$; **significant at $p < 0.10$.

with their fertility, women's labor force participation, and occupational prestige than it does for their intermarried counterparts. Intermarriage appears to distance the Jews involved by making whatever Jewish identity they have less relevant to their day-to-day lives. Although one can argue that this distancing may indeed be a motivation for intermarriage, we also show that intermarried Jews do not appear to start out significantly differently than intramarried Jews: many were exposed to at least some formal Jewish education, although for fewer years than their intramarried counterparts. But the Jewish capital that they have accumulated may actually make some of their secular achievement more difficult: among intermarried men and women, the stronger their ethnic attachment to Jews, the lower is their occupational prestige. Investment in social capital that conflicts with their marriage circle might actually be one reason for their lower occupational achievement.

Their overall weaker Jewish identity does not result in family behavior that is more similar to that of the broader population than the family behavior of their intramarried counterparts, but it does result in greater similarity to the broader population in patterns of occupational achievement.

We need data that follow the patterns of Jewish identity, first-marriage decisions and dynamics, divorce, and remarriage longitudinally, so that the role of changing Jewish identity and its effect on secular behavior in day-to-day life can be better understood, for both American Jewish men and women.

PART III

Conclusions

CHAPTER 11

Conclusions and a Look to the Future

DOES GENDER MATTER?

Whether or not it is an issue for American Jewish men and women, gender continues to differentiate them in terms of their family behavior, labor force participation, occupational achievement and rewards, expressions and strength of Jewish identity, and the extent to which their Jewish identity affects their family and economic behavior. Although both American Jewish men and women are distinguished by high educational and occupational achievement compared with their counterparts in the broader U.S. society, they have not achieved gender equality, and in some ways there is even more inequality among them than among their less educated counterparts in the broader society.

With regard to gender inequality in secular achievement, finding that American Jews have *not* achieved gender equality is important because in many ways American Jews embody the best chances for gender equality among all subgroups in the United States. In a subpopulation where nearly 90% of the women have the same education as their male counterparts, and nearly 60% of both men and women have at least an undergraduate college degree, one would expect similarity in labor force participation and occupational achievement. And American Jewish women do have high labor force participation rates and occupational achievement. Family roles should not pose as great an obstacle to occupational achievement as they do in the broader population, because American Jews tend to have smaller families on average. But perhaps in keeping with the cultural heritage of familism, American Jewish women tend to respond to family size—not necessarily by dropping out of the labor force (as they used to, according to Chiswick, 1986) but by curtailing their hours of employment. In fact, college-educated Jewish women with children are less likely to be employed full time than are less educated Jewish women with children under 18 at home. Jewish mothers respond in this way much more commonly than their husbands, placing them in the role of "secondary earner." Marriage facilitates this pattern, as Jewish mothers who are not currently married are more likely than married Jewish women to be employed full time. This pattern of being a "secondary earner" undoubtedly contributes to the lower occupational achievement of Jewish women compared with Jewish men. Their occupations are not less prestigious, but they earn less income. The disparity between men's and women's earnings is quite large, even when education and hours of employment are held constant. As is the case in the broader population, the disparity is greater among those with a college education, and because so large a percentage of the American Jewish population is college educated, the gender gap in income is greater than in the overall population. This lower income results in part from the differential occupations of men and women, common also in the broader population; but also contributing to an income gap may be a history of less career commitment, characterized by periods of part-time employment.

Perhaps this gender differentiation facilitates a division of labor within the family that entails commitment to the family coupled with many hours and much energy devoted to career. But it may be the norm because alternatives are too costly, especially when the supportive infrastructure makes it too challenging to arrange the division of labor differently. That is, unless men's and women's jobs truly provide equal rewards (income) for equal human capital, the value of most men's and women's family and economic time will not be considered equal (see also Chiswick, 2008, ch. 6). From the income data that we analyzed (although incomplete), it is apparent that American Jewish women are no better off than their counterparts in the broader society, and sometimes are even worse off, in terms of their income compared with that of American Jewish men in similar occupations. Furthermore, unless childcare for young children is provided at a reasonable cost, one parent is likely to remain home with a young child for at least some period of time; whose career is interrupted will be related to the respective values of each adult's time in the labor force versus time with the family—more often than not, it is the mother's career. So the economic conditions of the U.S. labor force reinforce a traditional familism that perpetuates a long-standing Jewish tradition: Jewish wives and mothers are the ones who scale back their careers for the good of the family.

Thus, the inequality in secular achievement that we find in the general American Jewish population is brought home within American Jewish couples. However, compared with couples in the broader U.S. white population, American Jewish couples are more homogamous in education, labor force participation, and occupation. Although husbands and wives do not make equal contributions to the household income, American Jewish wives in dual-earner couples appear to contribute a higher proportion of the earnings than do wives in the broader U.S. population. Because American Jewish couples are responsive to the number and ages of children in the household, with wives curtailing their hours of employment when there are younger children at home, their resulting average combined hours of work are on the average lower than are those of wives in the broader population. Wives also compensate for their husband's lower income or hours of employment by spending more hours in the labor force. Thus, the typical American Jewish wife's hours of employment fluctuate with family needs; American Jewish wives, as secondary earners, manipulate their labor force commitments to resolve role conflicts and to alleviate the overload accompanying multiple family and career demands. This pattern appears to be that of contemporary American Jews' traditional "familism," facilitated by their relatively high incomes.

These relatively high incomes do not characterize all American Jews. Divorced and remarried Jewish men are less likely to be in managerial/executive, business/finance, or professional occupations, and they have somewhat lower occupational prestige and annual earnings than men in their first marriages. As a result, remarried men are more likely to have wives with a similar or higher level of education, occupation, and income than they do. Intermarried men and women also tend to have less occupational and educational achievement than their intramarried counterparts, in first marriages as well as remarriages, but remarriage itself seems to have an effect in that remarried husbands are more likely to have wives with higher occupational status than themselves. It seems that intermarriage offers Jewish men higher economic status through their wives, particularly men who have lower educational and occupational achievement than their intramarried male counterparts. But in the remarriage, intermarriage, and first-marriage markets, American Jewish women appear to be more marriageable when they have a high education level and occupational potential. So here, too, we find that gender matters in the dynamics of remarriage and intermarriage.

Gender matters for Jewish identity. We found differences between Jewish men and women in the way they expressed their Jewishness and how strong a Jewish identity they had. Generally, women have stronger Jewish identity than men on a wide array of indicators expressing religious and ethnic, private (or personal) and public (or collective) identity. These gender differences are not explained by denominational preference, secular or formal Jewish education, or age. The biggest differences between men and women's Jewish identity have to do with the factor Belief, a private religious expression of Jewish identity. Jewish women's expressions of spirituality are more highly differentiated from those of men than are the more behavioral expressions of private religiosity measured by the factor Ritual, perhaps because women traditionally have been excused from some of the behavioral obligations expressing religiosity. Women also are more likely than men to understand Jewish identity as involvement in the activities of the Jewish community and to have a stronger ethnic connection to the Jewish "tribe" and culture. They also express more involvement in the public celebrations of Jewish identity. Such gender differences may be one reason for the centrality of Jewish women in perpetuating Jewish religion and ethnicity (see, e.g., Prell, 1999).

Gender differences in the various ways of expressing Jewish identity reinforce findings that women in other religions are more religious than men, as well as findings that women are primary carriers of ethnic identity. Because more men receive formal Jewish education than women, which is related to stronger Jewish identity (for both men and women), some of the gender gap in Jewish identity is reduced. But as women gain access to formal Jewish education, the gender gap in Jewish identity may grow.

One of the reasons for women's stronger identification with Jewishness may be the invigoration that the women's movement has brought to women's Jewish involvement and Judaism in general (Cohen, Hammer, and Shapiro, 2005; Prell, 2007b). In some areas of American Judaism, it is clear that men's Jewish identification and involvement are suffering (Fishkoff, 2008; Fishman and Parmer, 2008; but see also Shapiro, 2007). Although there is a consistent tendency for women to show greater religious involvement across many religions historically and in the United States, Fishman and Parmer (2008) suggest that such findings represent a change from the past for American Jews and particularly for non-Orthodox American Jews.

As we discussed with respect to gender and Jewish identity in Chapter 4, one of the explanations of women's greater religiosity (found not only among Jews) is that women have less of a structural stake in secular status (e.g., they participate less in the labor force and have lower occupational achievement than men). However, among the Orthodox and Conservative, women who are more personally religious (on the Ritual factor) are more likely to have occupations that confer higher status (managerial, business, or professional), are more likely to be in the labor force (Conservative and Reform/Reconstructionist), and are more likely to be employed more hours per week (among the unaffiliated). Our results therefore undermine this structural hypothesis. A clear conclusion is that gender continues to matter, and indeed matters more than ever, in contemporary American Jewish identity.

DOES JEWISHNESS MATTER FOR FAMILY AND ECONOMIC BEHAVIORS?

Perhaps an even more significant finding than our gender results is that Jewishness—in many forms—is related to family behavior and secular achievement, even when more conventional explanations of variance like education and age are controlled for. As we have indicated, there are ways in which the distinctiveness of American Jews from the broader U.S. population persists in terms of family behavior, education, labor force involvement, occupation, and occupational rewards of both men and women, and in the comparison between men and women. This in itself is something of a surprise, given increases in the educational level of the broader U.S. population, an increase in women's labor force participation overall, and changes in the economic structure which result in typically "Jewish" occupations being more common. Indeed, many of American Jewish women's family behavior and labor force participation rates have become more similar to those of women in the broader population. However, Jewish women continue to exhibit some signs of "familism" that are less characteristic of women in the broader population who have the same high levels of education. And the occupational differences between American Jews and the broader population remain wide for both men and women. The occupational niches of American Jews have changed somewhat even in the past decade; nevertheless, close to half of American Jewish men and women can be found in only 10 occupations (although which 10 differs between men and women). Goldscheider and Zuckerman's (1984) thesis that the American Jewish community was bolstered and reinforced by educational and occupational similarities and ties seems to be demonstrated by our findings.

Even stronger support for this thesis comes from our finding that the strength of Jewish identity is related to the familistic and economic behavior of both men and women, even after we control for more basic variables like age, education, and (in predicting labor force activity and rewards) familistic characteristics. Confirming our distinction between public and private expressions of Jewish identity, we found that expressions of private Jewish identity are more related to family behavior (also private) than are expressions of public Jewish identity. Reinforcing the notion that women are more religiously oriented than men, we found that their religious identity, as well as ethnic identity, was related to some of their family behavior, whereas among men, only their ethnic identity was related to some of their family behavior. Furthermore, women's family behavior was more likely to be related to some aspect of their Jewish identity than was men's.

The fact that there is an independent relationship to secular achievement, for the most part positive, suggests that the American Jewish community is not completely secularized; its particularistic investments in Jewish social and cultural capital often are related to higher secular achievement, especially for men. This means that Jewish identity does not become irrelevant even when a respondent does not identify with one of the main denominations. We cannot say that Jewish identity has a relationship to secular achievement only among the Orthodox; and we do not find that religious identity (as opposed to ethnic) has its main influence among the Orthodox as opposed to the other denominational groups. In fact, it is much more the case that ethnic identity is related to secular achievement, suggesting that reference groups and social norms may be part of the mechanism by which Jewish identity is related to secular achievement. It may be in its ethnic (rather than religious) function that the Jewish community exerts its primary influence on more secular aspects of contemporary life.

Such findings clearly reinforce Goldscheider and Zuckerman's (1984) "transformation" thesis—that Jewish identity and cohesiveness are at least reinforced if not maintained by the occupational and communal associations of Jews, perhaps as much as but certainly in addition to the religious centers of Jewish life. Thus, identification with an organized denomination is not a prerequisite for identifying oneself as Jewish and having one's Jewishness be related to one's everyday life.

We also found that some family behavior appears to influence religious identity: thus, ethnic feelings of attachment to the Jewish people appear to be weakened by multiple marriages, particularly when the spouse in higher-order marriages is not Jewish. Furthermore, denominational preference differs by marital status (especially being divorced, remarried, and/or intermarried), and we suspect that the divorced, remarried, and intermarried feel more comfortable in Reform or Reconstructionist congregations or not being affiliated with any denomination (i.e., marital status influences the denominational preference rather than the other way around).

These relationships between expressions of Jewishness and secular patterns of family and economic behavior undermine the notion that religion and ethnic identity are separate from secular behavior. Rather, American Jewish patterns of family and economic behavior are influenced by and influence patterns of American Jewishness. This phenomenon is not confined to women, whose Jewish identity is stronger than men's, but can be found across the spectrum of American Jews. The relationship is, however, stronger for intramarried Jews and Jews affiliated with the more traditional Orthodox and Conservative denominations, especially in terms of economic behavior.

Just as we found Jewish identity and denominational preference to be related to familistic behavior, age cohort and education retain similar relationships with family behavior, as in the broader population. Thus, religious and ethnic influences on family behavior appear to coexist—or even compete—with other social influences, sometimes being more important, sometimes as important, and sometimes less important. Also, early patterns of familistic behavior have an important influence on subsequent familistic behavior. For example, early marriage, which is related to Jewish identity and, for women, being Orthodox, has a strong effect on age at birth of first child, and this is the strongest predictor of a woman's fertility. Thus, Jewish identity not only directly affects a particular family behavior, but also affects it indirectly through past influences on family behavior, which increases its importance.

These interrelationships between Jewishness, family characteristics, and economic behavior indicate the continuing importance of multiple expressions of Jewishness and their reinforcement through nontraditional venues such as common occupations and their accompanying social and cultural networks.

Denominational preferences are reflected in different patterns of family behavior and as a result in different patterns of women's labor force participation and occupational achievement. Denominational groups tend to differ with respect to labor force and occupational achievement, particularly among women, and particularly in comparisons of Orthodox and non-Orthodox Jews. It should be noted, however, that among women in particular, ethnic Jewish identity has different relationships to secular achievement in different denominational groups. Thus, among the Orthodox, personal ethnic Jewish identity is weaker among women who are more involved in the labor force. Among Reform and Reconstructionist women, there is also a negative relationship between personal ethnic identity and labor force involvement. But among Conservative women, personal ethnic identity is higher among those who are active in the labor force. Therefore the impact of the Jewish community does not seem to be unified.

Some of the denominational differences among women can be explained when we control for family characteristics. Some of the denominational differences among men can be explained by the somewhat lower educational attainment among Orthodox men. Denominational groups appear to exert two kinds of influence on secular achievement: they reflect norms about familism, which are related to age at marriage, age at birth of first child, and number of children, which in turn are related to women's labor force involvement and subsequent occupational achievement. They also reinforce high secular achievement, particularly among men. Many of the denominational differences can be explained by variations in the strength of Jewish identity in its various forms. Therefore, when we control for expressions of Jewish identity and denomination, expressions of Jewish identity are more closely related to secular achievement than is denominational preference.

Cohen and Eisen (2000, p. 192) conclude that "Jews no longer seek American integration. They have in full measure achieved it, and as a result can consider options . . . once viewed as threatening to Gentile acceptance." Perhaps the extent to which American Jews allow their secular behavior to relate to their Jewish identity is another sign of accepting their Jewishness and allowing it to permeate their lives. Although their work was not based on a representative sample of American Jews, Cohen and Eisen (2000, p. 196) found that "the Jews we met tend to place Jewish commitment at or near the center of that which is enduring in their 'self-concept.'" The extent to which we find Jewish identity related to the secular aspects of the lives of American Jews whom we study reinforces the notion that Jewish identity is part of their central "self-concept" and not compartmentalized to symbolic or fragmented religious experiences.

DOES JEWISHNESS INCREASE GENDER INEQUALITY IN SECULAR ACHIEVEMENT?

One argument that has been advanced regarding the spillover from inequality in traditional public religious roles is that stronger Jewish involvement in traditional Judaism may result in greater inequality in educational and occupational achievement. However, our findings suggest that Jewishness does not increase gender inequality in secular achievement more than it does through its familistic effect, which does result in gender differences in family roles and consequent labor force involvement. On the contrary, gender equality in education and occupational achievement between husbands and wives is more common among the Orthodox than other denominational groups. It is also more common among the intermarried. What the two groups have in common is a somewhat lower educational and occupational achievement among men; there is also a greater concentration of Orthodox women than women of other denominations in professional occupations, which contributes to the findings. As we found in our analysis of the 1990 National Jewish Population Survey, there is no evidence that traditional Jewishness increases gender inequality in secular achievement. Nor is there evidence that stronger Jewish identity is related to any sort of "marriage penalty" against American Jewish women's educational or economic achievements. On the contrary, women's higher education and potential occupational achievement appear to be attractive in the American Jewish marriage market. Although there is a "child penalty" in terms of labor force involvement, it seems to have decreased somewhat since 1990.

We would like to be able to show the ways in which American Jews' secular achievement is changing, the directions of gender equality or inequality, the distinctions of American Jews from the broader population, and how Jewishness is related to family behavior and secular achievement. We can point in some directions, but not in a definitive way. Our ability to do so is circumscribed by a number of parameters. There are several comparisons we can employ to show change in a cross-sectional sample such as ours. The first is a comparison of age cohorts. We undertook such a comparison in a number of places in our analysis. However, because American Jews finish their education late (often in their 30s, because they undertake graduate and professional training), marry late (also often in their 30s), and have children late (also often in their 30s), it is difficult to separate life-cycle effects from cohort effects. That is, if we compare the 25–34 age group with the 55–64 age group, we cannot be sure whether those in the younger age group have completed their education, started a career, or finished (or even started) having children. The 35–44 age group is involved in intensive raising of young children, more so than the 45–54 or older age group. The 65 and older age group is beginning to retire, and it is difficult to compare their secular achievement with that of younger cohorts. That leaves us with a comparison of 45- to 64-year-olds—not a very definitive group for determining trends. In most of our analyses of secular achievement, age (cohort) did not have a significant relationship with the dependent variables, suggesting that there are not major changes from the younger to the oldest cohort once education and family characteristics are controlled for.

A second type of comparison is between the current analysis and that performed using the 1990 sample. For example, we saw that there are many ways in which the differences between American Jews and the rest of the white population in the United States have narrowed since 1990. Educational differences, particularly among women, are diminishing and are reflected in narrower differences in labor force participation rates and hours of work. Especially when age, education, and family roles are controlled for, we find increasing similarity from 1990 to 2000–01 between American Jewish labor force participation patterns and those of the broader population, especially among women. However, occupational distinctiveness remains and does not appear to be narrowing (also confirmed by Chiswick 2007).

Compared with 1990, there is somewhat more educational homogamy among American Jews, and fewer "traditional" differences defined by husbands having more education than their wives. These trends toward homogamy, and less traditionalism, mirror trends in the broader society. The pattern of dual earning has become more common among American Jews since 1990, aligning American Jews with the overall society.

But on some measures of secular achievement, such as occupation and income, we run into more difficulties in making a comparison between the two time periods. The U.S. Census changed its classification codes from 1990 to 2000 in such a way that it is difficult to make precise comparisons between the two years, except in a very general way (U.S. Bureau of the Census, 2003b). The 1990 NJPS did not collect data on individual earnings, so that we could not compare American Jewish wives' contributions to household income in 2000–01 with those in 1990.

Similarly, because the 2000–01 NJPS expanded the measurement of Jewish identity to such an extent, our analysis of how Jewishness is related to secular achievement is quite limited. We found, in 1990, for example, that "the relationship between Jewishness and labor force participation is mainly indirect, through accepted patterns of gender differentiation in the family" (Hartman and Hartman, 1996a, p. 293). But that is not what we found in our current analysis. We discovered that several aspects of Jewish identity had direct effects on educational achievement, labor force participation and hours of employment of women, occupational distribution, occupational prestige, and income—even when family characteristics, education (for the labor force variables), and age were controlled for. But we are hesitant to conclude that Jewishness is becoming more central to American Jews' lives (secular or otherwise), because of the differences in measurement and in analysis. We do think this is a trend worth considering in future research and in the analysis of other data sets, whether they be local or national.

IMPLICATIONS FOR FUTURE RESEARCH

Concern has been raised over the extent to which the 2000–01 NJPS is representative of the American Jewish population, as we noted in our introductory chapter. This concern extends, for example, to whether the mean annual earnings that we present are truly representative of the earnings of American Jews. We do not have a solid affirmative answer to this. With regard to earnings, we would exercise considerable caution in generalizing to all American Jews. And this concern is one of the main reasons we do not feel comfortable engaging in an extensive analysis of the changes that occurred between 1990 and 2000–01.

But when it comes to relationships between Jewish identity and earnings or occupational prestige, or gender differences in expressions of Jewish identity, we feel more confident that such relationships are likely to be representative of American Jews and that our analyses can at least lay a foundation for further research. One of the strengths of this data set is the potential it provides for analyzing the relationships between many different expressions of Jewish identity and other types of behavior.

Have all types of Jewish identity been taken into account in the 2000–01 NJPS survey? Here we would venture to say no. We are aware of several contemporary developments in expressions of Jewish identity that are not tapped by the questions in this survey—expressions that are particularly relevant to gender and Jewishness (see also Kaufman, 2005). For example, one of the most interesting transformations that has taken place among Orthodox and Conservative women is the prevalence of women's prayer groups, as well as their increasing participation in study groups for women (or allowing women to participate in more traditional institutions of learning). Rosh Chodesh (first of the month) groups, organized by and primarily for women, are becoming much more common in many congregations and signal women's increasing participation in public religious roles. This development has been documented in ethnographic studies (see, e.g., El-Or, 2002). However, these expressions of Jewish identity are not queried in the NJPS. As such, the NJPS can be criticized for focusing on the "concepts and paradigms most meaningful to men's lives" (Davidman and Tenenbaum, 1994, p. 143); that is, it includes the public religious behavior more common to men, but not the behaviors more apt to reflect women's involvement in public religious roles.

Furthermore, the NJPS lumps religious and ethnic activities (e.g., a Bible study group is lumped with a book club), making it difficult to differentiate religious and ethnic public activities. Having accurate information about ethnic activities is particularly important for understanding gender differences in Jewish identity. Previous research suggests that women's ethnic commitment to Jewish identity is more exclusive than men's (Davidman and Tenenbaum, 1994). From the NJPS, however, we know nothing about the interface between Jewish ethnicity and work relationships (e.g., whether respondents care if they have Jewish colleagues at work or whether they tend to lunch with Jewish colleagues at work), whether the Jewishness of the residential environment influences what schools they send their children to, or how important it is that their neighbors are Jewish. Because interpersonal relations are so important to women, these might be key questions for understanding men's and women's respective roles in the assimilation process among Jews, as well as in the maintenance of a cohesive ethnic identity.

In studies of contemporary religious identity in the United States, there is much discussion of the privatization or individualization of religion and religious beliefs. Here is another example in which the current data set falls short of what is desirable. Only one question in the survey clearly expresses this orientation by asking about resistance to outside authority ("I am bothered when told the right way to be Jewish"). Indeed, it loaded by itself on the fourteenth factor of the 14-factor solution. But one indicator out of more than 80 is not enough for a proper analysis of this individualistic orientation to being Jewish. It is possible that this is not a central orientation of Jews[1] or that there simply were not enough questions to adequately represent respondents' orientation to this expression of Jewish identity. Are respondents bothered when told the "right" way to pray? To eat? To observe rituals? To contribute money to the welfare of other Jews? Does the problem have to do with who is telling them the "right" way to be Jewish (fellow Jews, rabbis, authorities in Israel)? We do not know, because the orientation was not systematically covered by the questionnaire, and therefore we could not adequately analyze this aspect of Jewish identity.

So in addition to sampling issues and non-responses, there are gaps in the survey questionnaire we used for our analysis, which might be corrected with more careful attention to the theoretical bases of the questions as well as contemporary developments. Such criticism should not detract from our analysis of the existing data; we believe we have contributed to a better understanding of contemporary American Jews with our research. But it should be taken into account in the design of future research on this population.

In addition, some of the issues we raised would be better addressed with different research designs. To study the gender dynamics of family strategies in coping with childrearing and occupational advancement, longitudinal analysis of labor force involvement, fertility, and occupational changes would be much more helpful in unraveling patterns of dual earning and how they change over the life course. We discerned a pattern of wives being "secondary earners." To what extent does this affect wives' occupational achievements? To what extent are the changes in wives' labor force involvement a result of conscious decision making with which each spouse is satisfied? To what extent are the patterns carryovers from traditional roles? Without a better understanding of these dynamics, it is difficult to predict the kinds of changes we will see in the future. Perhaps women's labor force involvement has reached a saturation point, as long as traditional childrearing arrangements are dominant. Perhaps there is dissatisfaction with this "secondary earner" arrangement, in which case change may be more likely. Without knowing the decisions made at each point in time and how the partners feel about these changes, we are limited to the kinds of analyses presented here. And, in fact, we cannot know how much gender matters without understanding how couples feel about the inequalities in their lives.

Such understanding also calls for more in-depth, qualitative interviewing. We have several good examples of such research design, including Cohen and Eisen's (2000) and Horowitz's (2000) work, and more is needed to ascertain the role Jewishness plays in Jews' secular lives. Some observational analysis and perhaps focus groups would also help us to understand the mechanisms by which denominational norms have an impact on individual behavior, evidence of which we highlighted throughout our analysis.

PRACTICAL IMPLICATIONS

Some of you who have reached this point in our book are wondering whether our research has any practical implications. We'd like to think so. We will focus on the following six points:

1. *The failure of American Jews to achieve gender equality in their economic roles and in the family division of labor.* Although it is at a high level, Jewish women's education has not reached the same level as men's; and despite Jewish women's training, their tendency to scale back their labor force involvement for family reasons may interfere with greater occupational achievement and rewards. An infrastructure of support in the Jewish community for working women, such as childcare, would ease the tensions in dual-career families and perhaps make it possible for highly qualified Jewish women to obtain more return for their labor force investment.

   Our findings with regard to the labor force in general are actually mirrored by findings of gender difference in Jewish communal organizations: "Despite the fact that Jewish women are highly qualified to assume leadership of the Jewish community, focus groups revealed women have not yet achieved parity in the board room, in the synagogue or in key positions of professional leadership" (Cohen et al., 2005, p. 5). Community organizations would do well to confront the "glass ceilings" in their own organizations, and help harness the talent and leadership of qualified women for their own benefit.

2. *Jewish families' continuing commitment to high-quality family life and childrearing.* Although American Jews marry later than other Americans, start having children later, and have fewer children, their commitment to the family is evident in several of our findings. The lower rate of divorce, the longer duration of first marriages, the way Jewish mothers respond to having a child under the age of 3 at home, the pattern of secondary earning, by which Jewish wives' labor force involvement fluctuates according to family need—these are all indications of commitment to the family. Although some see family values unraveling, we would perhaps favor the

glass half-full approach and suggest that the family strengths of the Jewish community should be reinforced and supported through both institutional infrastructure (such as childcare support) and opportunities to acknowledge the Jewish family's strengths and strategies.

3. *Women's juggling of familial obligations and career opportunities and commitment.* Marriage makes it possible for mothers and wives to scale back their hours of employment and to care for young children. This may not always be in the family's best economic interest. In about 20% of families in which both spouses are employed, wives earn more than their husbands. Does the traditional pattern undermine the family's economic prospects? This is an issue that should be addressed; sometimes a nontraditional pattern may work better for a family's interests.

   Also, about 12% of Jewish mothers with children at home are not married. They may need even more support than two-parent families.

   Like women in the broader society, Jewish women find that balancing a career and a family is not easily accomplished, and there are no recipes for guaranteeing success. Recognizing the possible family constellations among American Jews, and analyzing ways in which the community can support these situations, is incumbent on the Jewish community leaders.

4. *The importance of Jewishness in secular activities.* A most important finding of our research is that Jewishness matters to American Jews in their secular activities. We think this is an indication that Jewishness is important to American Jews, that it helps to guide their mundane orientations in addition to filling spiritual needs. Its influence on family behavior is divided between religious and ethnic influences; its influence on labor force involvement and achievement is tied to a greater extent to ethnic influences. We think this demonstrates the continuing (or renewed) importance of the Jewish community in influencing norms of behavior and orientations. One practical suggestion that derives from this is that the American Jewish community may be receptive to learning more about what Jewish tradition and contemporary Jewish thinking have to say about family behavior, labor force involvement, and occupational commitment. Opportunities to discuss contemporary dilemmas with respect to these issues may well fall on receptive ears.

5. *The interaction of intermarriage, secular achievement, denomination, and Jewish identity.* American Jewish men who have married non-Jews on average have lower educational and occupational achievement than their intramarried counterparts; part of their motivation for intermarriage may be to gain social status, as their marriages, especially if they are remarriages, are more likely than those of their intramarried counterparts

to be marriages to women who have the same or higher educational and occupational achievements as theirs. This raises the question of whether the normative expectations of high education and economic achievements have pushed these sons away from the Jewish community and, if so, whether this is desirable.

Intermarried Jews are more likely not to identify with any particular denomination, or to identify themselves as Reform or Reconstructionist. Their Jewish identity tends to be weaker than that of those who express a denominational preference, and Jewish identity is not as closely related to their family behavior and secular achievement. Although none of this is unexpected, our empirical results confirm that this is a process of weakening ties to Jewishness and its impact.

6. *Denominational differences, especially between the Orthodox and the non-Orthodox, and the unaffiliated and the affiliated.* Paradoxically, we found that the very ways in which American Jews are more distinctive from the broader U.S. population do not correspond with the ways in which traditional Judaism or stronger Jewish identity affects family behavior and to some extent economic achievement. One reason for this is the very different patterns found among Orthodox Jews as compared with non-Orthodox Jews. The early marriage, the relatively early years of childbearing, and the large number of children in Orthodox families stand in stark contrast to the delayed marriage, delayed childbearing, and small families of the majority of American Jews. This different family pattern may be related to the somewhat lower educational attainment of Orthodox Jews, as well as their somewhat different occupational niches. Some of this behavior (such as early marriage, especially for women) is motivated by their religious commitment. However, most of it is related to ethnic identity and to practical considerations (e.g., which spouse has more education and therefore a higher earning potential, how many young children need care at home).

What was striking to us is that Jewish identity, particularly ethnic identity, affects all denominational groups' secular behavior. However, each denominational group may be exerting somewhat different influences because of its composition and its expectations about family and secular behavior. We find, indeed, evidence of how the myriad varieties of contemporary American Jewishness (Fishman, 2007) maintain some of their variety. And we find evidence that even those who have not found a denominational group to identify with continue to relate their secular behavior to their Jewish identity. Bringing these connections into public discourse, so that Jews find strength in their diversity and in their communality, would seem to be a worthwhile endeavor.

In conclusion, we set out to further pursue our studies of gender (in)equality among American Jews. What we found was a much more nuanced picture of how gender, Jewishness, denominational preferences, family behavior, and secular achievement are interconnected in a dynamic way. Undoubtedly, these interconnections will continue to evolve as the surrounding contexts develop. We look forward to following these developments.

Statistical Tables

Table A-1 Occupational Distribution for American Jews and Non-Hispanic Whites (Ages 25 and Over), by Gender and Education

Gender	Education	Occupation								Total
		Managerial/ executive	Business/ finance	Professional	Technical	Service	Sales	Office/ administrative support	Blue Collar	(n, thousands)[a]
Jews										
Men	High school or less	14.0	2.9	24.6	2.5	6.8	23.4	5.4	20.6	100.0 (106)
	Some college	16.2	5.5	28.5	4.0	9.0	25.0	4.2	7.7	100.0 (161)
	B.A.	14.2	13.2	32.9	4.3	2.3	22.8	5.3	5.1	100.0 (331)
	M.A.+	11.3	7.6	63.1	2.7	1.7	8.8	2.3	2.3	100.0 (367)
Women	High school or less	14.5	8.2	8.3	2.0	7.3	19.2	37.4	3.1	100.0 (96)
	Some college	14.2	4.6	17.7	5.1	7.8	21.6	23.1	5.9	100.0 (204)
	B.A.	16.1	9.7	42.5	5.5	3.0	12.1	9.9	1.1	100.0 (321)
	M.A.+	8.3	3.3	74.7	3.7	2.1	4.2	3.4	0.3	100.0 (298)

Non-Hispanic
whites

Men	High school									
	or less	7.2	1.1	1.7	1.2	12.2	7.9	5.7	62.9	100.0 (24,036)
	Some college	12.7	3.4	8.9	4.4	11.6	13.0	8.1	37.9	100.0 (16,992)
	B.A.	21.2	10.1	27.6	3.4	5.7	15.8	6.0	10.2	100.0 (11,207)
	M.A.+	19.6	7.2	56.1	1.8	2.5	5.8	2.9	4.2	100.0 (6,762)
Women	High school									
	or less	4.7	2.6	2.4	4.1	26.0	14.3	28.5	17.6	100.0 (20,140)
	Some college	7.9	5.4	12.5	8.5	14.1	11.6	33.9	6.0	100.0 (17,472)
	B.A.	12.0	9.3	40.6	6.3	5.4	9.7	14.6	2.1	100.0 (10,067)
	M.A.+	11.6	5.2	60.8	3.4	3.0	3.9	5.4	1.0	100.0 (5,491)

Data sources: U.S. Census, 2000; NJPS, 2000–01.

[a]NJPS data weighted by person-weights provided with dataset.

Table A-2 Occupational Distribution of American Jews and Non-Hispanic Whites (Ages 25 and Over), by Gender and Age

Gender	Age	Managerial executive	Business/finance	Professional	Technical	Service	Sales	Office/administrative support	Blue Collar	Total (n, thousands)[a]
Jews										
Men	25–34	11.5	7.8	40.2	5.8	5.4	19.4	4.5	4.3	100.0 (199)
	35–44	15.7	9.8	44.9	2.9	5.0	11.5	2.9	7.3	100.0 (207)
	45–64	14.2	8.3	42.6	2.8	3.0	20.3	2.2	6.6	100.0 (456)
	65+	9.4	9.8	44.1	2.8	0.0	16.9	10.8	6.2	100.0 (106)
Women	25–34	14.0	8.0	44.8	4.4	4.5	9.6	11.5	3.2	100.0 (196)
	35–44	10.9	7.1	46.4	4.3	4.6	13.7	10.6	2.4	100.0 (215)
	45–64	14.3	4.9	43.9	4.7	4.5	11.9	13.9	1.9	100.0 (434)
	65+	10.8	8.2	33.6	1.8	1.0	19.0	25.6	0.0	100.0 (76)
Non-Hispanic whites										
Men	25–34	8.8	3.8	14.7	3.2	11.8	10.2	6.6	40.9	100.0 (14,313)
	35–44	13.1	3.6	14.2	2.7	9.0	10.1	5.6	41.6	100.0 (17,292)
	45–64	14.7	4.6	15.6	2.4	8.4	10.8	6.1	37.4	100.0 (22,858)
	65+	14.8	5.2	14.6	1.9	11.7	13.8	7.0	30.9	100.0 (4,533)
Women	25–34	7.1	5.8	20.1	5.8	17.7	11.8	23.2	8.5	100.0 (13,158)
	35–44	8.4	5.5	19.5	6.5	15.8	10.6	24.0	9.7	100.0 (15,701)
	45–64	8.1	4.6	20.3	5.9	14.1	11.1	26.9	9.1	100.0 (20,774)
	65+	5.9	3.1	13.6	4.0	19.0	16.2	29.1	9.1	100.0 (3,537)

[a]NJPS data weighted by person-weights provided with dataset.

Data sources: U.S. Census, 2000; NJPS, 2000–01.

Table A-3 Occupational Distribution for American Jews and Non-Hispanic Whites (Ages 25 and Over) with College Degree, by Gender and Age

| Gender | Age | Occupation | | | | | | | | Total |
		Managerial/ executive	Business/ finance	Professional	Technical	Service	Sales	Office/ administrative support	Blue Collar	(n, thousands)[a]
Jews										
Men	25–34	8.5	10.4	40.4	6.5	3.5	19.3	6.6	5.0	100.0 (149)
	35–44	13.3	11.9	53.0	2.7	2.0	10.7	1.7	4.8	100.0 (151)
	45–64	14.8	9.7	49.0	2.8	1.5	17.1	2.1	2.9	100.0 (331)
	65+	10.6	8.8	57.2	1.8	0.0	9.6	10.4	1.6	100.0 (67)
Women	25–34	12.5	8.4	55.0	5.7	2.4	9.6	6.1	0.2	100.0 (150)
	35–44	9.8	8.9	55.1	5.0	3.2	8.7	7.7	1.7	100.0 (159)
	45–64	14.0	4.9	61.8	3.8	2.5	6.3	6.0	0.6	100.0 (270)
	65+	12.0	2.4	58.4	1.6	1.1	12.9	11.7	0.0	100.0 (36)
Non-Hispanic Whites										
Men	25–34	15.1	9.4	38.4	4.0	6.1	12.8	5.7	8.0	100.0 (4,133)
	35–44	22.6	8.5	37.6	2.7	4.3	12.0	4.4	7.9	100.0 (4,980)
	45–64	22.7	9.1	37.9	2.3	3.8	11.5	4.5	8.2	100.0 (7,551)
	65+	17.7	9.9	41.0	2.0	4.0	13.0	5.4	7.1	100.0 (1,305)
Women	25–34	11.0	9.9	46.0	5.3	5.7	8.5	11.9	1.6	100.0 (4,489)
	35–44	13.2	8.7	47.8	5.7	4.7	7.5	10.3	1.9	100.0 (4,610)
	45–64	11.7	6.0	54.2	5.0	3.5	6.7	11.2	1.6	100.0 (5,828)
	65+	8.3	5.0	50.3	4.2	4.7	10.3	15.3	1.9	100.0 (632)

[a]NJPS data weighted by person-weights provided with dataset.

Data sources: U.S. Census, 2000; NJPS, 2000–01

TABLE A-4 Questions with High Loading on Jewish Identity Factors, Principal Components Varimax Rotation

Factor	Loading on factor
Factor 1: The meaning of being Jewish	
1a: Activity	
Learning about Jewish history/culture	.508
Celebrating Jewish holidays	.739
Supporting Jewish organizations	.656
Having a rich spiritual life	.592
Being part of the Jewish community	.742
Caring about Israel	.483
Attending synagogue	.806
Observing *halacha*	.737
1b: Universal Morality	
Connecting to family's heritage	.498
Remembering Holocaust	.710
Leading ethical/moral life	.550
Making the world a better place	.609
Countering anti-Semitism	.498
Factor 2: Ritual	
2a: Ceremony	
Held/attended *seder* last Passover	.737
Current synagogue/temple member (any household member)	.624
Ever belonged to synagogue/temple	.648
Mezuzah on any door of home	.615
Number of nights lit candles last Chanukah	.582
Attended synagogue/temple the past year (respondent)	.715
2b: Ritual	
Observe Jewish rituals/practices	.521
Fast on Yom Kippur	.465
Comfortable attending Orthodox services	.164
Frequency of lighting Sabbath candles	.315
Factor 3: Tribalism	
3a: (Personal) Tribalism	
Importance of child's future spouse being Jewish	.876
Importance of grandchildren being raised Jewish	.852
Importance of child's future spouse converting to Judaism	.785
Importance of having friends to share Jewish ways	.685
Closest friends Jewish	.668

3b: Exceptionalism

Jews in America: cultural group	.770
Jews in America: ethnic group	.639
Jews in America: worldwide people	.705
Jews in America: religious group	.630

Factor 4: Culture

Past year: read Jewish book for Jewish content	.701
Past year: listened to Jewish audio media	.683
Past year: saw Jewish movie/video	.511
Likelihood of looking for Jewish places of interest when traveling	.699
Adult Jewish education attendance/sponsorship	.618
Past year: read Jewish print media	.683
Ability to read Hebrew	.517

Factor 5: Belief

Belief in God	.724
Being Jewish: believing in God	.698
Ever pray using own words	.594
Importance of religion in life today	.810
Extent personally religious	.796
Judaism guides important life decisions	.737

Factor 6: Organizations

Past year: dues-paying member JCC/YM/YWHA	.767
Past year: dues paid to any Jewish organization (not synagogue/JCC)	.716
Past year: attended JCC/YM/YWHA program	.718
Contributed to Federation	.563
Observed Jewish mourning/memorial ritual	.516

Factor 7: Attachment to Israel

7a: Attachment to Israel

Number of visits to Israel	.703
Familiarity with social/political situation in Israel	.672
Level of emotional attachment to Israel	.657
Family or close friends are living in Israel	.662

7b: Israel's Role Central

Jews in U.S./Israel share common destiny	.868
Jews in U.S./elsewhere share common destiny	.844
Israel is spiritual center of Jews	.580
Israel needs support of American Jews	.527

NOTES

1. An Introduction to Gender and American Jews and the Significance of the Inquiry (pages 1–9)

1. With the exception of Jews who claimed they were also adherents of a "non-compatible" religion such as a Christian denomination. (For more details, see United Jewish Communities, 2003d.)

2. Education Patterns: The Foundation of Family and Economic Roles (pages 13–24)

1. However, the differences are statistically significant, with χ^2 significant at $p <$ 0.01.
2. Differences in the education of the different age groups are significant ($p <$ 0.01) for both men and women.
3. $\chi^2 <$ 0.01 for gender differences in each of the age groups 45 and over.
4. The dissimilarity coefficient tells us the amount of dissimilarity, but only the comparison of the actual data can tell us the direction of difference.

3. Family Patterns of American Jews (pages 25–43)

1. The percentage of those cohabiting may well be underreported, as it relied on respondents' volunteering the information. This proportion represents only those who voluntarily characterized their marital status as "living together" (rather than never married or divorced, for example). Others may also be living together, but do not consider this their marital status. Most of those who reported "living together" as their marital status were single (never married) and between the ages of 25 and 34.
2. Our numbers differ slightly from those of the United Jewish Communities' (2003c) initial report, which focused on the answers of respondents under the age of 50 (see United Jewish Communities, 2003c, pp. 8–9, for a definition of their sample).

4. Labor Force Participation and Occupational Achievement (pages 44–87)

1. According to the NJPS, the majority (more than 90%) of Jewish children up to 3 years of age are in childcare or preschool, and the majority (94%) of 4- to 5-year olds are in kindergarten or preschool, but this is often for only a limited portion of the day, which may preclude outside employment for at least one parent.

2. Boushey (2005) attributes the lack of increase in women's labor force participation rates to the state of the economy, suggesting that women are more greatly affected by it than men because they are less likely to be in secure or tenured positions, and are more likely to be part-time workers. Although we do not have information on seniority for the Jewish population, clearly women are more likely than men to be part-time workers, so the reasoning would seem to apply to Jewish women as well.

3. The scores are adapted from Carl Frederick's work at the University of Wisconsin, Madison, per an e-mail communication with Robert Hauser (of the University of Wisconsin, Madison), December 4, 2005.

5. Dual-Earning Patterns of American Jews (pages 88–117)

1. Looking only at married wage and salaried employees, the 2002 National Study of the Changing Workforce found the proportion of such employees in dual-earner couples was 78% (Bond, 2002, p. 3). Among Jewish couples with at least one spouse employed, 71.2% were dual-earner couples, a somewhat smaller proportion. Perhaps this is because a larger proportion of American Jews remain in the labor force at older ages than does the broader population and/or because of the larger proportion of Jews at younger ages who are still completing their education (more detailed tabulations from the NSCW were not available to confirm this).

2. Apparently there is some selectivity among men answering the income question, such that those who do report their earnings on the survey have higher income than those who do not report their earnings (Chiswick and Huang, 2006); therefore, absolute values of income may be somewhat skewed.

6. Gendered Patterns of Jewishness (pages 121–151)

1. All factor analyses performed were principal components Varimax rotation.

2. The questions that did not share variance make for an interesting digression. The following were excluded: use of the Internet to obtain Jewish-related information; agreement that American Jews have a greater responsibility to rescue Jews than non-Jews in distress; agreement that "I have a special responsibility to take care of Jews in need around the world"; agreement that the fact that "I am a Jew has very little to do with how I see myself" (the direction of responses was reversed, but still the variable did not have enough commonality to be included); doing volunteer work for a Jewish organization; familiarity with the United Jews of America Federation campaign; and agreement that Jews in the United States are a nationality. We suspect that the responses to these variables are confounded by some other influences and therefore do not express mainly or only Jewish identity. For example, because Internet use is related to educational level and age, the responses are probably confounded by these additional influences on Internet use; responsibility for other people's welfare may be

confounded by personal wealth; and so on. Therefore, these variables do not have as much commonality with other variables that more clearly indicate Jewish identity without the confounding influence of other characteristics.

3. It is interesting that responses to "being Jewish: countering anti-Semitism" have high loading on this second factor. Heilman (2003–4, p. 64) suggests, "Often, the people who are attracted to these activities [combating anti-Semitism] are those who need some common enemy to make them feel they are part of the Jewish community." As such, it fits with the symbolic commitment of those attached to the "moral community" of Jews rather than those for whom being Jewish reflects a more active and daily commitment.

4. The survey also included a question about keeping kosher outside the home; however, it was asked only of people who kept kosher at home and therefore excluded a substantial portion of the sample. We did not feel we could make the a priori assumption that all people keeping kosher outside the home also kept kosher inside the home, and therefore did not include this indicator in our analysis. Similarly, the question about refraining from the use of money on Shabbat was asked only of those who kept kosher and lit Shabbat candles, and we did not feel we could assume that all others did not observe this.

5. See note 2 for this chapter, about the exclusion of a similar variable, using the Internet to obtain Jewish-related information.

6. The results also show that "subjective" indicators (how a respondent feels about a certain aspect of Jewish identity) often have high loading on the aspect of Jewish identity to which they relate rather than loading on a separate "subjective" factor of how a person feels about being Jewish. A few leftover subjective questions of a more general nature loaded on one of the last factors, but they did not explain enough variance to be included as a separate factor.

7. See Howe and Strauss, *Generations* (1992), on the characteristics of an "idealist" generational cohort, of which baby boomers are an example.

8. This figure is somewhat higher than that reported by Cohen (2004), probably because ours is a somewhat narrower definition of the sample than his, which included more Jews whose current identification with being Jewish is more tenuous.

9. According to the NJPS data, 82.5% of men and only 26.6% of women had a Bar or Bat Mitzvah. However, only respondents who had formal Jewish education were asked the question, so men and women who did not consider their training for Bar/Bat Mitzvah "formal" did not have the opportunity to respond. This makes the question less reliable than other estimates of Jewish education, so we do not use it in further analysis.

10. The way that these questions were asked is somewhat problematic (see Cohen, 2004), so we will not dwell on further analysis of them.

7. How Jewishness is Related to Family Patterns of American Jews (pages 152–171)

1. Of course, there are other steps: dating or otherwise seeking a mate, cohabiting, and sometimes having a child before marrying. However, the data on dating or

cohabiting in this survey are not comprehensive enough for us to determine how many couples dated or cohabited before marriage, for how long, and whether this indeed was their first step toward marriage. Only 2% of the women in the sample had children before their first marriage, too few to analyze. So we start with the first data that we have for most of the sample.

2. Some continue their education at a later age, presumably after marriage, as we discussed in Chapter 2 (as "lifelong learning"). Unfortunately, the current data set does not enable us to determine the age at which a degree was earned, or whether those in school as adults are studying to obtain a degree. Without at least this basic information, we cannot determine how many Jews actually receive degrees after they are married.

3. Only two women in the sample (less than 0.1%) reported having their first child after the age of 45. Only six women (0.3%) had their last birth after age 45.

4. Because age at birth of first child is most strongly predicted by age at first marriage, we skip over this step of family behavior to simplify the already complex presentation.

8. How Jewishness is Related to Gendered Patterns of Secular Achievement (pages 172–202)

1. Note that the dissimilarity coefficient is calculated on the detailed educational distribution, and not on the dichotomy of whether the respondents are college educated or not.

2. We confined our analyses to these family characteristics, as we had data for both men and women. Data on age at birth of first child, number of live births, and age of youngest child were collected only from female respondents, and so were not included. We considered including number of times married, but found it had an insignificant influence. Chapter 10, on intermarriage, includes more analysis based on number of times married.

9. How Jewishness is Related to American Jews' Dual-Earning Patterns (pages 203–229)

1. Income was not directly controlled for because of the number who did not answer the question; the resulting sample would be smaller and skewed toward those who did answer the question.

10. Intermarriage and Gendered Patterns of Secular Achievement (pages 230–249)

1. Intermarriage itself is not an indication that the marriage partners were in a different marriage market than Jews who married Jews. From Cohen and Eisen's research (2000), it seems that perhaps they were not. Indeed, it would be worthwhile to study the differences between marriage markets of inter- and intramarried Jews.

11. Conclusions and a Look to the Future (pages 253–268)

1. Indeed, other questions that a priori would be expected to share this "individualism" did not load as highly on that factor as on others, such as "ever pray using own words."

REFERENCES

Accenture. 2007. *Expectations and Achievement: Empowering Women from Within.* New York: Accenture. Retrieved March 23, 2008, from http://www.accenture .com/Global/About_Accenture/ExpectationsAchievementWithin.

Alba, Richard. 2006. "On the Sociological Significance of the American Jewish Experience: Boundary Blurring, Assimilation, and Pluralism." *Sociology of Religion* 67(4):347–58.

Alexander, Bobby C. 1987. "Ceremony." *The Encyclopedia of Religion* 3:179–183. New York: Macmillan.

Ament, Jonathan. 2005. "American Jewish Religious Denominations." United Jewish Communities Report Series on the National Jewish Population Survey 2000/ 01, Report 10 (February).

Ammerman, Nancy, and Wade Roof, eds. 1995. *Work, Family and Religion in Contemporary Society.* New York: Routledge.

Baskin, Judith, ed. 1991. *Jewish Women in Historical Perspective.* Detroit: Wayne State University Press.

Baum, Charlotte, Paula Hyman, and Sonya Michel. 1976. *The Jewish Woman in America.* New York: Dial Press.

Becker, Penny Edgell, and Heather Hofmeister. 2001. "Work, Family and Religious Involvement for Men and Women." *Journal for the Scientific Study of Religion* 40(4):707–22.

Becker, Penny Edgell, and Phyllis Moen. 1999. "Scaling Back: Dual-Earner Couples' Work-Family Strategies." *Journal of Marriage and the Family* 61(4):995–1006.

Bellah, Robert, Richard Madsen, William Sullivan, Ann Swidler, and Steven Tipton. 1985; updated 1996. *Habits of the Heart: Individualism and Commitment in American Life.* Berkeley: University of California Press.

Bellas, Marcia L. 1992. "The Effects of Marital Status and Wives' Employment on the Salaries of Faculty Men: The (House) Wife Bonus." *Gender and Society* 6(4):609–22.

Benokraitis, Nijole V. 2002. *Contemporary Ethnic Families in the United States: Characteristics, Variations, and Dynamics.* 4th edition. Englewood Cliffs, N.J.: Prentice-Hall.

Berger, Michael S. 2005. "Marriage, Sex and Family in the Jewish Tradition: A Historical Overview." In Michael Broyde and Michael Ausubel (eds.), *Marriage, Sex and Family in Judaism* (ch. 1). New York: Rowman & Littlefield.

Berger, Peter. 1967. *The Sacred Canopy.* Garden City, N.Y.: Plenum.

Bernasco, W. 1994. *Coupled Careers: The Effects of Spouse's Resources on Success at Work.* Amsterdam: Thesis publishers, Amsterdam. Cited in Smits, Ultee, and Lammers (1996).

Bielby, William, and Denise Bielby. 1989. "Family Ties: Balancing Commitments to Work and Family in Dual-Earner Households." *American Sociological Review* 54(5):776–89.

Blau, Francine, Mary Brinton, and David Grusky, eds. 2006. *The Declining Significance of Gender?* New York: Russell Sage Foundation.

Bond, James. 2002. *The National Study of the Changing Workforce (NSCW).* No. 3: *Dual-Earner Couples.* New York: Families and Work Institute.

Boushey, Heather. 2005. "Are Women Opting Out? Debunking the Myth." Briefing Paper, Center for Economic and Policy Research, Washington, D.C. http://www.cepr.net/documents/publications/opt_out_2005_11_2.pdf.

Bramlett, Matthew D., and William D. Mosher. 2002. "Cohabitation, Marriage, Divorce, and Remarriage in the United States." *Vital Health Statistics* 23(22). (National Center for Health Statistics.)

Brodkin, Karen. 1999. *How Jews Became White Folks and What That Says about Race in America.* New Brunswick, N.J.: Rutgers University Press.

Browning, Don S., Bonnie J. Miller-McLemore, Pamela D. Couture, K. Brynolf Lyon, and Robert M. Franklin. 2000. *From Culture Wars to Common Ground.* Louisville, Ky: Westminster John Knox Press.

Buchman, Claudia, and Thomas A. Diprete. 2006. "The Growing Female Advantage in College Completion: The Role of Family Background and Academic Achievement." *American Sociological Review* 71(4): 515–41.

Burstein, Paul. 2007. "Jewish Educational and Economic Success in the United States: A Search for Explanations." *Sociological Perspectives* 50(2):209–28.

Casanova, Jose. 1992. "Private and Public Religions." *Social Research* 59(1): 17–58.

Chao, Elaine, and Kathleen Utgoff, 2005. *Women in the Labor Force: A Databook.* Washington, D.C.: U.S. Department of Labor, Report 985 (May).

Chenu, Alain, and John Robinson. 2002. "Synchronicity in the Work Schedules of Working Couples." *Monthly Labor Review* (April):55–63.

Cherlin, Andrew J. 2005. *Public and Private Families: An Introduction.* 4th edition. New York: McGraw-Hill.

Chiswick, Barry. 1986. "Labor Supply and Investment in Child Quality: A Study of Jewish and Non-Jewish Women." *Review of Economics and Statistics* 47:4.

———. 1999. "The Occupational Attainment and Earnings of American Jewry, 1890–1990." *Contemporary Jewry* 20:68–98.

———. 2007. "The Occupational Attainment of American Jewry, 1990 to 2000." *Contemporary Jewry* 27:80–111.

Chiswick, Barry, and Jidong Huang. 2008. "The Earnings of American Jewish Men: Human Capital, Denomination, and Religiosity." *Journal for the Scientific Study of Religion* 47(4):694–709.

Chiswick, Carmel U. 2008. *The Economics of American Judaism.* New York: Taylor & Francis.

Christiano, Kevin. 2000. "Religion and the Family in Modern American Culture." In Sharon K. Houseknecht and Jerry G. Pankhurst (eds.), *Family, Religion, and Social Change in Diverse Societies* (43–78). New York: Oxford University Press.

Christiano, Kevin, William H. Swatos, and Peter Kivisto. 2002. *The Sociology of Religion*. Lanham, Md.: AltaMira Press.

Cohen, Steven M. 2004. *Jewish Educational Background: Trends and Variations among Today's Jewish Adults*. New York: United Jewish Communities Report.

———. 2005. "Non-Denominational and Post-Denominational: Beyond the Major Movements—Two Tendencies in American Jewry." *Contact: The Journal of Jewish Life Network* (Summer):7–8 (Steinhardt Foundation, Waltham, Mass.).

———. 2007. "The Differential Impact of Jewish Education on Adult Jewish Identity." In Jack Wertheimer (ed.), *Family Matters: Jewish Education in an Age of Choice* (34–58). Waltham Mass.: Brandeis University Press.

Cohen, Steven M., and Arnold Eisen. 2000. *The Jew Within: Self, Family, and Community in America*. Bloomington: Indiana University Press.

Cohen, Steven M., and Laurence Kotler-Berkowitz. 2004. *The Impact of Childhood Jewish Education on Adults' Jewish Identity: Schooling, Israel Travel, Camping and Youth Groups*. New York: United Jewish Communities.

Cohen, Tamara, Rabbi Jill Hammer, and Rabbi Rona Shapiro. 2005. *Listen to Her Voice: The Ma'yan Report*. New York: Ma'yan, the Jewish Women's Project.

Coleman, Marilyn, Lawrence H. Ganong, and Mark Fine. 2000. "Reinvestigating Remarriage: Another Decade of Progress." *Journal of Marriage and the Family* 62:1288–1307.

Coltrane, Scott, and Randall Collins. 2001. *Sociology of Marriage and the Family: Gender, Love and Property*. 5th edition. Belmont, Calif.: Wadsworth/Thomson Learning.

Crompton, Rosemary. 2006. "Class and Family." *Sociological Review* 54(4):658–77.

Current Population Survey, Annual Social and Economic Supplement. 1968–2005. Washington D.C.: Department of Labor, Bureau of Labor Statistics, Table 23.

Davidman, Lynn, and Shelley Tenenbaum. 1994. "Toward a Feminist Sociology of American Jews." In Lynn Davidman and Shelley Tenenbaum (eds)., *Feminist Perspectives on Jewish Studies* (ch. 7). New Haven, Conn.: Yale University Press.

Demmitt, Kevin. 1992. "Loosening the Ties That Bind: The Accommodation of Dual-Earner Families in a Conservative Protestant Church." *Review of Religious Research* 34(1): 3–19.

de Vaus, David, and Ian McAllister. 1987. "Gender Differences in Religion: A Test of the Structural Location Theory." *American Sociological Review* 52:472–81.

Diner, Hasia. 2003–4. "Multiple Outsiderness: Religious, Ethnic, and Racial Diversity in America." *Contemporary Jewry* 24:29–50.

Dollinger, Marc. 2003–4. "Jewish Identities in 20th Century America." *Contemporary Jewry* 24:9–28.

Edgell, Penny. 2006. *Religion and Family in a Changing Society*. Princeton, N.J.: Princeton University Press.

Edlund, Jonas. 2007. "The Work–Family Time Squeeze." *International Journal of Comparative Sociology* 48(6):451–80.

Ellwood, David, and Christopher Jencks. 2004. "The Spread of Single-Parent Families in the United States since 1960." Faculty Research Working Papers Series

RWP04–008. Harvard University, John F. Kennedy School of Government. Available online: www.hks.harvard.edu/inequality/Seminar/Papers/ElwdJnck.pdf.

El-Or, Tamar. 2002. *Next Year I Will Know More*. Detroit: Wayne State University Press.

Eshleman, J. Ross, and Richard A. Bulcroft. 2006. *The Family*. 11th edition. Boston: Pearson Education.

Ferber, Marianne, and Emily P. Hoffman. 1997. "Are Academic Partners at a Disadvantage?" In Marianne Ferber and Jane Loeb (eds.), *Academic Couples* (ch. 7). Urbana: University of Illinois Press.

Fishkoff, Sue. 2008. "Where Have All the Young Men Gone?" *JTA; http://ww.jta.org/cgi-bin/iowa/news/print/20080507/Gender2.html*, accessed May 13, 2008.

Fishman, Sylvia Barack. 1993. *A Breath of Life: Feminism in the American Jewish Community*. New York: Free Press.

———. 2004. *Double or Nothing? Jewish Families and Mixed Marriage*. Hanover, N.H.: Brandeis University Press.

———. 2005. "Choosing Lives: Evolving Gender Roles in American Jewish Families." In Dana E. Kaplan (ed.), *The Cambridge Companion to American Judaism* (237–52). New York: Cambridge University Press.

———. 2006. *The Way into the Varieties of Jewishness*. Woodstock, Vt.: Jewish Lights Publishing.

Fishman, Sylvia Barack, and Daniel Parmer. 2008. *Matrilineal Ascent/Patrilineal Descent: The Gender Imbalance in American Jewish Life*. Waltham, Mass.: Brandeis University, Cohen Center for Modern Jewish Studies and Hadassah-Brandeis Institute.

Fox, John, and Carole Suschnigg. 1989. "A Note on Gender and the Prestige of Occupations." *Canadian Journal of Sociology* 14:353–60.

Furseth, Inger, and Pal Repstad. 2006. *An Introduction to the Sociology of Religion: Classical and Contemporary Perspectives*. Burlington, Vt.: Ashgate.

Geffen, Rela Mintz. 2007. "How the Status of American Jewish Women Has Changed over the Past Decades." Jerusalem Center for Public Affairs No. 16, January 15. Retrieved March 19, 2008, from http://www.jcpa.org/JCPA/Templates/ShowPage.asp?DBID=1&TMID=111&LNGID=1&FID=385&PID=0&IID=1454.

Gelissen, John. 2004. "Assortative Mating After Divorce: A Test of Two Competing Hypotheses Using Marginal Models." *Social Science Research* 33:361–84.

Gershuny, Jonathan, Michael Bittman, and John Brice. 2005. "Exit, Voice, and Suffering: Do Couples Adapt to Changing Employment Patterns?" *Journal of Marriage and Family* 67:656–65.

Gilbert, Neil. 2005. "Family Life: Sold on Work." *Society* (March/April):12–17.

Gitelman, Zvi. 2003. "The Meanings of Jewishness in Russia and Ukraine." In E. Ben-Rafael, Y. Gorny, and Y. Ro'I (eds.), *Contemporary Jewries: Convergence and Divergence* (ch. 13). Leiden: Brill.

Glass, Jennifer, and Valerie Camarigg. 1992. "Gender, Parenthood, and Job–Family Compatibility." *American Journal of Sociology* 98:13–151.

Glenn, Susan. 1990. *Daughters of the Shtetl: Life and Labor in the Immigrant Genera-tion*. Ithaca, N.Y.: Cornell University Press.

Goldscheider, Calvin, and Alan Zuckerman. 1984. *The Transformation of the Jews*. Chicago: University of Chicago Press.

Goldstein, Joshua R., and Catherine T. Kenney. 2001. "Marriage Delayed or Mar-riage Foregone? New Cohort Forecasts of First Marriage for U.S. Women." *American Sociological Review* 66(4):506–19.

Greeley, Andrew, and Michael Hout. 2001. "Getting to the Truths that Matter." *American Sociological Review* 66(1):152–58.

Gregory, Elizabeth. 2008. *Ready: Why Women Are Embracing the New Later Mother-hood*. New York: Basic Books.

Hartman, Moshe, and Harriet Hartman. 1996a. *Gender Equality and American Jews*. Albany, N.Y.: SUNY Press.

———. 1996b. "More Jewish, Less Jewish: Implications for Education and Labor Force Characteristics." *Sociology of Religion* 57(2):175–94.

———. 1999. "Jewish Identity, Denomination and Denominational Mobility." *So-cial Identities* 5:279–311.

———. 2001. "Dimensions of Jewish Identity among American Jews." In S. Del-laPergola and J. Even (eds.), *Papers in Jewish Demography 1997* (239–260). He-brew University of Jerusalem, Institute of Contemporary Jewry, Jewish Popula-tion Studies No. 29.

———. 2003a. "Changes in the Education of American Jews, 1990 to 2000/ 01." Paper presented at the Eastern Sociological Society Meetings, New York (February).

———. 2003b. "Gender and Jewish Identity." *Journal of Contemporary Religion* 18(1)37–61.

———. 2003c. "How Survey Research Shapes the Understanding of Jewish Iden-tity." Paper presented at the Association for Jewish Studies Annual Meeting, Boston (December).

———. 2006. "Gender Similarity and Difference in Jewish Identity and Involve-ment." Paper presented at the American Sociological Association Annual Meet-ing, Montreal (August).

Harville, Michael, and Beth Rienzi. 2000. "Equal Worth and Gracious Submission: Judeo-Christian Attitudes toward Employed Women." *Psychology of Women Quarterly* 24:145–47.

Hauser, Robert, and John Warren. 1997. "Socioeconomic Indexes for Occupations: A Review, Update, and Critique." Center for Demography and Ecology Working Paper No. 96–01. University of Wisconsin, Madison.

Heilman, Samuel. 2003–4. "American Jews and Community: A Spectrum of Possi-bilities." *Contemporary Jewry* 24:51–69.

Heineck, Guido. 2004. "Does Religion Influence the Labor Supply of Married Women in Germany?" *Journal of Socio-Economics* 33:307–28.

Herman, Simon. 1977. *Jewish Identity: A Social Psychological Perspective*. New Brunswick, N.J.: Transaction Books.

Hertel, Bradley R. 1995. "Work, Family and Faith: Recent Trends." In Nancy Ammerman and Wade Roof (eds.), *Work, Family, and Religion in Contemporary Society* (81–122). New York: Routledge.

Heschel, Susannah. 2004. "Gender and Agency in the Feminist Historiography of Jewish Identity." *Journal of Religion* 84(4):580–91.

Hill, E. Jeffrey, Nicole Timmons Mead, Lukas Ray Dean, Dawn M. Hafen, Robyn Gadd, Alexis A. Palmer, and Maria S. Ferris. 2006. "Researching the 60-Hour Dual-Earner Workweek: An Alternative to the 'Opt-Out' Revolution." *American Behavioral Scientist* 49(9):1184–1204.

Himmelfarb, Harold. 1982. "Research on American Jewish Identity and Identification." In Marshall Sklare (ed.), *Understanding American Jewry* (56–95). New Brunswick, N.J.: Transaction Books.

Hochschild, Arlie. 1989. *The Second Shift*. New York: Avon Books.

Horowitz, Bethamie. 2000. *Connections and Journeys: Assessing Critical Opportunities for Enhancing Jewish Identity*. Revised edition. New York: UJA-Federation of New York.

Hout, Michael. 1982. "The Association between Husband's and Wife's Occupations in Two-Earner Families." *American Journal of Sociology* 88:397–409.

Howe, Neil, and William Strauss. 1992. *Generations: The History of America's Future*. New York: Harper.

Huffman, Matt. 2004. "Gender Inequality Across Local Wage Hierarchies." *Work and Occupations* 31:323–44.

Hull, Isabel. 1996. *Sexuality, State, and Civil Society in Germany, 1800–1815*. Ithaca, N.Y.: Cornell University Press.

Hunter College Women's Studies Collective. 2005. *Women's Realities, Women's Choices*, 3rd edition. New York: Oxford University Press.

Hurst, D., and F. Mott. 2003. "Jewish Fertility and Population Sustenance: Contemporary Issues and Evidence." Unpublished manuscript.

———. 2006. "Secular Pay-Offs to Religious Origins: Gender Differences among American Jews." *Sociology of Religion* 67(4):439–63.

Hyman, Paula. 1995. *Gender and Assimilation in Modern Jewish History: The Roles and Representation of Women*. Seattle: University of Washington Press.

Johnson, D. Paul. 2003. "From Religious Markets to Religious Communities: Contrasting Implications for Applied Research." *Review of Religious Research* 44(4):325–40.

Kadushin, Charles, Benjamin Phillips, and Leonard Saxe. 2005. "National Jewish Population Survey 2000–01: A Guide for the Perplexed." *Contemporary Jewry* 25:1–32.

Kalmijn, Matthijs. 1994. "Assortative Mating by Cultural and Economic Occupational Status." *American Journal of Sociology* 100:422–52.

Kalmijn, Matthijs, Anneke Loeve, and Dorien Manting. 2007. "Income Dynamics in Couples and the Dissolution of Marriage and Cohabitation." *Demography* 44(1):159–79.

Kaufman, Debra. 1999. "Embedded Categories: Identity among Jewish Young Adults in the United States." *Race, Gender, and Class: American Jewish Perspectives* 6(4):76–87.

———. 2005. "Measuring Jewishness in America: Some Feminist Concerns." *Nashim: A Journal of Jewish Women's Studies and Gender Issues* 10:84–98.

Kaplan, Marion. 1991. *The Making of the Jewish Middle Class: Women, Family, and Identity in Imperial Germany.* New York: Oxford University Press.

Katz, Jacob. 1973. *Out of the Ghetto: The Social Background of Jewish Emancipation, 1770–1870.* New York: Schocken.

Klaff, Vivian. 2006. "Defining American Jewry from Religious and Ethnic Perspectives: The Transitions to Greater Heterogeneity." *Sociology of Religion* 67(4):415–38.

Kotler-Berkowitz, Laurence. 2006. "An Introduction to the National Jewish Population Survey 2000–01." *Sociology of Religion* 67(4):387–90.

Kreider, Rose M. 2005. "Number, Timing, and Duration of Marriages and Divorces, 2001." Washington, D.C.: U.S. Census Bureau, Household Economic Studies (70–97).

Lefkovitz, Lori, and Rona Shapiro. 2005. "Ritualwell.org—Loading the Virtual Canon, or: The Politics and Aesthetics of Jewish Women's Spirituality." *Nashim: A Journal of Jewish Women's Studies and Gender Issues* 9:101–125.

Lehrer, Evelyn. 1995. "The Effects of Religion on the Labor Supply of Married Women." *Social Science Research* 24:281–301.

Lipset, Seymour Martin, and Earl Raab. 1995. *Jews and the New American Scene.* Cambridge, Mass.: Harvard University Press.

Luckmann, Thomas. 1967. *The Invisible Religion.* New York: Macmillan.

Martin, Steven P. 2000. "Diverging Fertility among U.S. Women Who Delay Childbearing Past Age 40." *Demography* 37(4):523–33.

Mayer, Egon. 2001. "Secularism among America's Jews." Paper delivered to the Association for Jewish Studies, Washington, D.C., December.

McGuire, Meredith. 2001. *Religion: The Social Context.* 5th edition. Belmont, Calif.: Wadsworth/Thomson Learning.

McLaughlin, Steven, Barbara Melber, John Billy, Denise Zimmerle, Linda Winges, and Terry Johnson. 1988. *The Changing Lives of American Women.* Chapel Hill: University of North Carolina Press.

Mueller, Charles W., and W. T. Johnson. 1975. "Socioeconomic Status and Religious Participation." *American Sociological Review* 40:785–800.

Muñoz, Sara. 2007. "Does It Pay to Work Long Hours?" *Wall Street Journal,* June 26.

Nakao, Keiko, and Judith Treas. 1994. "The 1989 Socioeconomic Index of Occupations: Construction from the 1989 Occupational Prestige Scores." GSS Methodological Report No. 74. Chicago: National Opinion Research Center (quoted in Hauser and Warren, 1997).

NCES (National Center for Education Statistics), 2007. *Digest of Education Statistics: 2006.* Washington, D.C.: NCES Publication No. 2007–017.

Newcombe, Nora. 2007. "The Truth of the Mommy Wars." *Chronicle of Higher Education* 54(8): B20.

Nock, S. L. 2001. "The Marriages of Equally Dependent Spouses." *Journal of Family Issues* 22:756–77.

O'Leary, Richard, and Fjalar Finnas. 2002. "Education, Social Integration and Minority–Majority Group Intermarriage. *Sociology* 36:235–54.

Ozorark, E. W. 1996. "The Power but Not the Glory: How Women Empower Themselves Through Religion." *Journal for the Scientific Study of Religion* 35(1):17–29.

Padavic, Irene, and Barbara Reskin. 2002. *Women and Men at Work*. 2nd edition. Thousand Oaks, Calif.: Pine Forge Press.

Pankhurst, Jerry, and Sharon K. Houseknecht. 2000. "Introduction: The Religion–Family Linkage and Social Change—A Neglected Area of Study." In Sharon K. Houseknecht and Jerry G. Pankhurst (eds.), *Family, Religion, and Social Change in Diverse Societies* (1–42). New York: Oxford University Press.

Phillips, Benjamin T., and Sylvia Barack Fishman. 2006. "Ethnic Capital and Intermarriage: A Case Study of American Jews." *Sociology of Religion* 67(4): 487–505.

Phillips, Bruce. 1991. "Sociological Analysis of Jewish Identity." In David Gordis and Y. Ben-Horin (eds.), *Jewish Identity in America* (3–23). Los Angeles: University of Judaism.

Prell, Riv-Ellen. 1999. *Fighting to Become Americans: Assimilation and the Trouble between Jewish Women and Jewish Men*. Boston: Beacon Press.

———. 2007a. "Family Formation, Educational Choice, and American Jewish Identity." In Jack Wertheimer (ed.), *Family Matters: Jewish Education in an Age of Choice* (3–33). Lebanon, N.H.: Brandeis University Press.

———(ed.). 2007b. *Women Remaking American Judaism*. Detroit: Wayne State University Press.

Raley, S., M. Mattingly, and S. Bianchi. 2006. "How Dual are Dual-Income Couples? Documenting Change from 1970 to 2001." *Journal of Marriage and the Family* 68:11–28.

Rayburn, Carole. 2004. "Religion, Spirituality, and Health." *American Psychologist* 59(1):52–3.

Rebhun, Uzi, and Shlomit Levy. 2006. "Unity and Diversity: Jewish Identification in America and Israel 1990–2000." *Sociology of Religion* 67(4):391–414.

Robert, Peter, and Erzsebet Bukodi. 2002. "Dual Career Pathways: The Occupational Attainment of Married Couples in Hungary." *European Sociological Review* 18(2):217–232.

Rosenfeld, Rachel, and Kenneth Spenner. 1992. "Occupational Sex Segregation and Women's Early Job Career Shifts." *Work and Occupations* 19:424–49.

Saxe, Leonard, Elizabeth Tighe, Benjamin Phillips, and Charles Kadushin. 2007. "Reconsidering the Size and Characteristics of the American Jewish Population: New Estimates of a Larger and More Diverse Community." Steinhardt Social Research Institute Working Paper Series: Understanding Contemporary American Jewry, No. 013107b, Waltham, Mass.

Schumm, Walter R. 2004. "Islam and the 'Universal' Gender Difference in Religious Commitment: A Brief Report in Response to Stark (2002)." *Psychological Reports* 94(3, pt. 1):1104–6.

Schwartz, Christine, and Robert Mare. 2005. "Trends in Educational Assortative Marriage from 1940 to 2003." *Demography* 42(4):621–46.

Sered, Susan Starr. 1994. " 'She Perceives Her Work to Be Rewarding': Jewish Women in a Cross-Cultural Perspective." In L. Davidman and S. Tenenbaum (eds.), *Feminist Perspectives on Jewish Studies* (ch. 8). New Haven, Conn.: Yale University Press.

Shapiro, Rona. 2007. "The 'Boy Crisis' That Cried Wolf." *Jewish Daily Forward,* January 5; http://www.forward.com/articles/the-boy-crisis-that-cried-wolf/.

Sharot, Stephen. 1991. "Judaism and the Secularization Debate." *Sociological Analysis* 52(3):255–75.

———. 1997. "A Critical Comment on Gans' 'Symbolic Ethnicity and Symbolic Religiosity' and Other Formulations of Ethnicity and Religion Regarding American Jews." *Contemporary Jewry* 18:39.

Shellenbarger, Sue. 2008. *The Breaking Point: How Female Midlife Crisis Is Transforming Today's Women.* New York: Henry Holt and Co.

Sherkat, Darren E., and John Wilson. 1995. "Preferences, Constraints, and Choices in Religious Markets: An Examination of Religious Switching and Apostasy." *Social Forces* 73:993–1026.

Smith, Thomas W. 2005. *Jewish Distinctiveness in America: A Statistical Portrait.* New York: American Jewish Committee.

Smits, Jeroen, Wout Ultee, and Jan Lammers. 1996. "Effects of Occupational Status Differences Between Spouses on the Wife's Labor Force Participation and Occupational Achievement: Findings from 12 European Countries." *Journal of Marriage and the Family* 58:101–15.

Stanley, Sandra C., Janet G. Hunt, and Larry L. Hunt. 1986. "The Relative Deprivation of Husbands in Dual-Earner Households." *Journal of Family Issues* 7:3–20.

Stark, Rodney. 2002. "Physiology and Faith: Addressing the 'Universal' Gender Difference in Religious Commitment." *Journal for the Scientific Study of Religion* 41(3):495–507.

Steiner, Leslie. 2007. "Busting the Work-Life Myth." *Health* 21(8):156–58.

Swail, Watson S. 2002. "Higher Education and the New Demographics: Questions for Policy." *Change* (July/August):15–23.

Sweeney, Megan. 2002. "Two Decades of Family Change: The Shifting Economic Foundations of Marriage." *American Sociological Review* 67(1):132–47.

Sweet, Stephen, and Peter Meiksins. 2008. *Changing Contours of Work: Jobs and Opportunities in the New Economy.* Thousand Oaks, Calif.: Pine Forge Press.

Tichenor, Veronica J. 1999. "Status and Income as Gendered Resources: The Case of Marital Power." *Journal of Marriage and the Family* 61:638–50.

United Jewish Communities. 2003a. *The National Jewish Population Survey, 2000–01.* New York: United Jewish Communities (producer). Storrs, Conn.: North American Jewish Data Bank (distributor).

————. 2003b. *NJPS/NSRE 2000–01 Datafile User Guide.* Available online: http://www.jewishdatabank.org.

————. 2003c (updated 2004). *The National Jewish Population Survey, 2000–01: Strength, Challenge and Diversity in the American Jewish Population.* Available online: http://www.ujc.org/njps.

————. 2003d. *National Jewish Population Survey / National Survey of Religion and Ethnicity 2000–01: Study Documentation.* New York: United Jewish Communities. Available online: http://www.jewishdatabank.org.

U.S. Bureau of the Census. 2003a. Table F-22 retrieved November 26, 2006, from http://www.census.gov/hhes/income/histinc/f22.html.

————. 2003b. "The Relationship between the 1990 Census and Census 2000 Industry and Occupation Classification Systems." Technical Paper No. 65. Washington, D.C.: U.S. Bureau of the Census. Retrieved October 3, 2007, from http://www.census.gov/hhes/www/ioindex/tp65_report.html.

Waite, Linda, and Maggie Gallagher. 2000. *The Case for Marriage.* New York: Doubleday.

Walter, Tony, and Grace Davie. 1998. "The Religiosity of Women in the Modern West." *British Journal of Sociology* 49(4):640–60.

Webber, Jonathan. 1983. "Between Law and Custom: Women's Experience of Judaism." In P. Holden (ed.), *Women's Religious Experience: Cross-Cultural Perspectives* (143–162). London: Croom-Helm.

Weber, Max. 1963. *The Sociology of Religion,* trans. Ephraim Fischoff. Boston: Beacon Press (originally published in 1922).

Weeden, Jason, Michael J. Abrams, Melanie C. Green, and John Sabini. 2006. "Do High-Status People Really Have Fewer Children? Education, Income and Fertility in the Contemporary U.S." *Human Nature* 17(4):377–92.

Wegener, Bernard. 1992. "Concepts and Measurement of Prestige." *Annual Review of Sociology* 18:253–80.

Wegner, Judith R. 1988. *Chattel or Person: The Status of Women in the Mishnah.* New York: Oxford University Press.

Weinberg, Daniel. 2004. "Evidence from Census 2000 about Earnings by Detailed Occupation for Men and Women." Census 2000 Special Report CENSR-15. Retrieved October 17, 2007, from http://www.census.gov/population/www/cen2000/briefs.html#sr.

Weinberg, Sydney S. 1988. *The World of Our Mothers.* New York: Schocken Books.

Wertheimer, Jack. 2005a. *All Quiet on the Religious Front? Jewish Unity, Denominationalism, and Postdenominationalism in the United States.* New York: American Jewish Committee.

————. 2005b. "Jews and the Jewish Birthrate." *Commentary* (October):39–44.

————. 2005c. "What Is a Jewish Family? Changing Rabbinic Views." In Michael Broyde and Michael Ausubel (eds.), *Marriage, Sex and Family in Judaism* (ch. 9). New York: Rowman & Littlefield.

Wilson, Bryan R. 1966. *Religion in Secular Society: A Sociological Comment.* London: Watts.

Winkler, Anne. 1998. "Earnings of Husbands and Wives in Dual-Earner Families." *Monthly Labor Review* (April):42–48.

Winkler, Anne, Timothy McBride, and Courtney Andrews. 2005. "Wives Who Out-earn Their Husbands: A Transitory or Persistent Phenomenon for Couples?" *Demography* 42(3):523–35.

Winslow-Bowe, Sarah. 2006. "The Persistence of Wives' Income Advantage." *Journal of Marriage and the Family* 68:824–42.

Woocher, Jonathan. 1986. *Sacred Survival: The Civil Religion of American Jews.* Bloomington: Indiana University Press.

Woolever, Cynthia, Deborah Bruce, Wulff Keith, and Ida Smith-Williams. 2006. "The Gender Ratio in the Pews: Consequences for Congregational Vitality." *Journal of Beliefs and Value: Studies in Religion and Education* 27(1):25–38.

Wyatt, Ian, and Daniel Hecker. 2006. "Occupational Changes During the 20th Century." *Monthly Labor Review* (March):35–57.

Xu, Xiaohe, Clark Hudspeth, and John Bartkowski. 2005. "The Timing of First Marriage: Are There Religious Variations?" *Journal of Family Issues* 26(5):584–618.

Adult education, 20–22, 280n2
Age and cohort, 2; divorce and, 28–29,
    261; education and, 15–16; family
    roles and, 171, 259; Jewish identity
    and, 138–40; labor force participation
    and, 45–47, 278n1; occupational
    prestige and, 86; occupations, 73–74,
    272
Age homogamy, 94, 230, 233, 234
Age at first birth, 29, 280nn3,4;
    denominational variation in, 154, 157,
    165–66; education and, 30–31, 165–66;
    Jewish identity and, 161–64, 165–66
Age at marriage, 28–29, 30;
    denominational variation in, 154–57,
    165; education and, 30–31; Jewish
    identity and, 161–65; intermarriage
    and, 231–33
Antisemitism, 279n3

Baby boomers, 140, 279n7
Bar/Bat Mitzvah, 13, 133, 144, 146, 279n9
Becker, Penny Edgell, 105, 153
Berger, Michael, 152–53
Boushey, Heather, 45, 278n2

Census. See U.S. Census
Child penalty, 61, 80, 84
Childcare, 2, 51, 277n1
Childlessness, 26, 30, 38–40, 154, 155,
    233
Children. See Age at first birth; Number
    of children
Christiano, Kevin, 153
Coefficient of dissimilarity, 18, 277n4,
    280n1
Cohabitation, 277n1, 279–280n1
Cohen, Steven, 260, 280n1
Cohort. See Age
Conservative Jews, 125. See also
    Denominations
Cultural capital, 2, 3, 172, 230; Jewish,
    242

Cultural homogamy. See Homogamy,
    cultural
Current Population Survey, 8

Dating, 279–80n1
Davie, Grace, 122, 123, 124
Denominations, 3, 124, 125, 132–33, 153–
    56, 174–87, 267; dual earners and,
    204–12, 220–29; educational
    differences, 144, 175–77, 194, 195–
    200; family roles and, 154–61, 164–71;
    gender differences and, 2, 137–38, 141,
    146, 151; income and, 185–87; Jewish
    identity and, 124–25, 134–37; labor
    force participation and, 177–79, 194;
    measurement of, 132–33; occupation
    and, 179–85, 194
Denominational switching, 230
Diaspora experience, 25
Dissimilarity coefficient. See Coefficient
    of dissimilarity
Divorce, 28–29, 255; age cohort and, 28–
    29; denomination and, 154; education
    and, 30–35; Jewish identity and, 161–
    64; U.S. Jews compared to U.S.
    whites, 38–39, 42
Dual earners, 88–117; age and, 93–95,
    117, 205, 221; change in, 92, 93;
    denominational variation in, 204–12,
    220–29; education and, 91;
    educational homogamy and, 96;
    hours of employment, 88, 94–96,
    102–5; income of, 98–101; Jewish
    identity and, 203–4, 215–29; Judaism
    and, 91; number of children and, 101–
    6, 221; occupational homogamy and,
    96; occupational prestige of, 98, 112–
    15; occupations of, 96–98, 106–15;
    religion and, 90–91; U.S. Jews
    compared to U.S. whites, 92, 94

Economic homogamy. See Homogamy,
    economic

Edgell, Penny, 105, 153
Education, 13–24; adult, 20–22; age and, 15; changes in, 15–16, 22–23; denominational differences in, 144, 175–77, 194, 195–200; family roles and, 13, 27, 30–35, 171; gender differences in, 13, 15, 19, 253; intermarriage and, 231; labor force participation and, 47, 52–53; lifelong, 20–22; number of children and, 30–31, 40, 243; occupational prestige and, 260; occupations and, 13; U.S. Jews compared to U.S. whites, 17–19. *See also* Jewish education
Educational homogamy. *See* Homogamy, educational
Eisen, Arnold, 260, 280n1
Employment status, 210–11
Exceptionalism, 130, 136, 137, 216, 224, 241, 275. *See also* Jewish identity factors

Family roles/familism, 28–35, 43, 253; age cohort and, 28–30, 171, 259; change in, 4, 25, 26, 153; denominational variation in, 154–61, 164–71, 259–60; education and, 13, 27, 30–35, 171; ethnic differences in, 153; intermarriage and, 231–34, 242–43; Jewish identity and, 124, 161–71; Judaism and, 2, 26, 152; labor force participation and, 44–45, 48–53, 253–54; occupation and, 74–80; U.S. Jews compared to U.S. whites, 26, 36–43. *See also* Age at first birth; Age at marriage; Childlessness; Divorce; Marital status; Number of children; Remarriage
Family size. *See* Number of children
Feminism/Feminist movement, 1, 2, 4, 90, 256
Fertility. *See* Number of children
Fighting to Become Americans, 88
Fishman, Sylvia Barack, 3, 231–33, 267
Full-time employment. *See* Hours of employment

General Social Survey, 26
Goldscheider, Calvin, 227, 229, 258
Graduate education, 15, 16–17

Heilman, Samuel, 129, 219, 279n3
Hofmeister, Heather, 123
Homogamy: age, 94, 230, 233, 234; cultural, 91, 92, 117, 230, 233, 234; economic, 91, 92, 230, 254–55; educational, 35–36, 89, 96, 116, 233, 234, 247, 254–55, 261; educational, of U.S. Jews compared to U.S. whites, 42–43; income, 90; intermarriage and, 230; occupational, 89, 90, 96–98, 107, 116, 117, 235, 248, 254–55
Hours of employment, 2; couples,' 89, 216; denominational variation in, 200, 201, 206–10, 221–22, 224; dual earners,' 89, 206–10; education and, 253–54; family roles and, 49–51, 53; gender differences in, 2, 46–47; husbands,' 208–10; Jewish identity and, 216–18; marital status and, 49; number of children and, 206–10, 221, 253–54; wives,' 206–10, 216–17
Household income, 93, 98. *See also* Income
Human capital, 2, 100–101

Income, 80–84, 93, 278n2; comparison of husband's to wife's, 99–101, 218, 222–27, 240, 245–47; denominational variation in, 185–87, 212–14; education and, 200; family roles and, 81–84; gender differences in, 81–84, 254; intermarriage and, 235, 237–40; occupation and, 81–83, 254; wives' contribution to household, 99–101, 218, 222–23, 224–27, 245–47
Individualism, 153, 263–64, 281n1
Intermarriage, 5, 230–49, 255; education and, 231; family roles and, 231–34, 242–43; homogamy and, 233–34, 237–40; Jewish identity and, 240–49; labor force participation and, 234–35, 245; occupations and, 235–40, 245; remarriage and, 230–31, 237–40; spousal homogamy and, 230
Internet use, 278n2
Intramarriage, 230–49, 255. *See also* Intermarriage

Israel: attitudes about, 131; attachment to, 131. *See also* Jewish identity factors

Jewish education, 13, 125, 133; age and, 145–47; denominational variation in, 144–47; gender differences in, 13, 125, 144–50; Jewish identity and, 147–50

Jewish identity, 121–43, 147–51; age and, 138–40; denominational variation in, 124–25, 134–37; dual earners and, 215–29; ethnic expressions of, 125–26, 173–74; factor analysis of, 127–32, 264, 274–75, 278n1; family roles and, 3, 152–54, 161–71, 257; gender differences in, 122–24, 127, 133–34, 137–51, 255–56; hours of employment and, 216–18; income and, 190–91, 217–18, 222; Jewish education and, 147–50; intermarriage and, 240–49; labor force participation and, 187–90, 200–201; measurement of, 127–32; occupations and, 191; private and public expressions of, 126–27; religious expressions of, 125–26, 173–74; subjective, 279n6;

Jewish social capital, 125

Jewishness, 2, 3, 5, 121, 122, 128, 152, 172. *See also* Jewish identity

Labor force participation, 44–62, 177–79; age and, 45–47, 53–54, 278n1; changes in, 45, 278n2; denominational differences in, 177–79, 200; education and, 47, 52–53; family roles and, 44–45, 48–53; gender differences in, 46–47, 48–50; Jewish identity and, 187–90, 200–201, 244–45; marital status and, 48–49, 60–61; number of children and, 49–53, 56–58, 61; secondary earners, 88–89, 102–6, 116, 254, 264; U.S. Jews compared to U.S. whites, 53–62

Learning theory, 91

Lifelong learning. *See* Adult education

Marginality thesis, 3

Marriage market, 91

Marriage penalty, 80, 84, 117

Marital status, 28–29; education and, 30, 31–35; income and, 225; labor force participation and, 48–49, 60–61; occupation and, 112–15, 255

National Jewish Population Survey (1990), 8, 44, 195

National Jewish Population Survey (2000–01), 3, 5, 121; critique, 7–8, 262–63; methodology, 6

National Study of the Changing Workforce, 278n1

Nock, Stephen, 99

Number of children, 1, 2, 26, 30–31; age and, 30; change in, 30; denominational differences in, 157–59, 166–68, 205; dual earners and, 205–10; education and, 30–31, 40, 243; intermarriage and, 233, 243; Jewish identity and, 166–68, 243; labor force participation and, 205–7; marital status and, 40; occupations and, 74–80; U.S. Jews compared to U.S. whites, 39–40

Occupational prestige, 84, 90, 93, 98, 101, 107–9, 112–17; age and, 86; denominational variation in, 200, 214; education and, 200; gender differences in, 85, 214; intermarriage and, 245; measurement of, 84–85, 98; spousal differences in, 214

Occupations, 2, 62–66, 82, 86, 254, 255, 257, 270–73; age and, 73–74, 272; changes in, 4, 73–74; denominational variation in, 200–201, 211–12; education and, 67–73, 270–71; family roles and, 74–80; gender differences in, 72–73, 254; hours of employment and, 254; husband-wife combinations, 106–15; Jewish identity and, 191, 200; sex segregation in, 66–67; top 10 among U.S. Jews, 63–67; top 10 among U.S. whites, 63–66; U.S. Jews compared to U.S. whites, 63–67, 69–73, 76–80, 270–73

Organizations (Jewish), participation in, 6, 131, 133, 134, 148, 243–46, 248, 265, 275, 278

Orthodox Jews, 124–25, 151, 154–61, 169–70, 260. *See also* Denominations

Part-time employment. *See* Hours of employment

Policy implications, 265–67

Prell, Riv-Ellen, 5, 45, 50, 88
Preschool. *See* Childcare
Privatization of religion, 125–26, 152–53, 263–64

Reform Jews, 125. *See also* Denominations
Religiosity. *See* Jewish identity; Spirituality
Religious roles, gender equality in, 2
Remarriage, 31, 91–92, 159–60, 230–31, 237–40, 247, 255; denominational variation in, 159–60, 169; education and, 31–32, 237–40; intermarriage and, 237–40; Jewish identity and, 161–64, 169; occupations and, 112–15
Retirement, 46, 93–94
Ritual observance, 5, 130. *See also* Jewish identity factors

Sample, 6–7, 93
Secondary earners, 88–89, 102–6, 116, 254, 264
Secularization, 173–74
Self-employment, 210
Single mothers, 4, 30
Social capital, 2, 125, 230
Spirituality, 122, 126–27, 130–31, 151, 256
Spousal influence on occupational achievement, 89
Status harmonization, 230
Structural location thesis, 122–24, 174, 201, 256–57

Survey of Income and Program Participation (SIPP), 8, 25

Transformation of American Jews, 227, 258
Trends, 261–62
Tribalism, 130, 133, 142, 164–67, 194, 200, 216, 241, 244–46, 274. *See also* Jewish identity factors

Universal morality factor, 3, 129, 136, 241
U.S. Census, 8, 84, 85

Volunteer work, 278n2

Walter, Tony, 122, 123, 124
Weighting, 6
Wertheimer, Jack, 152, 154
Widowhood, 33–35
Women's employment: with older children, 57; with young children, 57, 58, 86, 265. *See also* Labor force participation; Hours of employment
Women's movement. *See* Feminism/Feminist movement
Women's roles: domestic, 25; family, 75, 76, 78, 79, 82; occupational, 76–79; religious, 6

Zuckerman, Alan, 227, 229, 258